Managing eHealth

The Palgrave Macmillan IESE Business Collection

The Palgrave Macmillan IESE Business Collection is designed to provide authoritative insights and comprehensive advices on specific management topics. The books are based on rigorous research produced by IESE Business School professors, covering new concepts within traditions management areas (Strategy, Leadership, Managerial Economics), as well as emerging areas of enquiry. The collection seeks to broaden the knowledge of the business field through the ongoing release of titles with a humanistic focus in mind.

Books available in the series:

Domènec Melé
MANAGEMENT ETHICS

Adrian Done
GLOBAL TRENDS

Javier Estrada
THE ESSENTIAL FINANCIAL TOOLKIT

Jordi Canals
THE FUTURE OF LEADERSHIP DEVELOPMENT

Magdalene Rosenmöller, Diane Whitehouse and Petra Wilson
MANAGING EHEALTH
From Vision to Reality

Managing eHealth

From Vision to Reality

A Tribute to Jean-Claude Healy

Edited by

Magdalene Rosenmöller
IESE Business School, Spain

Diane Whitehouse
The Castlegate Consultancy, Malton, UK

and

Petra Wilson
CEO, International Diabetes Federation, Brussels, Belgium

palgrave
macmillan

First published 2014 by
PALGRAVE MACMILLAN

Palgrave Macmillan in the UK is an imprint of Macmillan Publishers Limited, registered in England, company number 785998, of Houndmills, Basingstoke, Hampshire RG21 6XS.

Palgrave Macmillan in the US is a division of St Martin's Press LLC, 175 Fifth Avenue, New York, NY 10010.

Palgrave Macmillan is the global academic imprint of the above companies and has companies and representatives throughout the world.

Palgrave® and Macmillan® are registered trademarks in the United States, the United Kingdom, Europe and other countries

ISBN: 978–1–137–37942–9

A catalogue record for this book is available from the British Library.

A catalog record for this book is available from the Library of Congress.

Transferred to Digital Printing in 2014

Contents

List of Figures

List of Tables

List of Boxes

Foreword

It is my great pleasure to introduce this inspiring "tour de table" on eHealth, written by leading experts in the field. Their multi-faceted views show the increasing relevance of eHealth and the changes it is already making to health promotion and the healthcare landscape. More important, the insights brought together here can help citizens, health professionals, information technology (IT) people and policy-makers to plot a future course for the full exploitation of eHealth in Europe.

This book comes at a very timely moment. European eHealth strategy is accelerating its speed: it is building on a good knowledge base and the considerable existing capacity for innovation in eHealth. Numerous initiatives now deal with how to translate remarkable technology advances into reality. They are really adding value to patients, professionals and healthcare systems by improving health and organisational outcomes, user satisfaction and, last but not least, the efficient use of resources.

In order to achieve this level of progress, an appropriate degree of policy support and the engagement of all actors, not least individual citizens, are essential.

With Horizon 2020, and its ambitious changes to European Union (EU) research and innovation, these two developments are now materialising. For example, the European Innovation Partnership on Active and Healthy Ageing has been successful in bringing regional, and other, eHealth champions together to foster networking and an exchange of practical experience. The EU eHealth Action Plan, which is also looking ahead to 2020, focuses on making eHealth actually happen. It addresses some remaining challenges for eHealth, such as interoperability, deployment, digital skills and literacy, international co-operation and research and development.

Beyond that, the ongoing and future challenges must include big data, brain-related research, genetic developments, mobile health, nanotechnology, photonics and sensorial techniques, just to name a few. My own hope is that Horizon 2020 will focus on creating innovation in IT health tools, encouraging user-centred treatments and increasing the evidence available about eHealth's positive impacts.

This book opens with a wonderful account of the beginnings of eHealth in Europe, and the way in which early leadership on European eHealth actions was undertaken by Jean-Claude Healy of the European Commission and World Health Organization. Professor Healy worked tirelessly on the realisation of the eHealth dream, which – with his prescience and energy – enabled us to get as far as we have today.

True to this spirit, the European Commission continues to play its role in advancing healthy and active ageing in Europe, supported by information and communication technologies. If all citizens join forces, we will realise the huge potential promised by eHealth, revolutionising health and care for Europeans in a wide range of different fields.

Robert Madelin
Director, Directorate General for Communications Networks, Content and Technology (Connect)
European Commission
October 2013

Preface

A Tribute to Jean-Claude Healy, a visionary and founder of eHealth in Europe

Writing a tribute jointly from the perspectives of a daughter and a colleague is not easy. The role of a father in shaping the mind and spirit of a child is of course far more significant than his influence in professional life, and a collection of essays is not the place to reflect on the memories of a daughter. Yet the lasting impression of Jean-Claude Healy's work in eHealth can perhaps be compared to the nurturing gifts of a father to a child. A father supports the early steps of an infant, teaches core vocabularies and provides guidance on fundamental values, which go on to shape the adult who will then live an independent life.

"When I was five years old", reflects Claire-Marie Healy, "my father would bring me to the Museum of Modern Art in Saint-Etienne, France, where we used to live. We would look at the paintings together and play at guessing their titles. I was always coming out with suggestions closer to the artists' choices. To his greatest surprise, the connection between the vision of the world of artists and the innocent eye of a five-year-old seemed more natural and evident than that of an adult. Jean-Claude never stopped experiencing this state of child-like wonder and curiosity – reflected well in the twinkle of his eye. Putting judgements and rules aside, this enabled him to come up with (sometimes) crazy but innovative ideas. Whatever the situation, you were always creating together more than one solution to your problem."

With this collection of writings from friends and colleagues of Jean-Claude, the editors have sought to provide a small glimpse of the impact of that same sort of support, teaching and guidance that he gave to the discipline of eHealth.

It has been a huge honour to work on this book and to draw together these chapters. In the first part of the book, they seek to explore the development of eHealth policy; in the second part, to explore the impact of eHealth on the key players in healthcare; and, in the final section, to look at the way in which eHealth is now changing the provision of healthcare.

The purpose of this preface, however, is not to enter into the detail of this collection of papers, but rather to highlight some of the sentiments and emotions, which came to the fore as the authors and editors worked together.

If one were to draw out one word which was evoked by almost everyone who worked on this collection in recalling their memories of Jean-Claude, it is passion. Jean-Claude knew that passion was his driver, and firmly believed that everyone should possess it. He even referred to passion as his stabiliser: he advised that everyone needed at least three commitments to be happy – their work, their family and friends and their inner passion. Jean-Claude's enthusiasm for eHealth was infectious; it fuelled many ideas and launched many careers.

One colleague, Diane Whitehouse, reminisced when working on this collection about how Jean-Claude's vigour translated into his daily work, remembering how he could not abide a bureaucratic mentality or laziness or lethargy about the status quo. She recalled how he sought constantly to bring the future into the present and was always able to capture huge ideas simply and graphically. As many of his colleagues from the European Commission will remember, those graphics were then often the guide for a new tranche of work as they re-grouped around an idea which resulted from a weekend spent by Jean-Claude at home with his family. Jean-Claude would emerge refreshed on a Monday morning, ready to take his team forward with the next eHealth conceptual model or set of actions.

That human passion and engagement is also fondly remembered by Joan Dzenowagis of the World Health Organization (WHO). She recalls: "working with JCH, as he used to sign his messages, brought home to me the power of the human network. Above all, he treasured people as the ultimate source of knowledge: the experiences, relationships, insights, spirit and expertise that are passed on and shared, person to person. This for him…was the magic of the connected world."

That magical element is noted also by Denise Silber, who worked with Jean-Claude as a consultant on numerous occasions, in recalling that his vision and hard work, which did so much to give legitimacy and prominence to eHealth worldwide, was always delivered with a twinkle of the eye.

Similarly, Magda Rosenmöller evoked Jean-Claude's mix of vision, enthusiasm, hard work and sense of achievement that was so fundamental, not only for the eHealth world but also for all those who had the honour to enter his sphere of influence. Jean-Claude made plans for people's future, putting forward curious – and apparently impossible – objectives. The fact that he believed in people reaching whatever future they put their mind to had the potential to pull them much further forward than they had originally thought possible.

The collection of essays and memories presented in this volume is therefore not only a chronicle of the key achievements accomplished that have paved the eHealth journey, but is also a testament to the abiding impact of Jean-Claude's vision. This was perhaps crowned in 2005, at the Ministerial eHealth Conference, when Jean-Claude jumped to the podium with a big smile on his face exclaiming: "Habemus resolution". What we had was his masterpiece: Resolution 58.28 of the World Health Assembly, 2005, adopted unanimously. It urged the WHO Member States to take initiatives to promote eHealth, and requested the WHO to promote international collaboration and provide more electronic information and technical support to its members.

As his colleague Ilias Iakovidis noted in 2008, the eHealth community lost a free thinker, a true optimist and a humanitarian who worked tirelessly towards a new era of eHealth in Europe and beyond. With this collection, however, we do not seek to dwell on our loss. Instead, we celebrate the growth of eHealth, as both an academic discipline and a practical reality, which has done so much to change the face of healthcare over the past 20 years.

To recall one of Jean-Claude's own favourite quotations, we hope that this book will keep alive his passion and the twinkle in his eye, as he urged us all to be unreasonable in our demands of ourselves, whether he was speaking to us as a friend, colleague or father:

> The reasonable man adapts himself to the world; the unreasonable one persists in trying to adapt the world to himself. Therefore, all progress depends on the unreasonable man.
>
> George Bernard Shaw

Claire-Marie Healy and Petra Wilson,
29 November 2013

Acknowledgements

The idea for *Managing eHealth: From Vision to Reality* was born during a great eHealth gathering, the HIMSS World of Health IT, organised together with the EU Ministerial Conference in Barcelona 2010, where we discussed the idea with the editorial team and some of the contributing authors. Since then, numerous people have supported the initiative and helped to make this publication happen.

We are extremely grateful to all the authors for their personal engagement and the enthusiasm they bring to the eHealth arena and to this project. Together with their teams, they are involved in researching eHealth and healthcare, designing health policies, managing and providing healthcare, and/ or representing some of the many eHealth related stakeholders. They took the time to provide their joint experience, insights and evidence and help to make this volume so valuable for the reader.

We would also like to recognize the invaluable contribution of a series of different people who have provided editorial support during the period the book project has been ongoing: Christiane Haberl in the initial stage, Wendy Wisbaum bringing the project close to the finishing line and Marta Ribeiro and Lucile Danglas from CRHIM (Centre for Research in Health Innovation Management at IESE Business School) for their tireless support and enthusiasm for finally getting this publication out.

We would also like to thank Kiran Bolla and the team at Palgrave Macmillan for their advice and support, availability and above all, patience.

Notes on Contributors

Albert Alonso is a senior researcher at the Innovation Directorate, Hospital Clinic Barcelona. He holds a PhD in Medicine and a postgraduate degree on Management and Organisation of Information Systems. He has been a main contributor to the development of integrated care services at the Hospital Clinic and the area served by the hospital. At present, he is involved in Project Integrate that benchmarks existing approaches to integrated care models in Europe. He is vice-chair of the International Foundation for Integrated Care (IFIC), and a member and an active participant in the European Innovation Partnership on Active and Healthy Ageing action group (B3) on Integrated Care.

Jörg Artmann is a research consultant with Empirica Communication and Technology Research in Bonn, Germany, where he is working on eHealth innovation projects, in particular on the formulation of ePrescription guidelines for cross-border interoperability and the monitoring of eHealth implementation progress across the EU. He holds an MSc in International Relations from the London School of Economics and the Institut d'Études Politiques de Paris.

Birgit Beger is the Secretary General of the Standing Committee of European Doctors (CPME). Holding law and political science degrees from the Freie Universität Berlin, she is a qualified registered lawyer with the Brussels and Berlin bar. In Brussels, she has been working for over ten years in Public Affairs and Law, inter alia with the European Parliament, a law firm and European non-governmental organisations in the field of human rights, social policy and professional policy.

Niels Boye is a physician and specialist in Internal Medicine and Endocrinology and is currently working as a consultant at a major Danish hospital with clinical and ICT supported care of chronic diseases. He has been participant, evaluator and reviewer in several EU projects in ICT for Health and Ambient Assisted living for more than a decade and served two years in the Ambient Assisted Living Joint Programme build-up phase at the Central Management Unit in Brussels.

Célia Boyer is the executive director of the Health On the Net Foundation (HON) – a non-profit and non-governmental organisation that promotes and guides the deployment of useful and reliable online health information, and its appropriate and efficient use. She is recognised as an expert in quality

assessment of medical information on the Internet, and has since 2000 taken part in several projects at both European and international levels. Her latest achievement is her participation as a workpackage leader in the European Commission funded project Khreshmoi (http://www.khresmoi.eu/). The project started in 2010 and aims to develop a multi-lingual, multi-modal search and access system for biomedical information and documents.

Don Eugene Detmer is Professor Emeritus and Professor of Medical Education in the Department of Public Health Sciences at the University of Virginia and Visiting Professor at CHIME, UCL. He is a fellow of the American Association for the Advancement of Science and the American Colleges of Medical Informatics, Surgeons and Sports Medicine. Don is past President and CEO of the American Medical Informatics Association. He is a recipient of the American College of Medical Informatics Morris Collen medal and the Walsh McDermott medal from the Institute of Medicine.

Vanessa Díaz-Zuccarini is a lecturer in bioengineering at University College London. She holds an MEng degree (University Simon Bolivar, Venezuela) and a PhD in Automatic Control and Industrial Informatics (Ecole Centrale de Lille, France). She started working for Imagine, S.A., a consulting and software developer company and was awarded a European Fellowship to work on the coupling of biologically oriented lumped parameter models as boundary conditions for 3D models of cardiovascular applications at the University of Sheffield. Vanessa is currently the Principal Investigator of several European Union, EPSRC and Royal Society grants. She won the UCL Consultants Award in 2012 for her work in the project "DISCIPULUS", an initiative established by the European Commission in 2011 to set up a roadmap for the "digital patient".

Joan Dzenowagis is an international health policy specialist with experience at the country, regional and global levels in public health, policy and strategy development. At the World Health Organization for over 15 years, she has held posts in disease surveillance, information technology strategy and research, as well as managing an international public–private partnership in information and communication technologies and health. Currently she is responsible for eHealth governance and Internet affairs. Her work covers global and regional developments in new technologies in the health sector, ranging from eHealth policy and ethics to health information on the Internet.

Antoine Geissbühler is Professor of Medicine, Chairman of the Department of Radiology and Medical Informatics at Geneva University, Director of the Division of eHealth and Telemedicine at Geneva University Hospitals. He is also President of the Health On the Net Foundation, the past president of the International Medical Informatics Association and Fellow of the American College of Medical Informatics.

Nick Goodwin is Co-Founder and CEO of the International Foundation for Integrated Care (IFIC), a not-for-profit membership-based foundation dedicated to improving the science knowledge and application of integrated care across the world (www.integratedcarefoundation.org). He is Editor-in-Chief of its scientific periodical, the *International Journal of Integrated Care* (www.ijic.org). Nick also works as a Senior Associate at The King's Fund, London.

Avrille Hanzel is Senior Manager, mHealth Alliance, United Nations Foundation. Avrille brings over five years of experience in the non-profit sector to her role at the mHealth Alliance, where she provides overall management for strategic initiatives and internal operations of the Alliance. She has a diverse background in grant management, events and conferences, fundraising and project management support for in-country and global partnerships. Avrille holds a BA in Sociology and Anthropology from the University of Michigan.

Nicholas R. Hardiker is the Director of the ICN eHealth Programme and is Professor of Nursing and Health Informatics and the Associate Head (Research & Innovation) of the University of Salford School of Nursing, Midwifery & Social Work, UK. Nick has nearly 20 years' experience of theoretical and applied research in eHealth.

Chelsea Hedquist is the Senior Communications Officer at the mHealth Alliance. Before joining the Alliance, she spent three years working for the WHO Regional Office for Europe, based in Copenhagen. She previously worked for a DC-based education advocacy group, as a publicist for the Sundance Film Festival and as a radio reporter/executive producer. She graduated from Stanford University and received her master's degree in journalism from Columbia's Graduate School of Journalism.

Ilias Iakovidis is Acting Head of Unit of Digital Social Platforms, DG Connect, at the European Commission. He holds a PhD in Applied Mathematics and undertook postdoctoral training in biomedical engineering. From 1993 to 2010, he contributed to the European Union's research and policy developments as well as international co-operation in the eHealth domain. Currently, he leads the EU programmes on technological research and innovation in the areas of active and healthy ageing and integrated care. In 2001, he was elected fellow of the American College of Medical Informatics.

Tom Jones is Director, tinTree International eHealth Leadership and Development, South Africa; Director, TanJent Consultancy, UK; Senior Consultant, Strategy, Projects and Evaluation, Greenfield Management Solutions, South Africa. Tom developed the eHealth Impact tool based on cost benefit analysis, and specialises in eHealth economics and finance. He manages the tinTree Economic Evaluation Database. An accountant with a degree in psychology, he is a member of the Royal Society of Medicine and the Royal African Society. He works in Europe and Africa.

Dipak Kalra is Clinical Professor of Health Informatics and Director of the Centre for Health Informatics and Multiprofessional Education (CHIME) at University College London. Dipak is President of the European Institute for Health Records (EuroRec), a Director of the openEHR Foundation, and a Fellow of the British Computer Society. He is a British Standards Institute representative to CEN and ISO on electronic health record interoperability, and a strategic advisor to the European Commission on semantic interoperability.

Zoi Kolitsi has been involved in clinical work and research in the field of medical physics and biomedical engineering for 17 years. She is currently an affiliate member of the Information Security Lab of AUTH. She contributes to national eHealth through posts with the relevant health authorities and major EU co-operation initiatives including epSOS, eHGI and eSENS. She has led the CALLIOPE Thematic Network and also chairs the national Sectoral Standardization Committee for eHealth. Zoi holds a PhD in Medical Physics.

Ada Kwan is a consultant for the mHealth Alliance and a researcher in the Division of Health Economics at the Mexico National Institute of Public Health. Her research experience and interests are in multi-country economic, impact and efficiency evaluations primarily for HIV/AIDS interventions and pay-for-performance schemes in Africa. She has additionally contributed to research and policy work on the benefits of leveraging information and communication technologies to improve health. She obtained her MHS degree in International Health from the Johns Hopkins Bloomberg School of Public Health and her BSc degree in Neuroscience from the University of Michigan.

Patricia Mechael is the Executive Director of the mHealth Alliance, which is hosted by the United Nations Foundation, as well as a faculty member at the Columbia University School of International and Public Affairs and Earth Institute. She has been actively involved in the field of International Health for 15 years with field experience in over 30 countries primarily in Africa, the Middle East and Asia. She has worked on research, programme design and implementation, strategic planning and policy development for mHealth and eHealth initiatives as well as Reproductive Health and Women's Health and Rights. Prior to joining the mHealth Alliance, she was Director of Strategic Application of Mobile Technology for Public Health and Development at the Center for Global Health and Economic Development at the Earth Institute.

Josep M. Piqué has been a physician and investigator in the field of digestive diseases, acting as Chief of Gastronterology Service at Hospital Clínic Barcelona for 10 years. He has published over 300 papers and has acted as member of Research and Telemedicine Committee in The World Gastroenterology Organization. Since 2005, he has been involved in healthcare management at Hospital Clínic Barcelona, where he was appointed CEO in March 2011. He has been involved in a profound transformation of the Hospital Clínic's organisation, orienting it to improve healthcare process management, and research and innovation. He is also currently the president of MIHealth Forum of Fira Barcelona, and a member of the Board of Trustees of Biocat.

Mayoni Ranasinghe worked in multiple disciplines including paediatrics and sexual health in Sri Lanka for over five years before moving to Geneva, Switzerland, where she joined the Health On the Net Foundation (HON). She has a Master's in Public Health from the London School of Hygiene and Tropical Medicine. She currently resides in Toronto, Canada, where she continues to work for the HON.

Jean Roberts is Director (Standards) of the UK Council for Health Informatics Professions (UKCHIP) and a member of EU eHealth Stakeholder Group. She is an international health informatician with extensive multi-faceted experience in management of complex programmes and projects, in informatics and e-health business areas. She has worked in operational healthcare, commercial solution providers and consultancy, and in academia over her career. She has been active internationally in health informatics since 1974, being involved in the inaugural UK Current Perspectives in Health Computing event, the initial Medical Informatics Europe congress and chaired the global MEDINFO 2001 congress. She was also the first ever local NHS District Computer Services Officer in the UK. Jean obtained her first degree in Computer Science in 1971 and a doctorate in Health Informatics (2005) with a subsequent Post-graduate Certificate in Research Supervision (2008).

Magdalene Rosenmöller is Professor of IESE's Operations Management Department, University of Navarra, Spain. A German by nationality, she holds an MD (University Louis Pasteur, France), a PhD in Health Policy (University of London, UK) and an MBA from IESE Business School. Her main areas of expertise are health management, managing information technology and innovation in healthcare, European health and research policies and global health issues.

Niels Rossing is an MD affiliated with MedCom, the Danish Health Data Net. Niels was chief physician at the Copenhagen University Hospital until 1988 and was also a consultant on national hospital planning. Serving the European Commission from 1988 to 1994, he was in charge of the AIM (Advanced Informatics in Medicine) research and development programme. Following this, he was CIO of the Copenhagen hospitals until his retirement in 2002. In 1994, he became Honorary Fellow of the European Federation of Medical

Informatics. In 2010, he received the HIMSS Europe Award for leadership in eHealth.

Denise Silber is President of Basil Strategies digital health consultants and organizers of the *Doctors 2.0 & You* conference series in Paris. An international healthcare social media influencer, Denise pursues her mission to improve conditions for patients thanks to digital health through consulting, events, public speaking and writing. Denise is a graduate of Smith College and Harvard Business School.

Veli Stroetmann is a senior research fellow with empirica Communication and Technology Research in Bonn, Germany. She obtained an MD from the Academy for Medical Sciences in Sofia, Bulgaria, as well as a PhD in Medical Informatics. She is project co-ordinator or principal investigator for European Commission initiated studies on eHealth policies, strategies, validation and impact assessment of eHealth applications. She leads work on business modelling in a European Union Network of Excellence on semantic interoperability. She is an evaluator and consultant on various topics including comparative effectiveness research, cross-border interoperability, uptake and sustainability of integrated care for people with chronic conditions.

Mats Sundgren is Principal Scientist in Biometric & Information Sciences in AstraZeneca R&D. He has more than 26 years' experience in the pharmaceutical industry (in discovery, development, marketing and patents). He is currently working within the area of R&D strategy focusing on implementing strategies for bridging Health Information Technology with clinical research. He is Co-ordinator for the ongoing EHR4CR project as part of the IMI programme. He is a Senior Research Fellow at Chalmers University of Technology & IT University of Gothenburg, Sweden, in areas of Innovation Management, Medical Informatics and eHealth, and a member of the evaluation board for VINNOVA (the Swedish Governmental Agency for Innovation Systems).

Rainer Thiel is Senior Research Consultant with empirica Communication and Technology Research in Bonn, Germany. He holds a PhD in Political Science from the Free University Berlin. He leads the research on clinical and socio-economic impact as well as technology assessment in many Virtual Physiological Human projects. He is also responsible for eHealth and Digital Patient business and exploitation planning as well as public policy and political health systems research. He has been designing assessment frameworks for the application to innovative and disruptive health technologies and ICT infostructures.

Michèle Thonnet works for the Ministry of Social Affairs and Health, in Paris, France. She is a neuropharmacologist, with a PhD, and also graduated in applied mathematics and medical informatics, political science and public law from the Industrial Strategies Institute. Michèle is a health strategist with more than 20 years' experience and the author of over 190 papers. She contributes to eHealth strategy and policy developments at both national and EU levels. Currently she is a member of the strategic committee of the health technologies national network, and is the official representative of France, actively involved in European projects (such as CALLIOPE, epSOS, eHealth Innovation, SemanticHealthNet and e-SENS), as well as in international committees (OECD, HON). She leads the European Interoperability Roadmap of the eHealth Governance Initiative and is a member of the eHealth Network.

Diane Whitehouse is a founding partner of The Castlegate Consultancy, which specialises in research, policy and deployment in eHealth. She previously worked in the European Commission's DG Connect in these same areas of expertise. Her career has spanned action research, academic research/teaching, civic and human rights, policy formation and publishing. Her academic background covered information systems, organisational theory and behaviour and political science.

Michael Wilks is Forensic Physician, having worked previously as a general practitioner. He chaired the British Medical Association's Medical Ethics Committee for nine years, and was a chief officer of the BMA for three years. He was President of the Standing Committee of European Doctors (CPME) from 2008 to 2009: during his presidency, the CPME became – and continues to be – deeply involved in eHealth. Michael has been a member of the Executive Committee of the European eHealth Governance Initiative since its inception, taking the lead especially on issues of trust and acceptability for users of eHealth applications.

Petra Wilson is Chief Executive Officer of the International Diabetes Federation. She has a PhD in Public Health Law from Oxford University, UK, and over 20 years' experience in the eHealth sector as senior director in Cisco's Connected Health team, and previously as European Director of the European Health Management Association. She has also worked for the European Commission in its eHealth unit. Originally trained in law, Petra spent several years as a lecturer at Nottingham University, UK, specialising in healthcare law.

1
Introducing eHealth: Past, Present and Future

Diane Whitehouse, Petra Wilson and Magda Rosenmöller

Overview

As seen in the Preface, this book is intended as a tribute to the work of our friend and colleague, Professor Jean-Claude Healy. Jean-Claude Healy was at the origin of many of the early ideas in the 1990s and the first part of this decade, which formed the foundations of eHealth in Europe. Stimulating and building eHealth in Europe was one of his key objectives – indeed, a decade ago, "eHealth matters" were the opening words of the European eHealth Action Plan that stemmed directly from the work of Jean-Claude and his team (European Commission, 2004). Jean-Claude's heritage, his vision, and the initial building blocks put in place through his and his colleagues' work, is still manifest in Europe today, where eHealth continues to establish itself as a key enabler of safe and efficient health and care.

Yet today, there is still a lot to do to make eHealth a complete reality. Current European studies, as well as the European policy position, emphasise that the promise offered by information and communication technologies (ICT) in healthcare remains largely unfulfilled (European Commission, 2012). Policy planning is focused on identifying, addressing and overcoming such limitations as deployment, digital skills and literacy, international cooperation, interoperability, and research and development. Both here, and in terms of future challenges, the shift is very much towards the co-design and co-production of innovative initiatives (Goodwin, 2013; Loeffler et al., 2013). Technologies that remain challenges for the fields of health and care include big data, genetic developments, mobile health, and many more. The issues surrounding these topics are being looked at by the experts who write in this volume.

What is eHealth?

eHealth is an attractive, concise and easy-to-remember term for a very large, yet not always clear-cut, concept. Some see the term as occasionally ambiguous, and others as an evolving definition. These shifts in terminology have been explored from the early years of the 21st century onwards (see, for example, Whitehouse and Duquenoy, 2009; 2010; George et al., 2012). Overall, the definition of eHealth moved first from an encyclopaedic listing of applications (European Commission, 2004) to a concentration on "the relationship and connections between the data shared among institutions and users" (European Commission, 2007, p. 10). In 2010 – as seen in the 2010–2011 policy work of the European Commission – it transitioned to an even more all-encompassing description, which focused largely on the challenges of healthcare supported by ICT rather than on eHealth itself (European Commission, 2011a, p. 3):

> eHealth is the use of ICT in health products, services and processes combined with organisational change in healthcare systems and new skills, in order to improve health of citizens, efficiency and productivity in healthcare delivery, and the economic and social value of health. eHealth covers the interaction between patients and health-service providers, institution-to-institution transmission of data, or peer-to-peer communication between patients and/or health professionals.

The notion of eHealth comprises three separate elements. They are the three market-related notions of products, services and processes; the two organisational aspects of change management and personnel/user expertise; and the trio of expected outcomes – improved individual health status, healthcare delivery and the economic and social value of health.

For academics, discussion around the precise meaning of eHealth remains a matter of keen debate. This is occurring even at the very moment in time that increasing numbers of people are arguing that it is time to drop the "e" in eHealth (EHTEL, 2009; Ebels, 2012; Roberts, this volume). The trend is to concentrate on important challenges related to the two domains of both health and care. Indeed, as is evident in European policy documents, the focus is now on innovative healthcare for the 21st century, and personalising health and care in a wide variety of applied and scientific developments (European Commission, 2011a).

As co-editors, we decided to maintain the concept of eHealth for the scope, title and orientation of this volume. This was indeed the idea and the name that was adopted when much of the work described here began in the late 1990s. The notion of eHealth represents the book's point of departure (see, for example, the two chapters by Rossing and Iakovidis). It is, however, a moot point that eHealth – as a concept – may be disappearing rapidly from people's psyche and vocabularies. Indeed, the demise of the term may be considered to be an indicator that eHealth's ambitions have been achieved. It is now a term that is well embedded in people's consciousness. In the same way, the term eCommerce is no longer in use because nearly all commercial enterprises – as part of their mode of doing business – use some element of that former expression.

eHealth has been regarded as encompassing many different forms of technology (European Commission, 2004; 2011a). In this book, several authors base their work around the term eHealth and its progress over time (examples include the chapters by Joan Dzenowagis; Ilias Iakovidis; Zoi Kolitsi and Michèle Thonnet; Niels Rossing; and Birgit Beger and Michael Wilks). Contemporarily, technologies supporting new forms of care such as integrated care and person-centred care are tackled by Nick Goodwin and Albert Alonso, and Dipak Kalra and his colleagues. Electronic health records are the core subject of Don Dettmer's chapter, but the implication for personal or individual records is also taken up in the papers by Mats Sundgren and Vanessa Díaz-Zuccarini and colleagues, as well as from the hospital viewpoint (Geissbühler and colleagues). Other authors are more oriented towards particular technologies – the Internet, web, social media and social networks are all evident in the chapters by Celia Boyer and also Denise Silber, whereas mobile health (mHealth) is covered by Patricia Mechael and her co-authors. Two specific domains in the field of informatics are handled here: medical informatics by Niels Rossing, and nursing informatics by Nick Hardiker.

Scope, aims and goals

The scope of this book is threefold. It aims to capture the current policy debates by putting them in their historical context, review the ways in which all the appropriate actors are involved in using ICT to ensure access to high-quality yet economic healthcare provision, and cover actual practice through a range of inputs, case studies and examples. It also considers patients' empowerment and participation. The book offers useful insights into how to tackle the challenges facing the healthcare systems of many regions and countries throughout the globe, even if its primary focus is on the European Union. Together, these approaches provide a rounded context for the environment in which eHealth is being developed and implemented. In this sense, the volume is an "umbrella" book, one which – although it stays with the big picture and offers a holistic overview of ICT use in healthcare systems – also mines in depth many important, and more detailed, topics.

The book brings together a series of chapters written by more than 30 leading experts in their respective eHealth fields. Among the authors are eminent health policy and eHealth leaders at international, European and national levels; leading business school faculty; corporate executives; well-known hospital executives and researchers; healthcare professional leaders; and prominent individuals in non-governmental organisations and civic society.

The book has three main messages. First, it enables readers to gain a better understanding of the uptake of ICT in healthcare. It uses examples that show

how patients, physicians and healthcare providers all collaborate better in an improved and more efficient healthcare system as a result of using eHealth. It therefore covers a considerable number of good eHealth practices while it does not forget by any means the challenges that remain to the use of technologies in healthcare. Second, the book reflects its contemporary position between a great deal of work having been achieved while substantial work on transformation still needs to be done. The book's historical overview shows how healthcare has changed due to the introduction of ICT. It also indicates how healthcare will change in the future, and how these alterations can be managed to assure high value for patients, professionals and the system as a whole. It particularly points to what can be learned positively from the experiences of others. Third, the book illustrates how the work of healthcare professionals may change, and how its readers, as diverse stakeholders, might involve themselves pro-actively in that transition process by contributing to the developments that are about to happen.

Healthcare systems, and the ways in which they can be supported by state-of-the-art and future technologies, are very much on a journey of transition. Indeed, the transition will be ongoing: as one cycle of deployment and implementation reaches maturity, the next is forthcoming. Electronic health records – once considered revolutionary in their implications – are moving into far more common use, combined with the availability of mobile telephony (mHealth); the exploration of genetic data to predict and prevent disease and hereditary health conditions is becoming increasingly usual; and the notion of human beings wearing "chips in the[ir] head[s]" – to cite one of Jean-Claude Healy's favourite examples – is an organic continuation of the contemporary growth in the use of sensors, radio-frequency identifiers and networks (http://futuremed2020.com) (eHealth Task Force, 2011).

This book does not pretend, by any means, to cover the complete width and variety of practices in the field of eHealth that are present and upcoming. eHealth is such a comprehensive field that it would be impossible to cover all its aspects in such a modest volume. For example, to name but three, the challenges posed by interoperability, medical devices and procurement have not been examined here in any great detail. For this reason, this volume has a simple structure, which reflects its main themes: policies, people and practices. The logic behind each of these sections is outlined here by the three contributing editors.

Politics: Policies and Institutions

Examining critical success factors for the transformation of any key issues in society requires the right political climate, institutions and leaders who can help formulate and make policy. Policies provide both the framework and the drivers for progress in combination with the work of the people on the ground, who put the policies into practice. Healthcare supported by ICT is no exception to this general rule. eHealth has been driven forward by energetic people possessing insight and vision, by solid policy positions and documents, and by people who have committed to actions that have coalesced around these political directions.

Five chapters form the core of this first section of the book. The first chapter in this section is written by Niels Rossing, who has evoked his personal memories of the early years of what became eHealth in Europe, and specifically in the European Commission. Niels was the first individual tasked with heading up this domain, and he was also the direct predecessor of Jean-Claude Healy. Niels highlights the way in which a number of substantial elements in the health field have not changed dramatically over the past 25 years. Today, as in 1988, it is still anticipated that eHealth will improve and facilitate healthcare, and develop sustainable products and services through a close collaboration between academia and industry. Yet, in 2013, in addition to policy-makers, it is very much the citizens and patients themselves who are getting engaged and realising this potential!

Ilias Iakovidis, who was also an early colleague of Jean-Claude Healy, takes up the story of eHealth in Europe as from 1990. Over the last quarter century, the European Commission has contributed to the emergence of several generations of technologies in diverse domains of healthcare. Much of this work has been accompanied by the development of relevant policy instruments (from research programmes on diverse areas of eHealth research and innovation) and by noteworthy deployments in products, goods and services. This progress puts a number of European regions and Member States at the leading edge of societal and technological innovation. Many healthcare benefits are already, and will likely continue to be, the result.

From governments to governance: Joan Dzenowagis explores how this paradigm has shaped eHealth, and charts some of its key aspects worldwide. She traces the history of the path taken by eHealth inside the World Health Organization, through its various committees, task forces and assemblies: such was the organisation's determination to facilitate the use of technologies to improve healthcare standards worldwide. The expected results continue to be greater access to healthcare and improvements in its quality, effectiveness and efficiency. Jean-Claude Healy made a unique contribution to this initiative. Joan's is a very personal view of someone who worked closely and intensely with Jean-Claude Healy. Its wording shows the degree of passion and commitment to eHealth that this very unusual individual generated in his colleagues and the surrounding community. This willingness to take bold steps forward lays out an inspiring message for many other groups of stakeholders working in contemporary health-related fields.

Governance in eHealth has previously been a considerable challenge, argue Zoi Kolitsi and Michèle Thonnet. Yet, in recent times, there is a growing clarity about how to govern this field. Built over the course of years, increased cooperative work on ICT related to healthcare is taking place among the European Member States and eHealth stakeholders. New proposals for eHealth for the 2013–2020 timeframe are now on the agenda: new institutions have been created to service and support these next stages in eHealth policy development and deployment. More are on the agenda. Like many other authors in the book, these two women take both a historical and a future-oriented view of eHealth.

Shaping eHealth through legal actions is the concern of Petra Wilson. Her expertise in the legal aspects of eHealth dates from the late 1990s, when she worked in the European Commission to advance a sound policy understanding of the ethical and legal aspects of eHealth. Her chapter offers an overview of the way in which various court cases, that have alternatively challenged or supported the use of the Internet for health purposes, have had an influence in Europe. Eventually there has been a shift towards a Directive, which supports cross-border access of patients to healthcare throughout the Union (European Commission, 2011b). Petra explores the ways in which legal frameworks could facilitate a more expansive framework for healthcare-enhancing technologies.

The politics and institutions portrayed in this section of the volume are among the most influential in the healthcare field both globally and in terms of the European continent. They include the World Health Organization, the European Commission, the Council and Parliament and the relevant ministries of a set of the European Member States. Also included is an overview of legislation at levels that cover the European continent and, in many cases – most relevantly for the health sector – the individual nations. It is these countries that, ultimately, possess the mandate for tackling healthcare. They do not, however, always carry the responsibility for policy-making in the many other areas of legislation – such as data protection; security; mobile telephony and medical equipment – that affect directly the technologies used to provide and support healthcare.

Many of the policies described in this first section of the book – entitled *Politics: Policies and Institutions* – are directly derived from the era in which Jean-Claude Healy started to work so energetically in the field of eHealth. Many of the authors who write about European and world politics and policies knew him directly and worked with him closely. For this reason, in several of the chapters there are reminiscences of times past and the important role that Jean-Claude played in several major historical events. Overall, however, the texts in this section of the book bring us up-to-date while also covering the historical context and, at the same time, they indicate exciting potential directions for the broader future.

Last but not least, this section of the book provides a story about personal and professional collaboration, not simply institutional development. It involves deep insights into people and the way in which they work together. It highlights the point that the potential of eHealth, and real value in healthcare, can be created with enthusiastic and motivated people, a concept Jean-Claude instilled in everyone he met. By bringing groups of individuals into the foreground of policy-making, it serves as a prelude to the next section of the book, with its more targeted focus on *People: Professionals, Patients and Consumers*.

People: Professionals, Patients and Consumers

The second section of the book, which comprises six chapters, deals in broad terms with the people who form the infinitely rich network of stakeholders who collaborate together on eHealth.

Working together, a doctor and a lawyer, Birgit Beger and Michael Wilks outline the increasingly important role that eHealth plays in healthcare for health professionals who are attempting to put their work into practice. At the same time, they explain the challenges that eHealth can continue to present, particularly for physicians. They suggest remedies for various shortcomings in eHealth developments, including better planning with more secure funding and an improved representation and participation of all stakeholders in the development process. The authors show considerable insight, from the perspective of physicians, into the barriers to the development and deployment of eHealth solutions, and they provide guidance about how these can be addressed.

Informatics is the term most used in the following two chapters that also deal with other health-related professionals. Nurses are working actively to absorb the positive benefits that eHealth can provide. Beginning with the experience of the world-renowned 19th century nurse, Florence Nightingale, Nick Hardiker describes the growing importance of informatics to the nursing profession. eHealth continues to be incorporated actively into the fabric of nursing through education, training and professional development. The early take-up of informatics in nursing led to a recognition of the need to define a variety of standards, especially for clinical terminology. Consequently, the nursing profession has played a key role in the creation of national and international special interest groups to support the standardisation of terminology and the spread of information about how useful a role ICT can play in the field of healthcare.

Jean Roberts then looks at the development of the field of health informatics. She examines the widely varied professional backgrounds – from clinician to specialist in information technology (IT) – that health informaticians have and the complex settings in which they work. The challenge of establishing the foundations of a health informatics profession is further complicated by such phenomena as direct interaction with members of an increasingly eHealth-literate public, and the growth in mobile health technologies. Jean points to the current work being done by the United Kingdom's Council for Health Informatics Professions to devise continuing professional development programmes. These maintain the core competencies and skills demanded by health-related strategy, management, research and technology.

As people at large become more and more familiar with easy-to-use technologies that support their daily lives, it can be expected that patients – and ordinary people too – will increasingly view technology as just one means to monitor their health status. Diane Whitehouse and Magda Rosenmöller explore how patients will both use easier and smaller eHealth technologies, the "e" – electronics – that support health. They recognise that these technologies will become more and more intimate, and closer to people's bodies, minds and brains. Greater numbers of patients and people will become the real users of eHealth and provide the driving force for the future of eHealth.

The focus therefore turns, in the latter half of this section, towards the kinds of technologies with which patients, people, and consumers are becoming more and more familiar – the Internet, social media and mobile telephony. Celia Boyer describes how the diffusion of healthcare information across the Internet has resulted in benefits for a large number of people. She points out that these conclusions assume that the health-related information provided is both appropriate and of the highest quality, and that users can be certain that this is the case. Historically, Celia traces the establishment and adoption of the Health on the Net Foundation (HON), and its code that signals the trustworthiness of online healthcare information. She also outlines how HON will continue to evolve to accommodate future developments on the Internet.

Denise Silber presents the viewpoint of an enthusiastic proponent of Web 2.0 and social media. She sees them as the tools that present the best opportunity for ICT to offer broad and effective healthcare information and support to the largest number of people. Web sites and blogs deal with specific health conditions and feature user-generated content. Social media sites display a variety of health-themed forums: the resulting communities define themselves as, for example, patient-only, professional-only or a mixture of the two. It is therefore important to facilitate the responsible dissemination and exchange of information, and to provide platforms for innovation whether the users are patients or clinicians. Denise's personal memories of the role that Jean-Claude Healy played in the eHealth field are timely reminders of how much of a shift has taken place in the balance of relations between patients and clinicians since this work began in the mid-1990s. Habits and practices in the fields of health and eHealth have indeed changed substantially, and are continuing to do so.

Practices: New ways of working and other challenges

eHealth is driven forward by policies developed by people with real vision and insight; these stakeholders have important and meaningful roles to play. At the same time as they gaze forward into the future, they undergo real changes in their day-to-day experiences in many spheres of the society and economy around the globe. This section of the book concentrates on organisational, professional and work practices. It looks not only at how such principles and practices are being modified today, but also how more far-sighted technologies – those used in drug discovery and development, for example, and in personalised medicine – will change in the future. Eight chapters examine several different aspects of practice, and the variety of practices that are posed to individuals and institutions working in the eHealth field.

In the first chapter of this section of the book, Nick Goodwin and Albert Alonso make it clear that co-ordinated – integrated – care is an important component in any vision of sustainable, effective healthcare. After describing the considerable challenges in modelling such a complex entity, they outline the characteristics of an effective integrated care service. They then describe how ICT can support integrated care by improving communication, enabling information and knowledge to be shared, and supporting the self-management of long-term conditions. They suggest that the wider adoption of integrated care and its associated technologies requires a larger number of example cases than exists today – which have been comprehensively evaluated and judged successful. There is every reason to believe that the integrated care landscape is changing so as to promote increased change and innovation – given, for example, the launch of a large-scale pilot in this field in March 2013 (http://ec.europa.eu/information_society/apps/projects/factsheet/index.cfm?project_ref=325158).

The importance of communication and data sharing is echoed in the second chapter of this section, where Dipak Kalra and his colleagues look at person-centred care. The authors discuss the increasing level of involvement of individuals in the management of their own health, particularly in the context of chronic diseases. They examine how ICT can support the effective functioning of the Chronic Care Model to create an effective health management programme. Furthermore, ICT can accommodate the transition from self-care to integrated care, and maintain the expertise and involvement of health and social care professionals. Using a future-oriented scenario, the authors identify a set of key enablers for person-centred care, and they broaden the concept into one that engages patients as co-producers of their health. In conclusion, the chapter addresses the challenges that abound in scaling up those ICT solutions that support person-centred care.

Hospitals too are key institutions for healthcare. The use of eHealth both within and among hospitals, in conjunction with the wider health and care communities, is crucial. A leading academic and two health sector executives have co-authored the third chapter in this section of the book. They examine IT use in two specific hospitals: the Hospital Clínic, Barcelona, and the Hôpitaux Universitaires, Geneva. They provide examples of how highly integrated IT systems can be introduced into such institutions. These kinds of establishments, as well as healthcare providers, provide critical leadership in the introduction, implementation and expansion of eHealth. To achieve the full potential of IT, sound IT governance is paramount. Whereas this chapter examines practice at the level of hospitals, managing eHealth can also be a regional, national and international exercise.

Comparing and contrasting international systems is always a fascinating exercise. Electronic health record systems have now shifted in the United States of America to become a central pillar in national health policy, argues Don Detmer. His chapter examines how this transition in policy, technology and practice has emerged, and he reviews a number of health domains including care, research and education. He discusses future prospects and challenges, and even how to coordinate these efforts around the world. It is for this reason that current European–North American collaboration (USHHS–EC, 2010) is to be welcomed, a notion that has been emphasised in another setting in this volume by Jean Roberts.

eHealth is of increasing importance to the pharmaceutical industry: it offers considerable opportunities for the enhancement of clinical research. In Chapter 18, Mats Sundgren describes the way in which networked electronic health records can facilitate tremendous progress by various research platforms, especially in the field of drug discovery and drug development. Thanks to IT, by making such detailed information as phenotypes and individual or group genetic data available, medical treatments are becoming ever more personalised.

The fifth chapter of this section concentrates on the role that mobile technologies play in health. Patricia Mechael and colleagues are from the mHealth Alliance, which is hosted by the United Nations Foundation. They write of how mobile telephony is reshaping health, especially in terms of the possibilities that mHealth has to offer the developing world. Indeed, mHealth is particularly suited to strengthening the communication and information opportunities offered by eHealth. Its communications, mobility and widespread coverage ensure it can affect the health experiences of many members of the general population. Mechael et al. offer numerous examples of how mobile technologies operate in contemporary societies, with their focus on the emerging economies. They then recommend how to realise the full potential of mHealth.

For over ten years now, the personalisation, prediction and optimisation of treatments have been a major preoccupation in the European health field, as

Vanessa Díaz-Zuccarini and colleagues discuss. The focus has been especially on the side of clinical research. The European Virtual Physiological Human (VPH) initiative has proven to be a considerable success since its inspired early days. Today, the Digital Patient initiative is just one example of the contribution made by VPH to individualised, patient-centred medicine. Developed by researchers – in conjunction with a much wider range of stakeholders – the Digital Patient roadmap details how progress in physiological modelling could improve healthcare and lifestyle interventions and their quality and accuracy. It is now possible to foresee how advanced technologies can offer tremendous improvements to patients' health and the effectiveness of clinical teams.

Until a decade ago, evaluations of eHealth implementations were restricted in their handling of economic or financial issues: few assessments, for example, included either cost data or examined costs or benefits over time. However, since the launch of the first eHealth Impact (eHI) study in 2002, more than 50 economic evaluations on both good and weak economic performances have used the methodology that was the result of that study. Not only have these evaluations provided important and meaningful data, they also identify clearly which risks it is important to bear in mind when trying to make realistic deployment decisions in the eHealth field. Tom Jones identifies how the concept of socio-economic return now informs many decisions on eHealth investment in quality, access and efficiency, and is likely to expand its influence even further. Having such an important and sobering tool as eHI is particularly useful in a period of continuing socio-economic challenges. It is able to support decision-making about which technologies to commission, how to procure eHealth, with which stakeholders to work and how long it will take to achieve sensible expectations.

At the same time as one looks forward, it is always important therefore to maintain a steady realism about the present and the near future. A decade ago, mentioning money in the same breath as healthcare was often considered quasi-sacrilegious: yet, Jean-Claude Healy was not afraid of stepping into such contested ground. For this reason, the focus of the book's final chapter is on not only access to and quality of health and care, but also the practical axis of its efficiency and effectiveness: its economy.

The eHealth landscape is fast moving, at the same time as it faces certain barriers. At least two chapters in this final section of the book on practices are remarkably complementary insofar as they examine fields – drug discovery/development and the Virtual Physiological Human (VPH) – which have been under development for at least a decade, and yet which continue to promise great hopes for the longer-term future.

Taking an extensive timeline into the future has always been a wise move. In the period of 2003–2005, Jean-Claude Healy encouraged much crystal ball-gazing among Europeans, in the fields of research, telecommunications policy and health-related deployment. He hypothesised, at this early stage of reflection, that many eHealth and health-related innovations took on average some 17 years to come to fruition. It is, therefore, both fascinating and fun to examine certain longer-term visions and trends of the future. A quick foresight-oriented scan is taken of some recent insights into where the next stages of health and care may head.

Looking towards the future

It is important to offer a flavour of what possible futures might affect the health and social care systems of Europe whether we are talking about 2020, 2030, or indeed 2050. Certainly, it is important to look beyond 2020 (http://ec.europa.eu/digital-agenda/en/digital-futures). For this, it is important to draw on views emerging not only from Europe but also worldwide.

Today, many forms of academic and policy literature about healthcare focus on healthcare systems and organisations rather than on their underpinning technologies. In the mid-2000s, Michael E. Porter and Elizabeth Teisberg (2006), and Clayton Christensen and colleagues (2009), concentrated on the notion of the United States' (US) healthcare system in crisis and the need for major reform. These views were clearly being developed in parallel to expectations of policy- and regulation-related reform.

The first of these two books, *Redefining Health Care*, outlined a framework for redefining healthcare competition based on patient value. It offered a number of recommendations for hospitals, doctors, health plans, employers and policy-makers. To quote its publishing house, it suggested a "move to a positive-sum competition that will unleash stunning improvements in quality and efficiency." The second book built on Christensen's earlier groundbreaking insights into the nature of disruptive innovation (1997). Yet it was oriented, more specifically, towards patient works and personalised care combined with new business models and the reform of health insurance and other regulations. Somewhat more soberly, in 2012, Henry Mintzberg (Mintzberg, 2012) was keen to dispel many of the myths that surround healthcare and its management. He particularly critiqued the notions of "detached" social engineering, heroic leadership and healthcare as a business. Rather, he was inclined to "reframe" the healthcare sector. As a result, he explored approaches related to distributed management, bottom-up strategies, collaboration, care and a holistic, systems-based approach. Here, the message is clearly about process with a social orientation. Overall, Mintzberg made a compelling case for both healthcare institutions and authorities to "make their case for scale on social grounds" (2012, p. 7).

In the policy field, many countries and their institutions have examined what the future may bring in the health and care domains. At least among

Organisation for Economic Co-operation and Development (OECD) countries, given their socio-economic similarities, many of their analyses share resemblances. The focus is on changing demographics, particularly in relation to older adults; difficult economic circumstances; and increasing autonomy of patients combined with the availability of easy-to-use technologies. Even in countries which still have the experience of expanding youthful demographics, such as in Africa or Latin America, the three latter factors remain startlingly similar.

Just two of the more well-publicised examples are Australia and the United Kingdom, specifically England. In the first case, Australia concentrated on care for older adults; mental health; performance standards; primary, secondary and tertiary care; prevention; reform; stakeholder engagement; and the workforce. In the second case, England's National Health Service (NHS) Future Forum was set up as an independent group to "pause, listen and reflect" on the content of the country's Health and Social Care Bill, and to make a series of recommendations on the future modernisation of the country's health system (Field, 2011). The four key themes that the report highlights are all important: choice and competition, patient involvement and public accountability, clinical advice and leadership, and education and training (the report did not, however, focus on IT specifically). The King's Fund and Nuffield Trust came together to respond to the work of the forum. With their commitment well and truly anchored to the notion of integrated care, Goodwin and colleagues (2012) avow that: "The prize to be won is a health and social care system centred on the needs of individuals and patients and delivering the best possible outcomes." As we have seen earlier, this degree of insight into health and care over the next five- to ten-year period, and beyond, is crucial also for the European Union and its individual Member States.

Some researchers and policy-makers take a very specifically technological orientation. Eric Topol is just one example. A top US cardiologist, he claims in his latest book (2012) that, as yet, "the digital world has hardly pierced the medical cocoon". He cites examples for the potential of transformative technologies that include wireless health devices, miniaturisation, social networks and cloud computing, the personalisation of healthcare with its focus on the importance of genomics: all of which can help head towards "precision therapy". As one of America's eminent voices on the digital revolution in medicine, and a leading light in several medical institutes, he argues that although important innovations are close at hand, for radical transformations to take place in the democratisation of medical care this has to be demanded by consumers.

What is clear, above all, from these trends and from this volume of insightful essays, is that people and technology are going to continue to operate together in their own unique format, each influencing the other. Health and care, alongside many other spheres of social engagement, are influenced by this continuing degree of interaction. The 2014 focus on collaboration, co-operation, co-design and co-production is likely to set the scene for health and care in the future. As health and care move towards greater degrees of integration, we can expect that policies, people and practices will each in their own right – and together in combination – influence, via eHealth, the quality, accessibility and the economy of health and health systems.

References

Australian Government (2010), *A National Health and Hospitals Network for Australia's Future. Delivering the Reforms.* Barton AT 2600: Commonwealth of Australia.

Christensen, C.M. (1997), *The Innovator's Dilemma: When New Technologies Cause Great Firms to Fail.* Boston, MA: Harvard Business School Press.

Christensen, C.M., Grossman, J.H. and Hwang, J. (2009), *The Innovator's Prescription: A Disruptive Solution for Health Care.* New York: McGraw-Hill.

Ebels, P. (2012), Putting the "e" in e-health. eu*observer*.com 07.03.12 http://euobserver.com/e-health/115436. [Accessed 15 December 2013].

eHealth Task Force (2012), *Redesigning Health in Europe for 2020.* Luxembourg: Publications Office of the European Union.

EHTEL (2009), Moving eHealth beyond the "e" – EHTEL celebrates its 10th anniversary and looks ahead. *Navigator* VII (1): 1. http://www.ehtel.eu/publications/navigator/anniversary-navigator-february-2009. [Accessed 15 December 2013].

European Commission (2004), *e-Health – Making Healthcare Better for European Citizens: An Action Plan for a European e-Health area.* COM 356 final Luxembourg: European Commission.

European Commission (2007), eHealth Task Force Report 2007. European Lead Market Initiative for Europe: Brussels.

European Commission (2011a), *eHealth Action Plan 2012–2020 – Innovative Healthcare for the 21st Century.* Brussels: European Commission.

European Commission (2011b), Directive 2011/24/EU of the European Parliament and of the Council of 9 March 2011 on the application of patients' rights in cross-border healthcare. In: Official Journal of the European Union, Brussels.

European Commission (2013), *Investing in European Success. Horizon 2020. Research and Innovation to boost Growth and jobs in Europe.* Brussels: European Union.

Field, S. (2011), *NHS Future Forum. Summary Report on Proposed Changes to the NHS.* Department of Health, England. https://www.gov.uk/government/publications/nhs-future-forum-recommendations-to-government-on-nhs-modernisation. [Accessed 15 December 2013].

George, C., Whitehouse, D. and Duquenoy, P. (2012), "Assessing legal, ethical and governance challenges in eHealth", in George, C., Whitehouse, D. and Duquenoy, P. (eds) *eHealth: Legal, Ethical and Governance Challenges.* Springer-Verlag: Heidelberg and Berlin.

Goodwin, N. (2013), "Understanding integrated care: a complex process, a fundamental principle", *International Journal of Integrated Care* 13: e011.

Goodwin, N., Smith, J., Davies, A., Perry, C., Rosen, R., Dixon, A., Dixon, J. and Ham, C. (2012), *Integrated Care for Patients and Populations: Improving Outcomes by Working Together.* Report to the Department of Health and NHS Future Forum from The King's Fund and Nuffield Trust. London.

Loeffler, E., Power, G., Bovaird, T. and Hine-Hughes, F. (2013), (eds) *Co-production of Health and Wellbeing in Scotland*. Governance International: Birmingham.

Mintzberg, H. (2012), "Managing the myths of health care", *World Hospitals and Health Services* 48 (3): 4–7.

Porter, M.E. and Teisberg, E.O. (2006), *Redefining Health Care: Creating Value-Based Competition on Results*. Boston, MA: Harvard Business School Press.

Topol, E.J. (2012), *The Creative Destruction of Medicine: How the Digital Revolution Will Create Better Health Care*. New York: Basic Books.

USHHS–EC (2010), *Memorandum of Understanding between The United States Department of Health and Human Services and The European Commission on Cooperation Surrounding Health Related Information and Communication Technologies*, http://www.healthit.gov/sites/default/files/HHS_EC_MOU_CooperationHealthInfo_and_ComTechSigned.pdf. [Accessed 15 December 2013].

Whitehouse, D. and Duquenoy, P. (2009), "Applied ethics and eHealth: principles, identity, and RFID", in Matyáš, V. et al. (eds) *IFIP AICT 298*. Laxenburg, Austria: IFIP Press, pp. 43–55.

Whitehouse, D. and Duquenoy, P. (2010), "eHealth and ethics: theory, teaching, and practice", in Mirijamdotter, A. and Haftor, D. (eds) *Information and Communication Technologies, Society and Human Beings: Theory and Framework. Honouring Professor Gunilla Bradley*. Hershey, PA: IGI Global, pp. 454–465.

Part I

Politics – Policy and Institutions

2
On the Creation of AIM and Its First Six Years

Niels Rossing

Introduction

Medical informatics arose as a discipline in the mid-1960s, about 20 years before the European Commission launched its first research and technical development programme in the area, the Advanced Informatics in Medicine (AIM) in 1988. This chapter is a personal account of the first years of that research programme, during which the author was a member of the European Commission administration. The philosophy underpinning the field has remained almost unaltered since that time: medical informatics will improve and facilitate healthcare and develop sustainable products through a close collaboration between academia and industry. By 1994, the AIM community of stakeholders was a reality. Its leadership was handed over to Dr Jean-Claude Healy, who went on to drive its growth until he joined the World Health Organization (WHO) in 2004. The programme has grown steadily larger and stronger over the years: it has established some very visible landmarks along its path, and has been of great inspiration to both the European Member States and WHO.

The birth of medical informatics

In 1962, Professor Francois Grémy of Montpellier, France, coined the term "medical informatics". Thus, the potential of digital computing was recognised in the academic arena as an appropriate support for clinical and research work. However, its widespread use in daily healthcare practice was still one or two decades away: technical diagnostic specialities, such as radiology and clinical pathology, often acted as the gateways to recognition. By 1967, the time was ripe to create the forerunner of the International Medical Informatics Association (IMIA), which started as a technical committee of the International Federation for Information Processing. Professor Grémy became its first president. He also co-authored a very early report in the field called "Education in Informatics for

Health Personnel" in 1974. University institutes of medical informatics then appeared gradually during the 1970s and 1980s as medical informatics became an academic discipline in its own right. A complete patient-centred hospital information system was established by Jean-Raoul Scherrer already in the 1970s in Geneva, Switzerland. The European Federation of Medical Informatics (EFMI) was founded in 1976 after a meeting of national medical informaticians under the auspices of the World Health Organization (WHO). Another of the many pioneers in the field, Peter Reichertz of Hannover, Germany, became EFMI's first president.

Medical informatics becomes a programme of the European Commission

The potential of medical informatics for industry was first identified by the European Commission as early as 1985. In that year, a planning exercise was launched called the "Bio-Informatics Collaborative European Programme and Strategy". European medical informaticians and industrial representatives met under the auspices of Directorate General XIII (DGXIII), which then stood for Telecommunications, Information Market and Exploitation of Research.

On the Commission's side, the director was then in charge of the large Programme for Research and Development in Communication Technologies (RACE), and was interested in creating meaningful use of these new tools and a market for them. RACE ran parallel to the European Strategic Programme for Research and Development in Information Technologies (ESPRIT). A work plan for an EU feasibility programme – later to be named Advanced Informatics in Medicine (AIM) – was drafted and presented to Member States' experts in 1987. These experts, many meeting for the first time, had very different backgrounds: some had "local research council-induced scepticism" in their briefcases (myself included); others greeted the news with great enthusiasm. Few were researchers; all were affiliated in one way or another with their national ministry. Today one should excuse the scepticism and partial ignorance among the experts present because, on a small scale, the whole project was felt to be as adventurous as bringing a man to the moon!

On the first day, the group members met officially for work in Brussels with representatives of the Commission and were asked to elect a chairman and to go to work. The Commission staff then left the room, declaring they would return in a few hours. When they returned, we had of course not chosen a chairman, so the lead Commission official briskly stated that – as Denmark held the presidency of the Union at that moment – the Dane, Niels Rossing, would be the chairman.

After a series of meetings by the group over about half a year, the work plan for the AIM feasibility programme was put before the Council of Ministers.

It was adopted on 4 November 1988 as a part of the 2nd RTD Framework Programme, and ran for a two-year period with a budget of €20 million. This Exploratory Action was followed up in July 1991, as part of the 3rd RTD Framework Programme, with a community contribution worth €111 million.

In 1988, I was fortunate to be invited to join the Commission as head of unit to be in charge of AIM. I worked from the beginning with a few trained project officers (such as Gerald Santucci and Jesus Villasante), who were soon to be supplemented with some newcomers recruited either as *fonctionnaires* or as *experts nationaux detachés* (their names include Jaap Nothoven van Goor, Bill Baig, Mike Wilson and Jacques Lacombe). As the programme was consolidated, others joined from Denmark, Germany, Italy, Portugal and the United Kingdom. From France, as a national expert on a part-time basis, came the professor of physiology from St Etienne, Jean-Claude Healy. He was later to succeed me from 1994 onwards, and with great success. Another extraordinary person to join the team when the programme was in its second term, with a budget of €80 million for the four years of the 3rd Framework Programme, was the Greek, Ilias Iakovidis, who flew in from Canada, and who was later to go on to become Jean-Claude's deputy for many years before leading another unit.

What the AIM programme was about

Over my six years of work with the Commission, a number of development lines were pursued. The mantra was always: the relevant data should be stored safely, retrievable as uncorrupted information, and made available for the authorised health personnel and interested citizen, irrespective of time and place. Already from the beginning, a fight against isolated information silos was announced. The ultimate purposes were, and still are:

- Seamless and continuous care irrespective of speciality and health sector;
- Improved diagnostics (for example, pathology and medical images);
- Standardisation (a special committee, CEN 251, was established);
- Decision support;
- Support to medical research and education;
- Support to public health and related statistics;
- Empowerment of the patient in his/her local community;
- Minimum basic data sets.

Modelling was a key word for many project proposers, and so too were artificial intelligence, compatibility, interoperability, modularity and scalability. Data security was acknowledged and gradually became a major issue. The electronic patient record was tried out. New storage media, notably the smart card, was thought by some to be *the* panacea for healthcare; picture archiving and communication systems were invented, explored and marketed; the increasing bandwidth of broadband fibres was exploited by some cities for healthcare purposes. At the same time, AIM's mother programme, RACE, was propagating "fibres to the homes" and standardised communications according to the United Nations-agreed Electronic Data Interchange for Administration, Commerce and Transport (EDIFACT). This was piloted successfully in two communities in the Netherlands (Breda and Appeldorn) by Jan van Bemmel, and was later used as the key element in the Danish health communication system.

Programme organisation: Call for proposals, funding, and follow-up

The calls for proposals to the programme were normally for consortia that consisted of partners from at least two Member States and one partner from industry. Small- and medium-sized enterprises were encouraged to join the consortia. They were considered more flexible than large companies. Also, academic institutions could be partners. Usually 50 per cent of the accepted budget would be financed by the Commission. About 10 per cent of the applications for funding were successful, but even they would rarely receive the full amount of financing for which they had applied.

The procedures around selection of projects and consortia to be financed were already established in an extremely professional and successful manner, literally locking up evaluators in their hotels for a week or two to avoid any suspicion of wrongdoing. The final selection and the funding allocated had to be approved by a committee of national experts and chaired by the Commission. A certain element of horse-trading could take place at such meetings, but always in an open atmosphere. The performance over time of the chosen projects and the behaviour of the Commission were followed regularly by the same group of national "watch dogs".

The projects' deliverables were scrutinised by the Commission's services via the allocated project officers, and "*concertation* meetings", with the presence of many project participants, were held regularly in an effort to secure a certain coherence between projects within the same action line. A hotel at Place Rogier in Brussels was the usual venue for many of these events. And no doubt both the hotel and Brussels' "City 2" shopping centre (which was nearby) thrived from these events.

An annual technical review for all projects took place for their progress to be presented to a fairly large group of independent evaluators. That process was also formalised and, fortunately, had strict rules. A few consortia performed poorly. Then, a "red flag" procedure would start. It involved scrutiny of the project's progress (by highly specialised evaluators who often suggested drastic changes or an end to the project).

The AIM community

The consortia consolidated, and grew in number and participants. The industrial partners included both small- and medium-sized enterprises and large information and communication technology (ICT) companies. In those days, the number of large supranational European ICT companies shrank from 12 to 7, called "The Seven Sisters". They were under heavy pressure from companies on other continents. Therefore, one purpose for the Commission was, and still is, to pave the way for industries and stimulate the market, adding value to innovative industrial solutions.

The necessary industrial footprint was not always fully appreciated by projects' academic partners. They would sometimes claim that the existence of a European Union Research and Technical Development (RTD) programme would act as an alibi for their home administrations to cut their local educational budget, and that they therefore needed all the funding. However, usually it was quite easy to encourage them to see the benefit of developing a commercial exploitation from their brain work.

The Commission's services had to adhere to clear rules in a didactic manner vis-à-vis the consortia's pursuit of funding. We repeated over and over again the principle of subsidiarity, that is, the principle that "you do back at home what should be done there, and you leave Brussels to finance what comes above that." Many people claimed they did not understand this papal vocabulary, but in their hearts, they did.

Some of the many eminent academics I remember were Ab Bakker and Jan van Bemmel from the Netherlands; Francis Roger France and Georges de Moor from Belgium; David Ingram, Allan Rector, Colin Gordon and Mike Bainbridge from the United Kingdom; Stelios Orphanoudakis and Nico Palikarakis, Greece; Angelo Rossi Mori and Marcello Bracale, Italy; Otto Rienhoff and Karl Sauter, Germany; Joan Guyanabens, Spain; Roger O'Moore and Jane Grimson, Ireland; Hans Peterson, Sweden; Jytte Brender and Peter McNair, Denmark, and the team of health informaticians from Aveiro University, Portugal. By 1992, the number of individuals directly or indirectly involved across Europe via the Commission's programme was very large. The term "The AIM Community" was coined, and its membership actually extended to certain branches of the United States administration, as well as to Canada, Japan and Latin America.

The programme, which during the period I was in Brussels changed its name to "Health Telematics", thrived alongside other programmes like RACE and ESPRIT, the Standardisation Unit of the Commission, as well as in collaboration with other directorates, such as the ones dealing with health and consumer issues, and social affairs. WHO was also involved from an early point in time.

Handing over the reins and looking back

During my whole period in Brussels, I had been on leave from my position in Denmark. I was kindly asked to return in 1994, which I did after three months of contemplation.

My successor as head of unit, Jean-Claude Healy, had up until my departure only been employed part-time in the unit, which now had 10–12 project officers. He was project officer for relatively few projects, but had a formidable ability to create new networks, and to explore and exploit ideas and thoughts from other scientific and philosophical domains and make them work in what was to become eHealth. He established relations with the diplomatic corps in Brussels and with WHO in Geneva. So, when he finally took the job, I felt it to be in good and yet different, hands. His subsequent career and success fully justified that assessment.

I am sure that Jean-Claude had many fine moments while in office in Brussels. Yet the one I personally attended was when he worked for WHO in Geneva after having left the Commission. There he worked full-heartedly for what had then become eHealth. The moment was in 2005, in Tromsö, at the annual Norwegian Telemedicine Conference. Jean-Claude jumped to the podium with a big smile on his face exclaiming: "HABEMUS" – "WE HAVE IT". What we had was his masterpiece: Resolution 58.28 of the World Health Assembly, 2005, adopted unanimously. It urged WHO Member States to take initiatives to promote eHealth, and requested WHO to promote international collaboration and provide more electronic information and technical support to its Member States.

Bearing that moment in mind, I sincerely feel that the European Union activities in the eHealth domain have been fruitful and have delivered more than could be hoped for when, in 1987/1988, we set out to "put a man on the Moon". Things do not move fast. We have to remember Jean-Claude's own learning, namely, that it takes 17–20 years from the moment humans have invented something useful until it comes to full use for the benefit of humankind. I feel that statement to be justified because, until recently, I have had the good fortune to still follow, participate in, and benefit from European Union-supported activities, but from the other side of the table.

To me, the European Union Action Plan for eHealth from 2004 (European Commission (2004) and the European large-scale pilot project on transborder interoperability in eHealth (epSOS, 2013) are ongoing beacons on that long journey.

References

epSOS (2013), The European eHealth Project. http://www.epsos.eu. [Accessed 8 April 2013].

European Commission (2004), COM (2004) 356 final, *e-Health – Making Healthcare Better for European Citizens: An Action Plan for a European e-Health Area*. Brussels: European Commission. 30.4.2044. http://eur-lex.europa.eu/LexUriServ/LexUriServ.do?uri=COM:2004:0356:FIN:EN:PDF. [Accessed 8 April 2013].

3
European eHealth Agenda, 1990–2010

Ilias Iakovidis

Introduction

The European Commission has been supporting eHealth research and development (R&D) through Framework Programmes since 1989, for almost a quarter century at the time of writing this chapter, and has contributed to the emergence of new generations of technologies in several fields of healthcare. Policy instruments have been introduced by the European Commission at European Union (EU) level to support innovation and faster deployment of eHealth moving towards more person-centred and more sustainable health services. In particular, an enhanced and focused cooperation among the European Commission, European Union Member States and other countries, together with the relevant stakeholders, has been pursued since 2004 to ensure awareness and effective deployment of eHealth solutions. These research programmes and policy activities, along with the various national eHealth research, innovation and deployment activities, have put many Member States in a leading position with respect to the deployment of eHealth and the harnessing of the corresponding benefits. This success in EU investment is analysed in this chapter through three different activities: various phases in research and development; policy support to deployment; and cooperation among the different main stakeholders.

Research and deployment: Preparing for future generations of technologies

For almost a quarter of a century, the European Commission has supported more than 500 collaborative R&D projects in eHealth through a community financial contribution of over 1 billion. The overall aim has been to prepare future European generations of technologies that will be of use to Europe's health systems (and, in recent years, care systems). Whereas eHealth-related research was supported mainly by the European Commission's eHealth Unit, there have been other units, such as Future and Emerging Technologies, Micro and Nano-systems of the then Information Society Directorate General (DG),[1] which supported specific aspects of eHealth. This €1 billion worth of financial support does not include two other aspects of assistance given to the field by the European Commission (the significant funding to biomedical technologies under past BIOMED programmes and subsequent support to medical technologies funded by DG Research (Iakovidis, 2007), and the latest initiatives of DG Health and Consumer Protection).

Broadly, three phases of support can be distinguished: the early years, 1988–1993; the period 1993–1999 with its emphasis on networks and electronic health records; and the last period, which ran up to 2010 and focused on tools for patients and information and communication technology (ICT) for predictive medicine.

Early years: Tools for health professionals – making health delivery systems more efficient

The potential of what was then referred to as the health telematics industry was first identified by the European Community as early as 1985, when a planning exercise called the "Bio-Informatics Collaborative European Programme and Strategy" was launched. This early stage of the programme concentrated on the development of information and communication technology (ICT) tools useful to health professionals, with a view to making health delivery systems more efficient and effective. An Exploratory Action was adopted by the Council of Ministers on 4 November 1988 with a community financial contribution worth €20 million. This Exploratory Action was followed in July 1991 by the "Advanced Informatics in Medicine" programme, with a community contribution that was more than five times as large – €111 million.

Today, similar notions of capacity building through trials of smaller-scale initiatives before the implementation of large-scale approaches remain a common operating method in the EU.

1993–1999: Connectivity and health information networks

Building on this foundation, European Commission R&D projects during the 1990s focused mainly on the development of electronic health record solutions. They concentrated on the connectivity among all the points of care of a health delivery system at regional and national levels. The aim was to enable infrastructures that could allow fast access to vital information and sharing of information among health professionals to improve quality and efficiency of care, as well as make care more accessible to patients. The results of the R&D in electronic health records carried out during the Third and Fourth R&D Framework Programmes (http://cordis.europa.eu/ist/ist-fp4.htm) can be seen today in many European countries, regions and hospitals. Key examples from European countries and regions include MEDCOM, the Danish health network whose stated objective it is to "support efficient performance and a gradual expansion of the national eHealth infrastructure," and TicSalut in Catalonia in Spain, which remains heavily engaged in advancing the use of technology. At hospital level, the COHERENCE system of the Georges Pompidou hospital in Paris won the eEurope for eHealth Award (http://www.epractice.eu/ehealth2003) in 2003; the work of Geneva's University Hospital in Switzerland is also highly influential and noteworthy.

Currently, many countries cooperate in making their systems interoperable to support patient mobility and to create a single European eHealth market (for example, via the epSOS and Calliope projects: http://www.epsos.eu; www.calliope-network.eu).

1999–2010: Tools for patients – improving engagement and personalisation of healthcare

Following the initial focus on infrastructure for health professionals, activities over the first decade of this century have focused more on an intelligent patient-centred environment that supports personalised healthcare (and an environment with ambient intelligence for patients). Wearable, portable and implantable personal health solutions have been developed to provide better information regarding a person's health status directly to patients and health professionals. These systems support health monitoring (homecare), chronic disease management and disease prevention.

Building on previous achievements under the Sixth and Seventh R&D Framework Programmes (ec.europa.eu/research/fp6/; ec.europa.eu/research/fp7), many integrated projects have shown the benefits of patient-centred care on a larger scale. These projects have covered the whole system of patient monitoring either at home or on the move – from medical sensors to intelligent processing of bio-signals, alerts and medical (tele)services. Another project area has looked at the use of ICT to prevent medical errors in prescribing drugs and in optimising decision-making for treatments (http://ec.europa.eu/information_society/ehealth).

Recent large-scale pilots, such as the Renewing Health project, have been funded by the Competitiveness and Innovation Programme (CIP). This pilot started in the spring of 2010 (http://ec.europa.eu/information_society/activities/health/cip_ict_psp/index_en.htm) and was aimed at deploying and assessing the effectiveness of telemedicine services based on the outputs of previous R&D activities.

The long-term view: ICT for predictive medicine – towards the virtual physiological human

The convergence of ICT, biomedical sciences and nanotechnologies, as well as synergies among information technology (IT) fields, such as medical informatics, bioinformatics and neuro-informatics (biomedical informatics), and their impact on medicine, have been recognised and promoted by the European Commission since 2001 (http://bioinfomed.isciii.es; www.symbiomatics.org). The International Physiome project provided the basis for launching a new initiative in 2005 – the Virtual Physiological Human (VPH). The VPH concept and R&D roadmap was published by the European Commission co-financed project called STEP (www.europhysiome.org). Some insights from the VPH project are further discussed in Chapter 19.

Patient-specific models will be developed to assist in safer medical operations, development of personalised treatments and safer drugs. As a result, knowledge of physiology and diseases will be integrated from the level of molecule and cell to the levels of organs and systems. VPH is intended to constitute a global scaffold of medical knowledge and a toolbox for researchers. There is provision in the VPH Network of Excellence (http://www.vph-noe.eu/), which started in 2010, to coordinate work in this area on an international level. (http://www.biomedtown.org/town/biomed_town/VPH/petitions/institute/).

Policy support to deployment (2003–2010)

The research results of the early years of the European eHealth agenda gave rise, from 2003 onwards, to the first policy and deployment efforts at regional and national levels. This triggered the involvement of the European Commission in supporting policy development and larger-scale deployment. It included the start of the series of annual eHealth Ministerial conferences. It became clear that policy initiatives and high-level engagement of authorities, combined with the clear commitment of professionals and industry, were all necessary to overcome the barriers to the deployment of eHealth solutions.

Since 2004, the European Commission has played a leading role in policy support to eHealth deployment. In that year, it adopted the eHealth Action Plan with the aim of facilitating a more harmonious and complementary European approach to eHealth. Through this approach, health authorities and stakeholders began to work together closely to improve the provision of healthcare to European citizens. The 2004 eHealth Action Plan provided a tool to promote core ideas; organise *fora* for discussion; raise awareness of the importance of eHealth among users, patients and health care professionals and foster collaboration among industry players by addressing technical issues, interoperability and benchmarking.

The emerging political cooperation among Member States and with stakeholders led to cooperation on the implementation and deployment of interoperable eHealth systems. The large-scale pilot project epSOS (www.epsos.eu) was the first example of such massive cooperation.

More specific policy support followed in the period up until 2010, namely:

- The **Recommendation on Cross-border Interoperability of Electronic Health Record Systems** (COM, 2008a), was based on the premise that connecting people, systems and services is vital for the provision of good healthcare in Europe. It defines actions at four levels: political; organisational; technical and semantic. It also addresses issues relevant to monitoring, evaluation and raising awareness.
- The **Communication on Telemedicine for the Benefit of Patients, Healthcare Systems and Society** (COM, 2008b) proposed actions for supporting and improving access to telemedicine for EU citizens and healthcare professionals across Europe. This initiative aimed to:
  - increase confidence and acceptance of telemedicine services among users by encouraging the provision and dissemination of scientific evidence of its effectiveness and cost benefits;
  - bring legal clarity on existing EU legislation regarding telemedicine services and encourage Member States to improve the provision of telemedicine services; and
  - solve technical problems such as the lack of an adequate community-wide broadband infrastructure and the interoperability of telemedicine devices.
- The **eHealth Lead Market Initiative**, launched in 2007, was part of a Commission Communication (COM, 2007) and policy support programme to accelerate market development by removing barriers such as market fragmentation, lack of legal clarity and funding issues. A three-year eHealth-related action plan focused on lead markets aimed at:
  - reducing market fragmentation and lack of interoperability through standardisation, certification and CIP-funded pilots;
  - improving legal certainty and consumer acceptance by disseminating information, best practice and guidelines; and
  - facilitating access to funding through training workshops, improved cooperation and guidance on financing and procurement.
- The **Digital Agenda for Europe** (http://ec.europa.eu/digital-agenda/), started in 2010, has placed an emphasis on scaling up the interoperability and deployment of telemedicine services to enable a single market in eHealth and to provide patients with direct and secure online access to their health data.

Cooperation among the European Commission Member States and other stakeholders, and the link with European eHealth governance

The European Commission, Member States, industry and users together have contributed to a deployment strategy for eHealth. By coordinating their efforts, they developed an attitude of trust, which led to a better understanding of the existing barriers to deployment and of the ways to remove them. New interaction mechanisms among all these actors are emerging. This has led to the formation of a new eHealth Governance Initiative, which involves all these different stakeholders. The Council Conclusions on eHealth, adopted in 2009, built on the achievements that had been reached to that point, and outlined the conditions of the new cooperation mechanism (http://www.se2009.eu/en/meetings_news/2009/10/22/broad_consensus_at_high-level_meeting_on_ehealth).

- **Political commitment and leadership from professionals and users of eHealth systems were identified as key elements to further deployment of eHealth.** Ultimately, each of these elements is a *conditio sine qua non,* in order for eHealth to benefit patients, healthcare systems and society. By endorsing the first eHealth Action plan of 2004, the Council of the EU recognised the importance of working more closely together to face common opportunities and challenges in bringing benefits to people, health systems and economy from eHealth.

During the first years of operation, such cooperation relied on personal contacts and the commitment of individual civil servants. Personal contacts and commitment are essential to start up any successful business relationship. Often, however, particularly in national administrations, they are insufficient to ensure the longer-term sustainability and scalability of the results that the cooperation may bring to the administration.

With this in mind, the European Commission started a distinct "mechanism of cooperation" among national administrations. The mechanism consisted of large-scale pilots that were supported by the CIP. These large-scale pilots focused their attention on issues related to large-scale deployment, in which national administrations (or regional entities acting on their behalf) worked closely together. The final objective of these large-scale pilots was to achieve the benefits of economies of scale, defragment the market and foster the deployment of interoperable ICT solutions. At the time, eHealth and eGovernment were considered two particular areas in which such an approach could bring important benefits to both society and the market.

- **epSOS: An example of large-scale pilot collaboration.** epSOS was the first large-scale pilot co-funded by the European Commission in the area of eHealth. In 2008, the year of the launch of the project, 12 Ministries of Health (or regional authorities acting on their behalf) signed up to the pilot. In 2010, an additional 13 national administrations applied to join an extension of epSOS (known as epSOS II) and to be formally engaged in the project. In addition to the national administrations, epSOS also involved more than 30 ICT companies, represented by a single beneficiary, and research and/or competence centres that agreed to work together to meet the objective of the pilot. epSOS was based on specific use cases. They were linked to the deployment and validation in real-life settings of interoperable patient summaries and ePrescriptions. The project has also addressed horizontal challenges essential to implement such services, such as identification and authentication of users, legal issues, semantics and nomenclature and standardisation. epSOS set up an infrastructure based on a federation of national contact points to make its services operational. Such solutions were sufficient to enable its interoperability during the lifetime of the pilot. However, at times it has been uncertain what will happen to the infrastructure and the results of the project once the European Commission funding for the initiative ends. The project had to take a number of other, similarly important, decisions which have been necessary to meet its contractual obligations and test the feasibility of its services. To address this issue, the European Commission, in cooperation with the large-scale pilots' representatives, started to examine possible options to ensure the future and the long-term sustainability of these types of projects. Currently, there is an effort underway to join forces with the parallel developments and results from the eGovernment area in order to establish a viable framework for innovative and sustainable public services in EU.

- **High-level representatives of national administrations have agreed to cooperate more closely to create a long-term strategic vision to eHealth.** This type of cooperation is a necessary condition to address the underlying challenges in the deployment of eHealth in Europe and to enable patients and healthcare systems to benefit fully from eHealth solutions. With this objective in mind, during the period 2007–2010, under the leadership of a set of four EU Presidencies (Germany, Czech Republic, Sweden and Spain), the State Secretaries (and/or their equivalent level) decided to work more closely together. Their aim was to set the foundations of a new cooperation mechanism, and to identify the specific areas in which it is urgent for Member States to cooperate more closely or to take collective decisions at the highest possible policy level (see also Giorgio, 2012).

Such cooperation aimed at addressing cross-border interoperability issues. Member States have outlined the need for high-level discussions on the challenges they are facing individually in their countries to deploy eHealth so that lessons can be learned and possible common solutions can be implemented.

This approach is described well by the Council Conclusions on eHealth (Council, 2009) adopted in December 2009. They state that:

> "The Council CALLS UPON Member States and the Commission to:... build upon the political momentum created by the existing informal meetings

of State Secretaries and their equivalents, in order to develop, via the most efficient and suitable Member State led high-level mechanism, the governance, coordination and consolidation of on-going activities in the field of eHealth, in liaison with the European Commission, to bring forward eHealth deployment and actual use of interoperable eHealth services within and between national healthcare systems."

To respond to this call, the European Commission has made available funding to facilitate a European eHealth Governance Initiative. The aims include the scaling up of existing initiatives, dissemination of best practices of EU-funded projects and/or national deployment programmes and awareness of progress at ministerial level.

- **On what issues did the eHealth Governance Initiative decide to work first?** Since the first official meeting in February 2009, the State Secretaries have singled out areas in which cooperation is considered to be of great value. The four areas are identification and authentication; trust and acceptance; legal issues and technical issues, as explained below.
  - *Identification and authentication.* Issues such as the unique user identification and authentication (both patients and professionals), respecting the fundamental human right to privacy, had to be tackled first so as to enable identification across the "border" of healthcare professionals and institutions (such as a hospitals, general practices or pharmacies).
  - *Trust and acceptance.* As a key enabler, these two issues are very much linked to identification and authentication. Trust and acceptance in eHealth systems by patients and professionals is a matter that has to be considered equally important, if not more so, than the relevant technical and organisational challenges that prevent deployment of eHealth.
  - *Legal issues.* eHealth is a relatively new domain. Legal provisions originally not meant for eHealth systems are often applied to them. Major uncertainty remains in specific areas like telemedicine. Although the eHealth situation is partially addressed in national contexts, when specifically looking at European interoperability, there are a number of major outstanding challenges. The large-scale pilot epSOS has provided important findings that may help resolve these challenges. The objective of the eHealth Governance Initiative is to propose possible ways forward that could be implemented within the appropriate institutional framework at European and/or national level, according to the issues concerned.
  - *Technical issues.* Although technology is probably the "easiest" of the several challenges to be addressed, significant solutions still exist that would enable greater interoperability within and across national borders. The main hurdles in this area include the need to build on the legacy

systems of many Member States; to take care of the consequences of any technical decision linked to a specific terminology or standard; to recognise specifically the potential financial implications; and to face the difficulties in using an infrastructure that meets everyone's standards in terms of security, legality and technical feasibility.

Conclusion

The impact of EU involvement and investment on technological development and deployment and on national and European policies during the crucial two decades of 1990–2010 can be summarised in three ways:

- eHealth firmly became part of both national and international health policies. This is shown by the ministerial declarations made under the Swedish and Spanish Presidencies, together with the 2005 World Health Organization commitment to eHealth, which was based on the 2004 EU eHealth Action Plan.
- EU leadership – in raising the potential of eHealth – had significant spillover on the introduction of national eHealth programmes and policies in many Member States. The European Commission facilitated the creation of intergovernmental cooperation and instruments to tackle several important eHealth issues at EU level.
- The role of the European Commission has been key in supporting research and innovation in eHealth in a way that was not possible in many Member States. The EU enjoys a leading role globally with respect to its wide use of eHealth systems and services, due to the consistent and longstanding commitment made by the European Commission. This commitment is very much due to the strong cooperation of all the stakeholders involved. In particular, the cooperation with national and regional authorities has led to solid deployment strategies in innovative technologies to ensure ever-improving and sustainable health services.

eHealth applications and telemedicine services have been shown to improve the quality and efficiency of health services. At the same time, they provide Europeans with economic opportunities, such as jobs, that are being created by the emerging European eHealth industry, as well as innovation and growth. This field is currently estimated to be worth around €15 billion.

The impact of the European Commission over the quarter of a century that it has been supporting projects and developing policy has, of course, been due to many players, including elected politicians at both national and EU levels, Commission officials and their counterparts in national and regional administrations, as well as hundreds of dedicated researchers, industry representatives, users, health professionals and health authorities who have contributed to the spectacular developments in this field. All of these people have contributed to establishing eHealth as a new industrial pillar and as an indispensable tool in the hands of healthcare providers and patients.

The author would like to note that special recognition goes to several dozens of colleagues who, over the years, have dedicated their professional lives to keeping the European Commission in the foreground of these developments. In particular, I would like to recognise Jean-Claude Healy, whose personal dedication and passion gave so much to the field. He was able to build substantially on the foundation built by Niels Rossing, who preceded him as Head of Unit. Jean-Claude's legacy and initiatives were carried forward by his successor Gérard Comyn, who from 2004 to 2010, led the policy developments described here.

The 10 years during which Jean-Claude led the unit were the most crucial in its development and growth. The budget for R&D in eHealth increased fivefold and two main developments took place. First, the renewal of the research agenda introduced the new domain of biomedical informatics. Second, initial steps in EU eHealth policy development were taken, as seen through the eHealth Action Plan and a series of ministerial events. eHealth in Europe owes a great deal to his visionary approach. There is one thing that stands above all and those who worked with him clearly recognise that: his ability to bring the right people to action at the right moment. His legacy is bigger than the ideas and people he left behind. It is firmly embedded in this slowly maturing sector and still continues to guide the initiatives of EU eHealth Agenda.

Notes

The views developed in this chapter are those of the author and do not reflect necessarily the position of the European Commission.

1. DG is now DG CONNECT.

References

COM (2007), "A lead market initiative for Europe", 21 December, COM (2007)860 http://ec.europa.eu/enterprise/leadmarket/leadmarket.htm

COM (2008a), 2 July (Com (2008a) 3282) http://eur-lex.europa.eu/LexUriServ/LexUriServ.do?uri=CELEX:32008H0594:EN:NOT

COM (2008b), 4 November 2008 (COM (2008) 689) http://eur-lex.europa.eu/LexUriServ/LexUriServ.do?uri=COM:2008:0689:FIN:EN:PDF

Council Conclusions on Safe and efficient healthcare through eHealth (2009), http://www.consilium.europa.eu/uedocs/cms_data/docs/pressdata/en/lsa/111613.pdf

Giorgio, F. (2012), "European eHealth Governance Initiative – a new way forward" in George, C., Whitehouse, D. and Duquenoy, P. (eds) *eHealth: Legal, Ethical and Governance Challenges*, Heidelberg: Springer-Verlag, pp. 371–386.

Iakovidis, I, Le Dour, O., Karp, P. (2007), "Biomedical engineering and eHealth in Europe – outcomes and challenges of past and current EU research programs", *IEEE Engineering in Medicine and Biology Magazine* (impact factor: 2.06). 06/2007; DOI:10.1109/MEMB.2007.364925.

4
From Governments to Governance: An Emerging Paradigm in eHealth

Joan Dzenowagis

The information society: A social shift

A decade ago when the first World Summit on the Information Society (WSIS) began its deliberations, the tension between governments, the private sector and civil society was palpable. Never before had the stakeholders come together at the global level to discuss matters central to the development of an equitable Information Society. The vigorous debates and acrimonious negotiations on new processes of inclusion tested participants and the United Nations (UN) system in valuable ways. From those challenging beginnings came the Internet Governance Forum, a second Summit event and, most significantly, a growing demand that governments commit to work meaningfully in a multi-stakeholder model.

While stakeholder consultation has long been a tenet of policy formulation in many governments,[1] such an approach in the context of information and communication technologies for development (ICT4D, as it came to be known) was completely new. The adoption of a multi-stakeholder model in the global information and communication technologies (ICT) policy arena marked an important social shift. Opening up the dialogue to more dynamic, liberal and equity-oriented advocates, such as non-governmental organisations (NGOs) and academic institutions put them on a more equal footing with industry and governments. By the time of the second WSIS event in 2005, the loosely organised "ICT4D community" had evolved into a serious force for change. This evolution has had a profound impact, not only by improving the contribution and credibility of non-state actors, but also by directly influencing the debate on ICT in developing countries.

Dr Jean-Claude Healy, in his role as Senior Adviser at the World Health Organization (WHO), reflected at the time with this author on the societal changes and what they might mean for the future of eHealth.[2] This chapter tells the story of how the context of global ICT development and its values have come to shape the priorities, processes and, to a large extent, the relationships between many of the stakeholders in eHealth, including in developing countries. The conflict and debates in the years leading up to the WSIS process helped to open the doors for more of society to participate in what has increasingly become an interconnected world in eHealth. This chapter looks to the future and reminds us, as Dr Healy noted years ago, of our responsibility to take the broad view. Moving from "governments" to "governance" in eHealth is not an easy task, but it is one that is absolutely necessary to address the challenges ahead.

ICT in the development era

> *From trade to telemedicine, from education to environmental protection, we have in our hands, on our desktops and in the skies above, the ability to improve standards of living for millions upon millions of people.*
>
> Kofi Annan, United Nations Secretary General (Annan, 2003)

With these words, the then UN Secretary General Kofi Annan opened the first World Summit on the Information Society in Geneva in 2003. The 80 heads of state who were present emphasised in their own remarks the vital role of governments in building an Information Society, with ICT at its core. The Summit, or "the WSIS" as it was called, marked a historical shift. It was the beginning of an important push to incorporate ICT into the world's development agenda in a meaningful way.

The central role of ICT in development had first been introduced in the year 2000 in the United Nations Millennium Development Goals. Goal 8, Target 18 encouraged: "In collaboration with the private sector, make available the benefits of technology – especially information and communication technologies" (United Nations). It was a promising start and the excitement was evident, despite – or perhaps due to – the lack of a blueprint as to how to proceed. Action plans were developed and projects were launched, with big announcements, new partnerships and high expectations. However, public-private partnerships, which were heavily promoted but still relatively untested in this realm, were turning out to be to be difficult to manage and fraught with risk. There often proved to be a significant gap between the results anticipated and those achieved. What was promised by the private sector was less than what could realistically be delivered in low-income countries without an environment, enabled by governments, that included essentials such as sustainable financing, capable human resources and relevant regulations and policies. It was a time of experimentation and learning – sometimes costly – lessons for all concerned.

Well before the Millennium Development Goals were agreed, WHO had been interested in the potential for using ICT to advance health goals. Early exploration with eHealth projects was dispersed throughout the Organisation without a shared view on how it should be approached. In the broader community concerned with development, the general view of agencies, donors, governments, and even the private sector, was either that ICT had a limited role in health or that there were other priorities in low-income countries (Helmore et al., 2000). This way of thinking was typically framed as an "either–or" scenario of unacceptable trade-offs in health development objectives, and it was often asserted that new technologies were not appropriate for poor countries and institutions. Advocates on both sides debated the issue with strong opinions and little evidence to back them up.

Fortunately, the inclusion of Target 18, along with an innovative UN–private sector project led by WHO (Smith, 2003), opened the door to making the link between new technologies and their application to global public health. The term "digital divide" was coined, and its measurement shed light on the differences within and between countries. The result was a proliferation of reports, readiness assessments and now-classic projects using ICT to bridge the digital divide (Kuruvilla et al., 2004).

It was at this time that the International Telecommunication Union (ITU) approached the UN agencies to begin to plan the first WSIS event. As the specialised UN agency with a public health mandate, WHO was invited to participate, because health as a social good had the potential to benefit hugely from ICT. Health could also be a driver for ICT growth, as a concrete application of ICT, particularly in developing countries.

The initial organising meetings of the WSIS in 2002 invited the stakeholders in the ICT-development sphere. As members of the ITU,[3] governments and companies were welcome, whereas civil society had to insist on having its own seat at the table. For civil society, the concept of development extended well beyond its economic aspects to include social action, ethical values, human rights and justice. The NGOs also demanded transparency and inclusion. However, the ITU insisted that governments remain in the leading role and that, during certain discussions, non-ITU members excuse themselves from the meeting room. This attitude outraged participants as the request excluded not only civil society organisations but also the other UN agencies. For their part, the UN agencies responded decisively by exiting in protest and complaining loudly to their headquarters. It took months to restore an acceptable (if still provisional) way of working and for negotiations regarding the accreditation of civil society stakeholders to take place. A transparent, inclusive and multistakeholder discussion was not an easy sell in those days.

Of course, old habits are hard to break, and paradigms – whether scientific or political – are harder still. The political economy of ICT does not change merely by pointing out the injustices or their reasons. Following the shaky start, WHO participated fairly cautiously in the first Summit process.[4] Aligned with its sister agencies, the United Nations Population Fund and the Food and Agriculture Organization, WHO attempted to ensure that the development agenda was well served.

In the end, the outcome of the first Summit (held in Geneva, 2003) was better than its unruly start had predicted. The final *WSIS Declaration of Principles and Plan of Action* set out a common vision, a useful way forward and some novel next steps (WSIS, 2003). The numerous and lengthy debates, position papers, drafting sessions and negotiations attested to the divergent perspectives and the multitude of controversial issues that had to be addressed. The action line for eHealth highlighted a range of important challenges and goals, noting the foundations of access to knowledge, capacity development and connectivity for the health sector.

The WSIS process itself represented an inflection point in ways that are still to be fully understood. What was clear, however, was that the process of bridging the interests of rich and poor countries, industry, NGOs, international organisations and other actors in shaping a key global agenda had highlighted the need for ensuring effective governance mechanisms in creating public value using ICT.

eHealth at WHO: Towards a global strategy

It was shortly after the first Summit concluded in 2003, and as the second Summit was being prepared in 2004, that Dr Jean-Claude Healy arrived at WHO from the European Commission. The combination of the context of the WSIS and the new landscape of WHO was to shape Dr Healy's thinking in important ways. Although he had not participated in the first Summit, he was particularly curious about the political dimensions of the WSIS, and he resolved to participate in the second Summit. He asked many questions about the deep divisions that existed not only on substantive and social issues, but also on matters of process.

Dr Healy's assignment at WHO was no less than to guide the organisation in the preparation of its first eHealth Strategy. The goal was to raise the profile of eHealth and to fast track the strategy for approval by WHO's governing body, the World Health Assembly, at its annual meeting in May 2005. For WHO, a global strategy on any topic must highlight the potential, the challenges and the way forward. It must also be acceptable to all its Member States (of which there were 192 in 2004–2005). Dr Healy's stature and credibility from his days at the European Commission, his perceived objectivity as an outsider and his distinctive blend of intellect and charisma made him the ideal person to bring together in a single vision the diverse efforts on eHealth at WHO. The European Commission had just announced its eHealth Action Plan,[5] in which international collaboration on eHealth was highlighted as a key action point.

Dr Healy had been instrumental in its development, which helped make the case for his transition to WHO.

Dr Healy's experience at the European Commission did not prepare him, however, for the strong development focus and the divisive politics of an international organisation such as WHO. At the Commission, his work in eHealth had been leading-edge, market-oriented and carried the risk of failure. The eHealth, DG Information Society and Enterprise unit that he had run for many years was focused on identifying and funding innovative, forward-looking projects intended to shape and accelerate the growth of the health IT industry in Europe. By contrast, at WHO, the focus was on the thorny task of setting norms and standards on public health matters, as well as on co-ordinating and administering health programmes in over 100 low- and low-middle-income countries through the Organisation's regional and country offices. In WHO's complex environment, eHealth was not well understood and had a very low profile. There was every reason to expect that the strategy development process might fall short.

Dr Healy's early days at WHO were spent learning how the Organisation worked and considering the potential role it should play in eHealth. WHO was quite different in form and function from the European Commission. Gradually, Dr Healy came to appreciate its strengths: its convening power, its normative and neutral role and its global reach. Bringing together the different threads of eHealth at WHO required reaching out to all the technical programmes working in eHealth and inviting them to contribute to the strategy. Each cluster of departments and each of WHO's six regions appointed a representative to participate in the process. Programmes as diverse as communicable disease surveillance, disaster preparedness and response and noncommunicable diseases management prepared background papers on the use of ICT in their respective areas. These were discussed at bi-weekly meetings as the draft strategy gradually took shape. Dr Healy had carefully selected as his model the successful *WHO Strategy on Essential Medicines*. Clear, concise and high-level, it proposed action along five major lines. WHO's eHealth strategy was to follow suit. The consultation and drafting continued over approximately four months before being finalised for review: first by the WHO Executive Board in January 2005, then by the World Health Assembly in May 2005.

The World Health Assembly

The 58th World Health Assembly in May 2005 adopted Resolution WHA58.28 establishing an eHealth strategy for WHO (WHO, 2005). The resolution recognised that eHealth is transforming the delivery of health services and systems around the world, and urged Member States to plan for appropriate eHealth services in their countries. The resolution came at a pivotal time. Approved a mere half year before the second WSIS event in November 2005, its effect was immediate. In particular, it enabled WHO to come to the Summit as a committed partner in the effort to advance ICT for development.

The process of building awareness and endorsements from ministries of health during the WHA was also to have important implications as WHO built its own eHealth programme. Dr Healy's task was completed, but he felt that his work at WHO was far from over. He wanted to further explore some of the fundamental questions that had arisen during the strategy development process.

Revisiting governance

Since his days at the European Commission, Dr Healy had believed in the potential of an interconnected and intelligent world. He believed that the digital world would play a vital role in ensuring Europe's competitiveness, and that a resolute and realistic approach to funding and deploying eHealth based on sound policy would enable steady progress towards that end. He endorsed the active engagement of both public and private organisations in this endeavour. He encouraged stakeholder debate, and he understood that giving protagonists of different positions the opportunity to talk to one another led to greater understanding and respect. But a critical aspect was still unclear to him.

Specifically, how would developing countries navigate these new waters and how would their governments need to equip themselves for and engage in eHealth and in the Information Society? His participation in the second WSIS event, held in November 2005 in Tunis (WSIS, 2005), helped to answer that question. For Dr Healy, the WSIS underscored a new reality; that is, that the Internet had become a potent driving force in social and economic development. What was less clear was how developing countries understood their role in realising its potential, and how their values and needs might shape the Internet in unforeseen ways. For example, the conflict at the WSIS in Tunis over human rights violations and freedom of speech was deeply disturbing to him. He observed with concern the host government's constraints on certain NGOs, limiting their participation and ability to distribute their literature. He noted that the WSIS was not relevant to the local population, when bus drivers assigned to the event did not know what the Internet was. He took in the rhetoric on inclusion and access, and worried aloud about how this would play out in countries where basic rights were as yet unrealised.

A striking moment occurred in the WSIS opening session in Tunis where, one after another, heads of state delivered their official statements to the sea of delegates present and by broadcast to many others. The tedium of the overwhelmingly male and bureaucratically bland speakers was brought home to the audience when a civil society representative from the Global Knowledge Partnership took the podium. In contrast to the preceding speakers, the representative spoke articulately, passionately and without referring to her prepared text. Through her words and her presence, she embodied the "rest of the world", for whom the Internet was a lifeline and a promise. The power of her distinctive voice meant that Internet development, opportunities and access, and how all these elements affect diverse groups (including women), would emerge as one of the central issues in Internet governance. The lesson was not lost on Dr Healy. The episode reminded him of the importance of visible and powerful leaders, and of the need to frame salient issues in ways both intellectual and emotive.

WSIS successes and failures

Not every outcome of the WSIS was successful. A notable omission of the official WSIS final texts was a serious discussion of the political–economic context of the information society. Many of the statements submitted by stakeholders in the preparatory meetings described a vision of the information society as inclusive and open, stressing access, capacity building and equity. The WSIS discourse seemed to consider the global digital divide as a problem in its own right, rather than in the context of the larger development divide. Instead, access to information and ICT were promoted as main contributors to solving global inequities. Moreover, the assumption that the benefits of ICT diffusion would be equally distributed overlooked historical evidence; that is, that society has always experienced an unequal distribution of benefits from technology and there was no reason to believe that this era would be different.

The WSIS missed the opportunity to critically question whether the digital divide could be addressed within the prevailing development paradigm. Nor was there reference to existing international agreements in related domains.[6] Probably the biggest gap was that there was no exploration of an alternative conceptualisation of development.

In reality, the global information society was already well under way in 2003. But while the WSIS focus was on the nuts and bolts of building it, at the same time, shared social responsibilities also needed to be addressed. Indeed, the information society rather quickly revealed its serious and undesirable effects, such as the loss of privacy, criminal activity and cybersecurity threats. The mechanisms to address these should have been more adequately considered and framed at the WSIS.

Instead, the implementation of the WSIS recommendations was destined to be problematic. As long as the rules served the status quo, it would be wishful thinking to believe that the networked world would be inclusive, equitable and transparent. Civil society organisations – themselves not necessarily representative, democratic or accountable – would be challenged to change this.

On the positive side, it was inspiring to observe that civil society managed to make its presence felt. Its contribution was essential even if the Summit was never a multi-stakeholder decision-making forum. The Internet Governance Forum (IGF) that emerged from the WSIS (and continues to exist) reflects a genuine civil commitment and has become an influential international forum for policy dialogue. The issue of improving accountability and transparency in Internet governance is now relevant to many different stakeholders in the Internet community. The IGF has an important role to play in highlighting the impact of Internet policy on social, economic and human development and, going forward, its agenda no doubt will continue to reflect the salient and often controversial issues of the day.

The impact of WSIS

Since 2005, under the stewardship of several UN agencies,[7] the WSIS has been kept alive through regular stocktaking surveys and annual events such as the WSIS Forum. At the annual WSIS event in Geneva, May 2013,[8] more than 150 sessions were held, in the form of high-level dialogues, thematic and country workshops, ministerial roundtables, workshops and other sessions to highlight progress on the WSIS targets. ITU will host a "WSIS+10" high-level event in 2014 to highlight progress and reinvigorate the stakeholders through a preparatory process leading up to the meeting.

Of course, the digital economy continues to expand on a global basis. With ten years having passed since the first WSIS event, the early efforts to establish ICT indicators seem like distant history. From its origin in a technical working group on Measurement of ICT under the auspices of the UN ICT Task Force,[9] the regular assessment of ICT progress has become more sophisticated. It is now established in the international agencies,[10] with the regular publication of statistics and reports on the uptake of ICT in countries and sectors.

Along those lines, WHO established its Global Observatory for eHealth[11] in early 2005 as the World Health Assembly was about to consider eHealth.[12] Its first project was to undertake a global survey to map the status of eHealth around the world. WHO also analysed available ICT indicators, policies, expenditure in health, ICT and education and burden of disease. The eHealth unit developed country profiles to highlight the relative place of ICT in relation to health, for country and regional comparisons.

Dr Healy saw that examining the data in this way was breaking new ground and would represent a starting point for discussion of how eHealth development should be approached in countries. His experience at the European Commission had convinced him that the main problems to be addressed by eHealth were those of productivity, cost and quality, and that eHealth should be positioned as the engine of health sector reform. WHO's analysis convinced him that, for developing countries, access to care and quality of care should be the priorities, and that ownership of eHealth by governments must be complimented by outreach to stakeholders. He reviewed with great interest the data and conclusions, and insisted that the report be co-published with the EC (Dzenowagis, 2006).

Looking back, the 2005 WSIS led to some important outcomes. First, it focused attention on the increasing importance of ICT in development and economic growth. Second, it galvanised many new actors to participate in a global event, included through its regional preparatory processes, which caused considerable excitement and opened the door to new ways of engagement. Third, as a "Summit of Opportunity" it raised awareness, highlighted successes, facilitated partnerships and encouraged innovation.

Despite the progress in ICT adoption made so far, it cannot be assumed that all the gaps will disappear on their own as the diffusion of ICT continues. An open, inclusive Information Society that benefits all people will not emerge without sustained commitment, investment and political will. There are obvious social, economic and other barriers that affect a country's ability to take advantage of digital opportunities. This reality remains a social, economic and, ultimately, political challenge. A WHO-organised session at the WSIS in 2005 on "Avian flu and beyond" considered issues such as access to information, challenges for countries and the need for international collaboration, with contributions from international agencies, civil society, governments and donors. Ten years later, those themes remain as important as ever.

Dr Healy believed in the power of such events to catalyse change, as the WSIS had originally done. He also believed that such processes run their course, and that new initiatives must be regularly proposed, to capture and refocus attention as well as to allow the next rank of leaders to set the path and pace of change. It would have been Dr Healy's view today that the WSIS has run its course and that the real excitement has moved elsewhere.

Looking to the future: Effective governance mechanisms in creating public value using ICT

Dr Healy had shaped an era at the European Commission and saw the agenda for 2003–2014 as one of tackling the challenges of implementation. eHealth was the only way forward for health services and systems. He strongly believed in the power of ICT to reach every individual, and that the future of technology would enable the development of personalised medicine on a population-wide basis. He believed in the power of collaboration in eHealth, not just in meeting its technical challenges but also in solving real-world health problems.

In order for this to happen, eHealth solutions had to be available, affordable and suitable for a range of country contexts. The enabling environment had to be created. Examples of implementations had to be studied, and learned from, in a rigorous manner. Beyond the technical challenges, however, eHealth development will increasingly demand effective governance mechanisms to move forward on a collective basis. The WSIS advanced the notion of an Information Society. Today, the networked society is already a reality, well beyond the information society imagined a decade ago. The global uptake of mobile technologies has opened an important opportunity for participation, including in health. The linkages of public health, clinical practice and other health domains have become a reality as well as a shared challenge.

In some respects, Dr Healy foresaw this. For example, as an avid supporter of the application of grid technologies to health, Dr Healy pushed for tighter collaboration between scientific and ICT innovators. Today, through the use of "big data", such collaborations enable research and discovery from massive and distributed patient information databases. These collaborations not only benefit research and clinical practice, but can also include patients. They have the potential to save money in healthcare services, offsetting the cost of innovation through savings elsewhere. Although his work was focused on getting the technology right, at the same time he realised that legal and ethical issues could outstrip our ability to gain the benefits.

There are a number of challenges to be dealt with, such as governance of shared resources, the health Internet space, and viable and ethical business models that keep the consumer in mind. Exploiting big data requires intensified efforts to standardise methodologies and establish priorities for analysis. Public policy-makers need a much better understanding of how big data can enable healthcare that can be tailored to a patient's characteristics and needs. Privacy concerns need to be addressed in an atmosphere that takes account of the interests and needs of public health, patients, consumers and clinical research.

Going forward, eHealth should be used to strengthen patient engagement and should be promoted by patient advocates, payers and providers, as well as by researchers themselves. Healthcare needs safe, effective alternatives to randomised clinical trials that are costly and dependent on recruitment of a suitable cadre of patients. The incorporation of new forms of data for health should be encouraged and tested. There are considerable opportunities for patient engagement across the spectrum of health promotion and practice.

Mechanisms and platforms for collaboration should be facilitated. Further growth of personalised health rests on expanding patient monitoring and self-care. Health IT and mobile health innovators need feedback from individuals, providers and payers as they develop products. However, policy-makers still control the relationships among manufacturers, payers and providers. The need for competition and consumer protection should be balanced with the need to innovate to reduce healthcare costs and improve health outcomes.

Dr Healy understood the need for a long-term view, to invest in and develop the potential of innovative approaches. The healthcare system is still unsure of how to do this. It needs to develop new ways to test and adopt innovations that create significant value for patients and society, but which may not match the short time horizons for return on investment that now characterise our health systems.

Eight years after the eHealth strategy, the World Health Assembly in 2013 passed a new resolution on eHealth (WHO, 2013). The resolution highlighted the importance of eHealth standardisation and interoperability, the need for national eHealth strategies and a reliable and trustworthy health Internet. The resolution was an opportunity to bring eHealth into focus and to advance global health Internet affairs. Dr Healy would have been pleased. He would have at the same time been bolder, opening the door to discussions to push the eHealth agenda further than ever. In any case, it will be critical in the coming years to ensure that cross-border, regional and international efforts in eHealth work in harmony, and that all governments build their capacity to engage in this area.

The Healy legacy

Dr Healy was an extraordinary force for eHealth throughout his career and his time at WHO was no exception. Following the development of the WHO eHealth Strategy, he continued to advise, support and spark eHealth activities and to stress that eHealth should remain as cross-cutting as possible, rather than becoming an isolated programme. He promoted eHealth in invited talks to governments, industry association meetings and other settings, extending his tenure at WHO until mid-2006. He was a constant advocate of broad engagement with the private sector, insisting on transparency, efficiency and responsiveness to needs. He brought together industry leaders for exploration of common goals and approaches towards ensuring the benefits of ICT for all. On leaving WHO, he accepted an assignment to the newly launched UN Global Alliance for ICT and Development (UNGAID)[13] in New York, with an aim to observe first-hand how a decentralised ICT task force would function, and to contribute to elevating eHealth policy on the broader development agenda. Ultimately, he set his hand to drafting a short handbook for developing a national eHealth strategy, commissioned by the ITU. In the handbook, Dr Healy sought to convey to policy-makers in a concise manner the steps required to undertake a national strategy process.

True eHealth governance requires people to come together around shared challenges, towards joint solutions, innovation and bridging specialities to create new frontiers. To be successful, it needs leadership at all levels. Beyond vision, it needs the kind of personal characteristics that marked Dr Healy's unique style: involvement, dialogue and action.

Dr Healy was changed by his years at WHO. His vista, already broad, was opened still further by his exposure to a global organisation. In particular, he came to believe that some of the critical policy issues in eHealth go far beyond the technicalities of ICT and the regulation of industry. He came to understand the long-term risks of not building capacity and not engaging developing countries in global policy matters. Previously keen to drive markets, he no longer seemed to feel their strong pull in driving public policy.

Dr Healy would have loved to see the next wave of eHealth, influenced in large part through his doing: the push to develop national eHealth strategies, to engage globally in health Internet affairs, and a reimagining of governance towards ensuring public ownership, trust and confidence in eHealth for years to come.

Acknowledgement

This chapter is courtesy of WHO.©

The author is a staff member of the World Health Organization. The author alone is responsible for the views expressed in this publication and they do not necessarily represent the views, decisions or policies of the World Health Organization.

Notes

1. See for example: https://www.gov.uk/government/publications/consultation-principles-guidance; http://consultation.cabinetoffice.gov.uk/openstandards (Accessed 17 July 2013).
2. Dr Healy spent over two years in this role at WHO, on leave from the European Commission.
3. ITU has a membership of 193 countries and over 700 private-sector entities and academic institutions. http://www.itu.int/en/about/Pages/membership.aspx (Accessed 17 July 2013).
4. Preparatory processes leading up to the first WSIS Summit in December 2003: http://www.itu.int/wsis/index-p1.html (Accessed 17 July 2013).
5. Launched 30 April 2004; http://eur-lex.europa.eu/LexUriServ/LexUriServ.do?uri=COM:2004:0356:FIN:EN:PDF. (Accessed 17 July 2013).
6. Including the World Telecommunications Agreement and the TRIPS Accords.
7. ITU, United Nations Educational, Scientific and Cultural Organization (UNESCO), the United Nations Conference on Trade and Development (UNTAD) and the United Nations Development Program (UNDP).
8. http://www.itu.int/wsis/implementation/2013/forum/. (Accessed 17 July 2013).
9. The UN ICT Task Force existed from 2001 to 2005: http://www.unicttf.org/ (site no longer maintained; documents are archived). (Accessed 17 July 2013).
10. See, for example, reports of members of the UN Group on the Information Society; http://www.ungis.org/.
11. WHO Global Observatory for eHealth; www.who.int/goe/en.

12. The second WSIS preparatory process was already under way.
13. UN GAID press release: http://www.un.org/News/Press/docs//2006/dev2572.doc.htm. (Accessed 17 July 2013).

References

Annan K., Opening address to the World Summit on the Information Society, Geneva 2003: http://www.itu.int/wsis/geneva/coverage/statements/opening/annan.pdf. [Accessed 17 July 2013].

Dzenowagis, J. (2006), Connecting for health, WHO, Geneva. http://www.who.int/kms/resources/WSISReport_Connecting_for_Health.pdf. [Accessed 17 July 2013].

Helmore, E. and McKie, R. Gates loses faith in computers, Sunday (November 2000), http://www.guardian.co.uk/technology/2000/nov/05/billgates.microsoft. [Accessed 17 July 2013].

Kuruvilla, S., Dzenowagis, J., Pleasant, A., Dwivedi, R., Murthy, N. and Samuel, R. (2004), "Digital bridges need concrete foundations", *British Medical Journal* 328:1193, http://www.bmj.com/content/328/7449/1193. [Accessed 17 July 2013].

Smith, R. (2003), "Closing the digital divide", *British Medical Journal* 326:238. http://www.bmj.com/content/326/7383/238.1?variant=full-text. [Accessed 17 July 2013].

United Nations http://www.unmillenniumproject.org/goals/gti.htm. [Accessed 17 July 2013].

WHO, WHA58.28 (2005), http://apps.who.int/iris/bitstream/10665/20378/1/WHA58_28-en.pdf. [Accessed 17 July 2013].

WHO, WHA66.24 (2013), http://apps.who.int/gb/ebwha/pdf_files/WHA66/A66_R24-en.pdf. [Accessed 17 July 2013].

WSIS 2003 archive: First Phase of the WSIS (10–12 December 2003, Geneva), Geneva Declaration of Principles, WSIS-03/GENEVA/DOC/0004: http://www.itu.int/wsis/documents/doc_multi.asp?lang=en&id=1161|0. [Accessed 17 July 2013]; Geneva Plan of Action, WSIS-03/GENEVA/DOC/0005; http://www.itu.int/wsis/documents/doc_multi.asp?lang=en&id=1160|0. [Accessed 17 July 2013].

5
New Directions in eHealth Governance in Europe

Zoi Kolitsi and Michèle Thonnet

Introduction

Governance has been a challenge from almost the beginning of eHealth. However, gradually, models of governance in eHealth have emerged and have become clearer. Much of this progress has been fuelled by cooperative work among European Member States and eHealth stakeholders at the level of the European Union (EU). The CALLIOPE Network was representative of this kind of collaboration. It built on the wealth of national and regional strategies and implementation paradigms, was developed over several years and addressed multiple stakeholder visions. The EU eHealth Interoperability Roadmap laid the foundations for a common working model that has been exemplified in the large-scale pilot test addressing patients' access to services while outside their usual country of residence (epSOS – European Patients' Smart Open Services).

This chapter takes both a historical and a future-oriented view of this exciting area. It represents the view of the authors, yet draws substantially on work conducted by CALLIOPE, the eHealth governance initiative and, more recently, the eHealth Network. The authors, having both worked closely with Jean-Claude Healy during his years of service in the European Commission, reflect upon his lasting legacy in many of the initiatives reported, most of which post-date his time in the Commission, but whose foundation stones his work laid.

Co-operation in the European Union

European Member States are all facing similar challenges associated with ageing societies, increasing levels of chronic disease and financial pressures on the social security system. At the same time, demand for healthcare is rising and there is or will be an inevitable shortage of skilled health and care professionals. However, the story of the health of Europe's population is not limited to heath and care services. Much of Europe's health is dependent on social and environmental factors, as well as the daily attention that citizens are willing or able to pay to their own health and wellness. Similarly, for their own functioning and efficiency, the union's health systems depend on strategies and policy choices made by other public sectors. The health sector, in turn, has an impact on the functioning and efficiency of other sectors, such as the employment sector. Alongside these external factors, it is important to also note that the historical origins of national healthcare systems across the European Union (EU) vary: this is reflected in their contemporary structure, their work forces and their financing.

Nevertheless, despite such differences, European health and care partners have the common goal of achieving value for patients and an outcome that optimises the ratio of care effectiveness to cost. To offer two examples generally agreed by European health and care partners: enabling a seamless distributed care environment would eliminate duplication; an appropriate distribution of roles throughout the continuum of care would optimise the fit between needs and demand in a system that covers the whole social network – from tertiary hospitals to the home. Eventually, a re-distribution of labour across actors in the health systems will be necessary. This would call for fundamental changes in the way health and social care are administered and managed, and a fostering of professional management and governance so as to improve efficiency drastically in "health production" processes. The greatest challenge, however, is to manage the change process and master the complexity of a multi-disciplinary health environment that is built on deep-rooted beliefs and traditions.

eHealth has excellent potential to support this transformational change. Nevertheless, this potential can only be fully exploited if the eHealth tools, solutions and services that are used are both interoperable and usable. As a fundamental principle, the continuity of care is based on the fact that health and social care professionals share work along clinical pathways for integrated care and they also exchange information about patients, and with patients, at appropriate points in the care or treatment process. eHealth, therefore, requires that the legal and ethical issues that surround data protection and privacy are addressed properly, delivery processes are re-engineered appropriately and services are integrated around patient needs. In turn, these requirements call for supportive infrastructures, such as shared patient records. These challenges need to be addressed in synergy with other enablers, including standardisation and clinical governance, and through the fostering of security and quality cultures. Legislation and standardisation must then become facilitators of innovation by supporting the dynamics of change while providing full protection and legal and ethical certainty. The financial investment and the operational costs of interoperable eHealth is an opportunity cost competing with other costs in the sector. Hence, the economic aspect of eHealth is an essential component in all eHealth strategies at local, national and European levels. eHealth interoperability challenges are common to all countries. For many years, each country separately has tried to solve problems that are in fact common to many other countries. However, each country lacks the resources and skills needed to boost innovation and would benefit from a joint effort directed towards addressing common challenges together. Since 2004, the European Commission and European Parliament, together with Member States, in a long series of communications and reports, have highlighted the need and opportunities for common European action, through the "exploitation" of cross-border scenarios. EU co-operation can add value and help accelerate developments, especially in those areas such as standardisation, clinical evidence-based processes and exchange of best practices, which are less affected by regional differences; for this acceleration to be achieved, EU eHealth governance is needed.

Common European Union action – exploratory phase

Driven in part by the eHealth objectives adopted by the European Commission over the last few years, European national governments have taken important steps towards a collaborative approach to common eHealth challenges. An important milestone was the adoption of the Directive on the application of patients' rights in cross-border healthcare (European Parliament, 2011), which was transposed into Europe's national legislations by October 2013. Since 2011 (and made official in 2012), Member States' co-operation on eHealth has rested on the legal basis provided by Article 14 of the Directive on eHealth and the establishment of the voluntary Network of Member States ("the eHealth Network"). It is the work of this high-level governance initiative that is expected to advance eHealth policy towards the development and deployment of interoperable eHealth. This section presents the key EU initiatives, which preceded this important development.

The European Commission has long supported collaborative initiatives through both its policy and regulatory initiatives, as well as its research funding that have all been applied to the key priorities of citizen mobility and borderless healthcare. In particular, in July 2008, in support of the focus on eHealth interoperability, the Commission launched three interlinked initiatives:

- A recommendation on cross-border interoperability of electronic health record systems (COM, 2008), which put forward a number of recommendations for eHealth interoperability involving policy, social, legal and technical issues. At the same time, the recommendation addressed the creation of processes and structures to achieve interoperability in Europe on security, privacy and certification issues.
- epSOS, a large-scale pilot (www.epSOS.eu) and

- CALLIOPE, a European Thematic Network, representing collaborative approaches among Member States, national authorities, stakeholders and industry (www.calliope-network.eu).

The recommendation required EU partners to work together on addressing all the facets of interoperability challenges in a multinational, interdisciplinary environment. Process improvements, testing and adoption and use of open standards are pursued through close co-operation with national, European and international standardisation organisations. This, in turn, strengthened and bound together the European health information technology (IT) industry and stimulated new partnerships. The immediate benefits of this approach for the public sector and health authorities meant that they began to rely on open, interoperable and sustainable IT solutions.

Major stepping stones: epSOS and CALLIOPE

Two of the three initiatives named earlier have played a major role in enabling progress on eHealth interoperability in Europe.

Smart Open Services for European Patients (epSOS) is an EU large-scale pilot project that was focused initially on providing solutions for interoperable and shareable patient summaries and ePrescription services. This was to be piloted in a limited number of Member States. Once the foundations were established, epSOS extended its work to new use cases and included more countries. It managed to demonstrate that its technical and semantic specifications, as well as its legal interoperability approach, are extendable to other use cases and replicable in other Member States; these proposals themselves have led to greater openness and sustainability.

CALLIOPE supported this entire process by establishing an open, stakeholder-driven method, and defining a European eHealth Interoperability Roadmap ("the Roadmap"), which captured the knowledge and experience that emerged from epSOS and from external stakeholders. The Roadmap builds on the vision of a desired future for all the parties involved, provides a framework for making that future happen and proposes action – primarily at EU level – to be taken up in common so as to benefit national eHealth deployment efforts.

Standardisation is an indispensable element of national and regional eHealth implementation plans and roadmaps. Another important aspect is access, both to the standardisation process and to the resulting outputs for local use. The work on the epSOS pilot specifications and in the CALLIOPE standardisation task force demonstrated, however, that much additional support is needed to ensure that standards can be applied to real implementations. In turn, this insight highlighted the need for action at Member State and European levels to consider global and specific approaches to standardisation. The Roadmap and a set of epSOS recommendations were adopted as the main sources of input into the high-level governance process established under Article 14 of Directive 2011/24/EU.

The knowledge that emerged from epSOS and CALLIOPE has been supplemented in specific areas by other EU projects and, in particular, by the work performed in STORK and STORK 2.0, focusing on e-Identification (including identification of roles) and the Semantic Health Network of Excellence (www.semantichealthnet.eu). The European Commission has also funded studies that have explored several specific aspects of interoperability in depth. This has included: e-Prescriptions (Empirica EC study to be delivered by end of 2013), the SemanticHealthNet project; the eHealth technical interoperability framework in the light of the Standardization Regulation, and a legal study aimed at examining national laws on electronic health record systems and services in the EU Member States and how they interact with cross-border eHealth services and exchange of health data (Health for Growth Programme, results expected by the end of 2014).

A common working model

As its point of departure, epSOS took the European Commission recommendation on the interoperability of electronic health record systems, which was elaborated in close co-operation with the Member States and established a work plan aiming to concurrently address four areas of interoperability: legal; organisational; technical and semantic. These four types of interoperability were applied to a limited initial number of priority use cases.

This first epSOS pilot (2008–2012) established a number of legal foundations. These foundations supplemented the EU regulatory framework that existed at the time. The pilot also set up an organisational cross-border collaborative mechanism that permitted the development, implementation, testing and operationalisation of the technical specifications of the relevant cross-border eHealth services. Through extension to new use cases and countries, the epSOS pilot has further demonstrated the proof of concept of its collaborative working model, which was further processed and published in the CALLIOPE Roadmap. A commonly adopted, distributed working model or framework for the sharing and exploitation of health-related data, information and knowledge across sources, actors, languages and jurisdictions is a prerequisite to a collaborative approach. The common working model encompasses information and communication technology (ICT) infrastructure layer and eHealth info structure foundations that meet the requirements of both the national and the EU eHealth architecture, are future-oriented and seek to address both national and cross-border eHealth needs. In particular: the eHealth info structure layer contains all the necessary data structures, repositories, codifications, terminologies and ontologies, databases and registries, data interoperability, accessibility standards, stored information, rules, agreements, and tools for the collection and management of these data and for their exploitation; the eHealth services layer contains all the components and organised content reflecting the healthcare system priorities, which directly contribute to high-quality services and improved accessibility and cost containment. They include patient summaries, ePrescribing, chronic disease management, home monitoring, tele-consultation and tele-radiology. Typically, these services reflect the Member States' national priorities. Many of them are common to all EU Member States, and are therefore candidates for priorities that should drive common EU eHealth activities.

Good eHealth governance encompasses all these different layers and brings them together under a single umbrella national/EU strategy and leadership to drive eHealth deployment; a collaborative framework with all key stakeholders; policies and mechanisms for the adoption and use of standards; the safety and quality of the information generated; and data protection of shared personal data. The governance element also effectively addresses such challenges as incentives, financing models and the development of various partnerships and new business models. National, regional and EU level priorities may be expressed either as use cases or as integrated services. They will usually reflect health system priorities and aim at achieving specific objectives. Interoperability specifications are elaborated through the consideration of available standards for profile development or adaptation.

Need for European Union collaborative governance

In order to address eHealth interoperability challenges jointly in the EU, it is necessary for Member States to have a continuous collaborative process in place. This process should enable extensive synthesis around the national and regional diversity in eHealth in Europe and the many visions of the key stakeholders. Obviously, this co-operation needs to be organised at EU level; however, it also needs to have strong links to the various national policies and strategies, eHealth platforms and stakeholder communities.

Along these lines, a major challenge for the coming decade, during which eHealth is to be deployed widely into everyday health and care provisions, will be to encourage stakeholders to work together with public authorities towards this common goal. This will include facilitating effective collaboration between the policy level and the operational level. In fact, the breadth and complexity of the issues that need to be addressed, as well as the imperative for integrity that should underpin such a process, required appropriate EU collaborative governance for eHealth to be set up.

In December 2009, the Council of Employment, Social Policy, Health and Consumer Affairs (EPSCO Council) conclusions provided the mandate for

EU eHealth co-operation and the establishment of an eHealth high-level governance process in Europe. The establishment of Article 14 eHealth Network of Directive 2011/24/EU provides a unique window of opportunity to elevate these proposals to an appropriate level of political decision-making and national commitments. Thus, the CALLIOPE thematic network was succeeded by the eHealth Governance Initiative (eHGI) which, together with the European Commission, now supports the EU decision-making process on eHealth.

Today, EU-level governance is articulated at the following three levels: policy; strategy and operations. Each of these serves a number of different interlinked goals:

- At the policy level, the governance sets out the higher-level political objectives, and defines common priorities and policy measures to guide and steer developments. This layer is operationalised through the functioning of the eHealth Network, and its Multiannual Work Plan. Its mandate for action is provided in Article 14 of Directive 2011/24/EU.
- At the strategic level, the governance proposes concrete strategies for developing and implementing integrated, value-added eHealth services for EU citizens. This layer is presently supported by the eHGI. It is informed by an operational layer, which uses effective knowledge brokering mechanisms.
- At the operational level, the governance enables a process through which knowledge is harvested in a variety of areas of specific focus. These include electronic identification, information governance, data protection, safety and ethics, security policies and services; implementing the EU info structure and sustaining convergence services; addressing the implementation challenges of the new standardisation regulation; and maintaining the links with national stakeholder groups.

This EU eHealth co-operation and the further development, deployment and sustainability of cross-border eHealth services are also to be supported, in the future, by the Connecting Europe Facility. This facility is envisaged as both an EU governance framework and a form of targeted infrastructure investment at European level. It is expected to come into being in 2014. It will support the roll-out of high-performing, sustainable and joined-up trans-European networks in the fields of transport, energy, broadband and digital services, including for health. It is presently expected that health/eHealth will form a principal area of activity of the facility.

Towards sustainable European Union–wide eHealth services

Providing EU-wide eHealth services requires at least three fundamental fields to be clearly developed and laid out. They include the need for legal certainty,

EU governance and political commitment. Each of these individual domains is described in some detail below. This tripartite model of support underscores once again the legacy left by Jean-Claude Healy, who was instrumental in steering the work of the European Commission in eHealth away from a singular focus on technological research and development to encompassing also the wider political and legal frameworks to allow the technology to move from the researcher's bench to the care providers' hands.

The need for legal certainty

Since 2011, the EU legislative framework has made considerable progress in terms of creating clarity and an underpinning governance framework supportive of cross-border electronic services. These advances are expressed in the proposed Regulation on Data Protection (COM, 2012a), the guidelines on electronic identification for cross-border services (COM, 2012b), and the European Standardisation Regulation, which impacts primarily the adoption of technical specifications in the domain of ICT (European Parliament, 2012). However, it is important to note that none of these legal documents are health sector-specific. With the exception of the eID regulation, they are also not cross-border specific. One may argue, however, that although the setting forth of requirements for mutual acceptance and notification of eID schemes is voluntary, the eID regulation will eventually promote uniform criteria for national identification schemes. In this sense, these EU legal interventions create conditions for harmonisation in several areas that are critical to the functioning of cross-border eHealth services, and they supplement Directive 2011/24/EU, which regulates the way in which these services will be delivered and reimbursed. A secondary effect of these regulations is that they are likely to facilitate a greater cross-sectoral integration of electronic services supporting several other domains, such as the business life-cycle, e-procurement and e-justice, all addressed in the eSENS large-scale pilot test (Electronic Simple European Networked Services, www.eSENS.eu). The Legal, Privacy and Protection of Data (LPPD) working group of the eHGI has further considered the implications of sector-agnostic regulations for the health sector, as well as the role of the eHealth Network. This consideration took place in view of the need for additional legal prerequisites to make the functioning of cross-border eHealth services possible. The group has made a number of proposals, which are briefly presented below.

EU and national laws create the legal basis for interoperability. This articulation of EU and national legislation for eHealth in general, and cross-border access to electronic health records and ePrescriptions in particular, is referred to as legal interoperability. The EU and national legal frameworks define the conditions under which health data may be shared, making provisions for specific safeguards that need to be in place without, however, being prescriptive. Creating, adopting and implementing such safeguards for cross-border eHealth services is a prerequisite for deployment and sustainability which, in addition to legislation being in place, creates conditions for organisational interoperability.

European Union level governance

Whereas legal frameworks provide the needed legal basis, cross-border services will need to rely on the implementation and monitoring of safeguards for daily functioning. It is therefore necessary to agree, at the EU level, on a system of common policies, measures and monitoring mechanisms through which legislation is applied in practice. This may be referred to as EU information governance. It is clear, overall, that the foundations for EU eHealth governance have been built on the results of a targeted number of Europe-wide projects and initiatives such as epSOS, CALLIOPE, eHGI and the Semantic HealthNet (www.semantichealthnet.eu). The eHGI is instrumental in collecting evidence from, and holding consultations with, Member States concerning national capacities and priorities. What is needed is to propose a roadmap towards an eHealth governance framework for sustainable cross-border eHealth services. In the long term this proposal may be part of the broader operation of the Connecting Europe Facility, and, therefore, should also influence its development.

The role of the eHealth Network

The role of the eHealth Network is to "work towards delivering sustainable economic and social benefits of European eHealth systems and services and inter-operable applications, with a view to achieving a high level of trust and security, enhancing continuity of care and ensuring access to safe and high-quality healthcare" (Directive 2011/24/EU, Article 14). The network's Multiannual Work Plan (2012–2014) has an initial focus on interoperable patient summaries and ePrescriptions. It also includes a roadmap for achieving legal, technical and semantic interoperability through agreement and adoption of common measures including for e-Identification and authentication, in support of the implementation of the Directive 2011/24/EU. These efforts should all come together under a governance scheme. Hence, in particular, Priority 6 of the plan aims to deliver recommendations on the governance of the Connecting Europe Facility.

Final reflections

Nations and their regions have important influence on eHealth development. A clearer formulation of their ways of working together is critical to progress on eHealth in Europe. There appears to be ever-increasing agreement on the principles. Yet, concrete movement forward on actual working mechanisms is also an obvious future priority. It may be argued that the provision of cross-border eHealth services is a challenge of limited scope for national governments, which have the primary task of securing efficient, safe and high-quality healthcare for their own citizens. However, the recent co-operation experience in epSOS and other initiatives has demonstrated that cross-border eHealth provides an excellent opportunity for Member States to work together to address common challenges for national eHealth deployment. Hence, the value of EU-level co-operation reaches far beyond simply serving the interests of mobile EU citizens seeking care abroad.

It is evident that three conditions must be met for eHealth services to be sustainable. First, there must be a clear legal and organisational framework; next, national infrastructure and info structure layers must be in place; and third, a clear co-ordination and governance mechanism must exist. More details on each are laid out below.

- A clear legal and organisational framework.
  - This must regulate the participation of the parties, that will jointly establish conditions for eHealth interoperability and their identification and recognition as trusted nodes to the eHealth ecosystem; their duties and responsibilities would include adherence to requirements and safeguards, monitoring, audit and reporting.
  - This should be anchored on standardisation, including accreditation and certification processes, that encourages the choice and development of standards-based eHealth services and applications, and hence fosters the development of an open health IT market.
  - This supports and encourages health service innovation, which focuses on improving quality and safety of services and health systems sustainability; is anchored on clinical guidelines and standards for ICT-supported integrated care; and encourages the choice and development of standards-based integrated health and social care services as well as the development of appropriate models for their reimbursement.
- Infrastructure and info structure layers that are established at national level and also act as active nodes in their respective EU co-ordination networks, exchanging and sharing assets, knowledge and experiences that accelerate eHealth deployment.
- A co-ordination mechanism and clear governance for setting policies and maintaining the oversight of mechanisms for the adoption and use of standards for the safety, quality and protection of shared personal data. The governance mechanism should also effectively address incentives, financing models and development of partnerships and new business models at the national and the EU level to drive forward eHealth deployment.

National and subsidiarity issues are important. Yet, working towards EU-wide cooperation on eHealth remains a much-needed target. The starting point for the sustainability of these eHealth services, with regard to cross-border eHealth in particular, will always be the existing national/regional legal frameworks, and eHealth and eGovernment strategies and infrastructures. Directive 2011/24/EU provides a legal basis for the provisions of cross-border care. However, securing cross-border eHealth interoperability will in addition require a sustainable future in terms of the EU policy environment, where specific Interoperability Agreements (COM, 2010) may be reached. Such a policy environment can be made possible as part of the Article 14 eHealth Network and its associated EU governance. At this level, it is also necessary to agree on a common set of priorities for health challenges, eHealth services and use cases in which common effort and resources should be focused on EU-level collaboration.

Notwithstanding the need for the legal, technical and governance support structures highlighted here, the sector also needs the life blood of passionate engagement. Jean-Claude Healy gave so much of his personal passion to the early stages of the development of eHealth. In doing so, he inspired many others, include the two authors, to continue his good work, and ensure that in the 21st century healthcare will use all the benefits of ICT to drive safer, more sustainable and more accessible health and care services for all.

Acknowledgements

This chapter presents an overview of the EU eHealth governance concepts created in such initiatives as CALLIOPE, epSOS and the eHGI. It provides insights into all three of these initiatives.

References

COM (2008), European Commission Recommendation on cross-border interoperability of electronic health record systems, Brussels, 3282 final.

COM (2010), "Written interoperability agreements are concrete and binding documents which set out the precise obligations of two parties cooperating across an 'interface' to achieve interoperability". Source: European Interoperability Framework (EIF), 744 final, Annex 2 to the Communication from the Commission to the European Parliament, the Council, the European Economic and Social Committee and the Committee of Regions "Towards interoperability for European public services".

COM (2012a), Regulation of the European Parliament and of the Council on the protection of individuals with regard to the processing of personal data and on the free movement of such data (General Data Protection Regulation), 11 final.

COM (2012b), Regulation of the European Parliament and of the Council on electronic identification and trust services for electronic transactions in the internal market, 238/2.

Regulation of the European Parliament and of the Council (2012), 25 October on European Standardisation.

European Parliament and of the Council (2011), Directive 2011/24/EU of the 9 March on the application of patients' rights in cross-border healthcare.

6
The Emergence of EU Law and Policy on eHealth

Petra Wilson

A chance encounter

In 1995 I was invited to present a paper at the German Sociology of Law conference on work I had recently completed about the impact of the use of personal computers (PCs) in general practitioners' consulting rooms. As an academic lawyer, I was interested in understanding the confidentiality issues presented by the use of PCs, and the impact they were having on the patient–doctor relationship of trust. A chance encounter at coffee time lead to a life-changing move to Brussels: the agent of that change was Jean-Claude Healy.

Back in 1995, Jean-Claude was building up the European Commission team started by Niels Rossing some years earlier. He was bringing in new players so that together they could drive forward the European Union (EU) research fund for Advanced Informatics in Medicine. The aim was to address all the challenges that using information and communications technologies (ICT) in healthcare were raising. At the time Jean-Claude invited me to become a "Detached National Expert" in his team, he offered me a secondment to the European Commission from my teaching post at a British university. An academic lawyer had never been included in the team before: this choice marked a departure from the norm that was so typical of a man who always saw the bigger picture and understood the value of an inclusive and diverse team. Despite the initial job's apparent short-term time horizon, it also led to a further two decades spent in Belgium working in and around EU eHealth-related policy.

The reason Jean-Claude felt that a person with a background in healthcare law would be useful to the team is evident when one looks back at that time in history and considers the legal and policy canvas on which eHealth concepts were being sketched. In the following pages, I will set out the legal and policy context in which the new field of health telematics was being developed, highlight some of the key milestones that were passed along the way and end with an indication of where the journey might take us as eHealth is integrated into daily healthcare practice and as the concept of mHealth gains ground.

Healthcare policy in the European Union

The European Union (EU) is served by five primary institutions (Commission, Parliament, Council, Court of Justice and Court of Auditors) and secondary institutions including the Economic and Social Committee, the Committee of the Regions, the European Central Bank, the European Investment Bank and a number of agencies. (For an introduction to the EU institutions and law making, see Weatherill, 2012.)

The European Commission leads EU policy-making by proposing legislation and ensuring that adopted EU legislation is correctly transposed into Member States' code of law and is duly enforced. The European Commission's work on health is driven primarily by the Directorate General (DG) for Health and Consumer Protection, although the work of many other DGs has a significant impact on the way in which health services are delivered in the Member States, as well as a direct effect on the health and well-being of European citizens. In the area of eHealth, the main policy-making parts of the Commission are the DG for Health and Consumer Protection and the DG for Communications Networks, Content & Technology. The two DGs co-operate extensively on research and development. They contribute significantly to the development of eHealth solutions, although the former addresses policy more directly related to the use of such solutions.

The Council of the EU is the institution through which Member States meet directly. Depending on the issue on the agenda, each Member State is represented by the minister responsible for that portfolio. In total, there are nine Council configurations (or "councils of ministers") of which the one that takes the lead on health issues is termed the Employment, Social Policy, Health and Consumer Affairs Council (EPSCO). Healthcare issues are also discussed in other Councils such as the Competitiveness Council which deals with internal market, industry and research. No matter what configuration meets, the Council is a single body and, regardless of the Council configuration that adopts a decision, that decision is always a "Council Decision". Council decisions are prepared by a structure of some 250 working parties and committees comprising delegates from the Member States. The Council takes decisions by a vote of Ministers from the Member States.

In a great majority of cases, the Council takes decisions on a proposal from the European Commission in association with the European Parliament, either through the consultation procedure (for example, in the areas of agriculture, judicial and police co-operation, and taxation), the assent procedure or through co-decision (that is, on the internal market, and consumer affairs). As many health and health-related policies fall under the co-decision procedure, the European Parliament plays an equally important role in the shaping of health in the EU.

Healthcare law in the European Union

The route to policy is the same for all areas in which the EU has the right, or legal competence, to propose legislation – that is, the European Commission proposes an area for policy or regulatory development through a proposal to the Council, which then debates and possibly amends the proposal, passes it to the European Parliament, which further debates and amends it. Finally, a new legal instrument is adopted and duly implemented by the Member States.

The areas of law, which lie close to the origin of the Union, such as agriculture or the internal market, have had a long legal history. Health, however, is a relative newcomer on the European policy scene. It came on board only in 1992 when the Maastricht Treaty included a new article "encouraging cooperation between member states" and "if necessary, lending support to their actions" in the area of public health. This new legal competence was strengthened in 1997 with the establishment of the Amsterdam Treaty. Through the next Treaty, the EU was mandated to ensure "a high level of human health protection" in the "definition and implementation of all [union] policies and activities" and to work with Member States to improve public health, prevent illness and "obviate sources of danger to human health". However, the Amsterdam amendment maintained the subsidiarity principle for health: this provides that harmonisation of Member States' Health legislation is prohibited, and that the Union shall continue to respect fully the Member States' responsibilities for the organisation and delivery of their own health services and medical care. (For a detailed discussion on EU healthcare law, see Hervey and McHale, 2004.)

The present treaty article relevant to health is Article 168 of the Treaty on the Functioning of the European Union (TFEU) (European Union, 2010), which maintains this situation. Section 1 of Article 168 TFEU states:

> A high level of human health protection shall be ensured in the definition and implementation of all Union policies and activities. Union action, which shall complement national policies, shall be directed towards improving public health, preventing physical and mental illness and diseases, and obviating sources of danger to physical and mental health. Such action shall cover the fight against the major health scourges, by promoting research into their causes, their transmission and their prevention, as well as health information and education, and monitoring, early warning of and combating serious cross-border threats to health. The Union shall complement the

Member States' action in reducing drugs-related health damage, including information and prevention.

The current situation is therefore that the European Union has a limited mandate to adopt public health policy, while it must at all times respect the right of Member States to adopt national level measures to regulate the organisation and delivery of their health services.

The emergence of the European patient

However, healthcare does not exist in a vacuum; it is used by EU citizens who have the right to move within the EU for work or pleasure. It is this right of movement to provide or consume a service, which lies at the heart of the change in Europe's response to health policy, which has emerged since the late 1990s. The history of the change is charted below.

The EU Treaties accord all European citizens four fundamental freedoms: the freedom of movement of goods, capital, services and persons. (For a thorough discussion on the four freedoms, see Barnard, 2013.) The freedom of personal movement was initially construed as an objective applying only to workers. However, as EU integration has deepened, a wider interpretation has come to prevail, not least through Directives which provide rights of residency for students and retired people and allow free movement of EU citizens provided that they can show an adequate financial means to support themselves.

The free movement of persons is closely linked to the free movement of services, since it provides for professionals to practise anywhere in the EU in order to offer their services. The current rules lay down that, save for certain exceptions based on public policy, a provider of services is entitled to offer his or her services in any EU Member State or to offer such services to someone who travels from another Member State in order to avail him/herself of services outside the normal country of residence.

The development of the free movement of services and people with respect to healthcare is found in the interpretation of the European Court of Justice (ECJ) of the rights accorded to European citizens under *Regulation 883/2004 on the coordination of social security systems* (European Union, 2004). The Regulation, first adopted in 1971 (European Union, 1971) and updated in 2004, provides for a series of systems whereby European citizens can obtain health services in another Member State in an emergency when travelling either as tourists or on business (using the European Health Insurance Card), or when temporarily resident in another State as a student or worker.

Starting in 1996, the ECJ was called on several times to interpret the way in which this Regulation applied in specific healthcare cases. It is the interpretation of the ECJ that began to drive a change in EU health policy, and ultimately led to the adoption of EU health-related legislation.

Basing their cases on *Regulation 1408/71 on the application of social security schemes to employed persons and their families moving within the Community* (European Union (1971) updated to 883/2004 (European Union, 2004)), in 1996, two Luxembourgish men who had purchased orthodontic treatment and spectacles outside of Luxembourg went to the ECJ to claim reimbursement from the Luxembourg health fund (Case C-158/1996). The first was a Mr Kohll, the second a Mr Decker. In both cases, the parties had purchased health services or goods in another EU Member State without obtaining prior permission from their health insurance schemes (as provided for in the Regulation). Yet, they pleaded in the ECJ that their costs should be reimbursed. Mr Kohll argued that the prior authorisation system restricted him from purchasing orthodontic services in contravention of Articles 59 and 60 of the Treaty, whereas Mr Decker maintained that his right to spectacles was protected under Article 30.

The ECJ heard the cases jointly. It determined that the provisions of the Treaty covered access to health services and health goods. The Court stated that, although Regulation 1408/71 was valid, it was nonetheless a secondary law, placing health services within the reach of the Treaty. Consequently, the Court held that the Treaty provisions on free movement of goods and services applied to health goods and services, and therefore provided a means for obtaining health goods and services in another Member State.

Having established the principle, the Court next had to decide if the rules in Regulation 1408/71, which require the citizen to obtain prior authorisation before accessing such goods or services, were justifiable on the basis of public health or public policy. In each case, the lawyers for the country of Luxembourg argued that the requirement of prior authorisation was a justifiable restriction on the basis that it was necessary to ensure the financial balance of the social security system and to safeguard the quality of the services and goods delivered. The Court dismissed the first argument on the basis that as the reimbursement sought was at Luxembourg rates, the local insurer would not have to pay out more than if the services or goods had been obtained in Luxembourg. The Court did accept, however, that, in principle, the need to ensure a balanced medical and hospital service open to all might justify limits on cross-border access to certain types of health services. Luxembourg's second argument, that free access to health goods and services across internal borders should be limited on the basis of ensuring high quality, was dismissed on the grounds that the mutual recognition qualifications legislation provided adequate surety of the quality of health services providers in other EU countries. (For a detailed overview of Kohll-Decker, see Obermaier, 2008.)

Following these two landmark cases, which in effect started to create EU healthcare policy, a number of other citizens brought cases to the ECJ that tested the extent of the Kohll/Decker decision. In the Geraets-Smits/Peerbooms case (Case C-385/99) (which combined claims by Mrs Geraets-Smits and Mr Peerbooms), Mrs Geraets-Smits claimed that the treatment she received for Parkinson's disease in a specialist clinic in Germany should be reimbursed by her insurer. Her sickness insurance fund refused this on the grounds that satisfactory and adequate treatment was available in the Netherlands, and that the treatment provided in Germany conferred no additional advantage. Mr Peerbooms received special intensive therapy in an Austrian clinic after falling into a coma following a road accident. He was treated in Austria because he did not satisfy the requirements for the treatment in the Netherlands, where the treatment was available only to persons under the age of 25 years. Neither patient had obtained the prior consent for treatment outside the Netherlands.

In both cases, the Court observed again that Member States are free to organise their social security systems, and recognised that a prior authorisation scheme was generally legitimate. However, in each case the Court decided that the grounds given for refusing the prior authorisation were not justifiable and did not satisfy the principle of proportionality. The Court held that authorisation may be refused only if the patient can receive the same or equally effective treatment without undue delay from an establishment with which his sickness insurance fund has contractual arrangements.

In the Müller-Fauré/van Riet case (Case C-385/99) the Court further clarified that, in determining undue delay for access to hospital care, national authorities must take account of the patient's medical history and also their actual medical condition and, where appropriate, the degree of pain or the nature of the patient's disability, which might, for example, make it impossible or extremely difficult for him or her to carry out a professional activity. For the case of non-hospital care, the Court held that the principle of freedom to provide services precludes legislation, which requires the insured person to obtain prior authorisation for non-hospital care provided in another Member State by a non-contracted provider.

On the matter of the level of costs to be reimbursed, the Van Braekel case (Case C-368/98) provides that national legislation must guarantee that an insured person who has been authorised to receive hospital treatment abroad receives a level of payment comparable to that which he or she would have received if s/he had received hospital treatment in his/her own Member State, even if in some cases this might result in a patient obtaining reimbursement at the national rate which is higher than the actual costs incurred in another EU Member State.

It may be seen, therefore, from this series of cases that the European Court has decided quite firmly that:

- Health services are services within the meaning of the Treaty and that therefore the rules on freedom of movement to obtain such services apply

to European citizens seeking health services outside their own Member State;
- Member States have a justifiable interest in limiting free access to health services in other Member States if to do so is necessary for the planning and financial balance of health services;
- A system of prior authorisation may be used to facilitate planning of hospital based services, but not for non-hospital care;
- Prior authorisation must be granted if equivalent treatment cannot be offered in a reasonable time having regard to the specific characteristics of the patient.

Accordingly, through its case law, the ECJ has in practice changed health policy at EU level, and has provided the impetus for the European Commission to establish a route to proposing a Directive on cross-border care which codifies the case law. (For a detailed discussion of the case law and the ensuing policy, see van de Gronden et al., 2011.)

The emergence of eHealth law and policy

Following on from the case law discussed earlier, the EPSCO Council of 2006 adopted the *Council Conclusion on Common Values and Principles in EU Health Systems* (Council of the European Union, 2006). It called for an initiative on cross-border healthcare to ensure clarity about the rights and entitlements applying for EU citizens seeking treatment abroad. This call for clarity came as a direct result of the body of case law built up since 1996, which had created a patchwork array of rights. It was also built on the decision in 2006, which concluded that health would not be included in the *Directive on Services in the Single Market* (European Union, 2006). (For a full discussion on the emergence of EU patient mobility, see Rosenmöller et al., 2006.)

However, as noted earlier, there was no clear route for the Commission to put forward a proposal for a Directive on healthcare, at least in the field of healthcare, as Article 168 TFEU maintains that healthcare is a matter of Member State subsidiarity. The Commission therefore chose the internal market principles as the basis for the proposed future legislation to unify all the decisions of the ECJ. The Commission proposal was based on Article 114 TFEU, which provides that, if no other provision exists in the Treaties, Article 114 may be used to achieve the objectives of internal market (as set out in Article 26), to ensure that "the internal market shall comprise an area without internal frontiers in which the free movement of goods, persons, services and capital is ensured". Articles 26 and 114 TFEU together therefore provided the legal basis for the European Commission to propose legislation which would ensure that EU citizens could avail themselves of health services across the EU, and thereby ECJ case law could be formalised into a single Directive which would then be duly translated into individual Member States' legislation.

Accordingly, after many Council Committee meetings, European Parliament Reports and a large volume of lobbying during 2011, the *Directive on the application of patients' rights in cross-border healthcare* (European Union, 2011) was adopted. (A detailed discussion of the lengthy process can be found in Wismar et al., 2011.) It should be noted that the Directive, although based on the internal market provisions of the TFEU, maintains the principle of subsidiarity in healthcare through a reference made in recital 4 of the Directive, in which national legislation resulting from the transposition of the Directive on patient should not "result in patients being encouraged to receive treatment outside their Member State of affiliation".

The Directive indicates, however, two vital markers. It was not only a turning point in access to reimbursement when patients receive medical care in an EU Member State other than their usual state of residence, it was also the first time that eHealth, and the concept of care delivered by electronic means, was enshrined in EU law. The Directive does not lay down any hard requirements on eHealth, but it does mention the concept of access to healthcare by electronic means for the first time. It does so in recital 26, which notes that the right to reimbursement... *should apply to recipients of healthcare seeking to receive healthcare provided in another Member State through other means, for example through eHealth services*. The wording here is important, as it indicates that eHealth services have an equal standing, at least insofar as reimbursement rights are concerned, with healthcare services provided face to face.

The Directive is explicit on matters of eHealth in Article 14, which addresses the concept specifically. It also sets up the eHealth Network as the main decision-making body on eHealth at European level so as to provide a vehicle for representatives of the Member States to work together to define a common vision and strategy for eHealth across Europe. Its objectives, as set out in the Directive, are to:

> work towards delivering sustainable economic and social benefits of European eHealth systems and services and interoperable applications, with a view to achieving a high level of trust and security, enhancing continuity of care and ensuring access to safe and high-quality healthcare;

and specifically to draw up guidelines on:

(i) a non-exhaustive list of data that are to be included in patients' summaries and that can be shared among health professionals to enable continuity of care and patient safety across borders; and

(ii) effective methods for enabling the use of medical information for public health and research;

And further to

> support Member States in developing common identification and authentication measures to facilitate transferability of data in cross-border healthcare.

The eHealth Network started its work in 2012 and is scheduled to meet twice a year. At the time of writing, an early policy-related output has been the November 2013 report on patient summaries (eHealth Network, 2013).

The network is also being supported by two further groups: the eHealth Governance Initiative and the eHealth Stakeholder Group. The eHealth Governance Initiative (eHGI) is a Member State-driven mechanism to establish a governance structure for eHealth within Europe. Its mission is to enhance co-operation between Member States, develop a joint vision for eHealth, and create a mechanism linking the political level developed by the eHealth Network and the operational level in the Member States. The eHGI operates as a preparatory body for eHealth Network decisions. It is, however, a temporary measure, funded by research support funds, which will end its work in 2014 when a new, more permanent, group will be put in place to support the work of the eHealth Network. Alongside the Member State-focused initiatives, the European Commission has also set up a mechanism for stakeholders from industry, patients and healthcare professionals to offer their input into eHealth policy development. This group is known as the eHealth Stakeholder Group, and was established in February 2012.

This discussion shows that health law and policy-making have now been clearly established in the EU. Although at the time of writing we see only the early shoots of the new eHealth policy, it is clear that the EU has now embraced the principle of using ICT as a tool in the delivery of health and care services. The primordial position of face-to-face healthcare has also been shifted somewhat so that new models of care delivery can be set up.

The emergence of mHealth law and policy

The embracing of ICT in healthcare is not confined to the established eHealth solutions of electronic health records, electronic prescriptions and other solutions used and controlled by healthcare professionals. It has also opened the door to the use of tools and solutions used and controlled directly by patients or consumers, which brings with it a whole new array of policy and regulatory challenges.

As eHealth develops, it establishes new concepts of care delivery to patients on the move or at home. In fact, a major reason for the implementation of eHealth in many countries is to develop new ways to provide care in the context of demographic change. This change sees greater numbers of older patients with complex co-morbidities – that is, one or more conditions or diseases – who require care in their own homes. Similarly, the rise in non-communicable and chronic conditions, such as diabetes, has also prompted the policy-makers in many healthcare systems to look at new ways of monitoring and supporting patients in order to find more efficient and patient-centric models of care provision.

The development of home support and remote monitoring has led to the emergence of a new branch of eHealth, often referred to as mobile health or mHealth. The Global Observatory for eHealth in the World Health Organization defines mHealth as "medical and public health practice supported by mobile devices, such as mobile phones, patient monitoring devices, personal digital assistants (PDAs), and other wireless devices" (WHO, 2011). It further outlines that mHealth involves the use of a voice or short messaging service (SMS) as well as more complex functionalities such as 3G systems, global positioning systems (GPS) and Bluetooth technology.

At the time of writing, the mHealth concept is strongly linked with the use of "apps", often through smartphones. A 2013 study by the IMS Institute for Health Informatics (IMS, 2013) found that, in 2013, in the iTunes app store alone, around 43,000 health and wellness apps were available for free or charged download. The majority of these simply provide health or wellness-related information to patients or citizens. They are "passive" apps insofar as they do not collect any active information about their users. Some, however, are "active" and interact with devices like pedometers or blood glucose monitors so as to collect data about the user, and provide patient-specific advice based on the collected data. Although the IMS report notes that, in 2013, fewer than 1 per cent of the apps available in the iTunes store had a real medical monitoring functionality, academic and policy-maker interest in the potential legal challenges posed by apps with a real medical functionality is pronounced. Currently, several journal articles are dedicated to the regulatory challenges posed by such apps and by mHealth generally. The key challenges noted are in terms of data protection, when a device captures user-specific and user-identifiable data, and medical device regulation.

In terms of data protection it should be noted that, although the use of medical apps which collect identifiable user data is still limited, the proliferation of apps generally, as well as the very widespread use of smart phones, means that huge amounts of data are logged, indicating for example where phone users are located and to some extent what they are doing, and what information they are accessing on the Internet. Given this situation, the Data Protection and Privacy Commissioners meeting in Warsaw, Poland in 2013, at their 35th annual international conference, saw fit to issue a declaration urging policy and law makers to take seriously the privacy challenges of the "appification" of society (Mantovani et al., 2013).

In 2013, there is not yet any concrete proposal for EU-level legislation to deal with the data protection issues raised by mHealth. However, the very fact that the risks are evident has led many EU countries to hold back on promoting the use of "active" apps in healthcare. It is interesting to note though that the National Health Service (NHS) in England, for example, has established a library of NHS-vetted apps, which help people with such tasks as obtaining advice on their conditions, booking repeat prescriptions, accessing test results and finding the most appropriate NHS service. Again, at the time of writing, the European Commission is finalising a Green Paper on the legal issues raised by mHealth and health-related apps.

Similarly, the overlap between an mHealth app and a medical device is also being scrutinised for potential EU-level regulation. There is a long-established history of EU level legislation to regulate the quality and registration of medical devices. However, a European Commission Guideline, adopted in 2012, indicated that standalone software is a medical device if it has a controlling function, such as delivery, or if it directly guides decision-making. Scholars have argued that many mHealth apps could be considered as standalone software subject to regulation in the EU, as these can provide decision-triggering information. As noted by Papadopoulos and colleagues, EU regulators are struggling to keep pace with the growing development of apps (Papadopoulos et al., 2013). The authors argue, however, that the EU should adopt legislation, which both safeguards the public and at the same time supports innovation. In this way, such law would give patients, consumers and healthcare professionals confidence in the mobile health apps, which they might use every day, and thus allow this burgeoning field of EU innovation to flourish.

Postscript

Jean-Claude Healy did not live to see these latest steps, and for him mHealth was only a notion. However, his vision throughout the 1990s and the first decade of the 21st century paved the way for much of the innovation and excitement around the technologies that we now see. The healthcare community owes a great debt of gratitude to Jean-Claude for his passion, perseverance and powers of persuasion, which have all allowed the field of eHealth, and now mHealth, to develop and thrive.

References

Barnard, C. (2013), *The Substantive Law of the EU – The Four Freedoms*. 4th edn. Oxford: Oxford University Press.

Case C-158/1996 of 28 April 1998 (Kohll)
Case C-120/1995 of 28 April 1998 (Decker)
Case C-157/99 (Geraets-Smits/Peerbooms)
Case C-385/99 (Müller-Fauré/van Riet)
Case C-368/98 (Van Braekel)

Council of the European Union (2006), Council Conclusions on Common values and principles in European Union Health Systems, *OJ* C 146 22/6/2006 (1–3). http://eur-lex.europa.eu/LexUriServ/LexUriServ.do?uri=OJ:C:2006:146:0001:0003:EN:PDF. [Accessed 2 December 2013].

eHealth Network (2013), *Guidelines on minimum/non-exhaustive patient summary dataset for electronic exchange in accordance with the cross-border Directive 2011/24/EU*, Release 1.0, 19 November 2013. http://ec.europa.eu/health/ehealth/docs/guidelines_patient_summary_en.pdf. [Accessed 2 December 2013].

European Union (1971), Regulation (EEC) No 1408/71 of the Council of 14 June 1971 on the application of social security schemes to employed persons and their families moving within the Community, *OJ* L149 5/7/1971 (2–50). http://eur-lex.europa.eu/LexUriServ/LexUriServ.do?uri=CELEX:31971R1408:en:HTML. [Accessed 2 December 2013].

European Union (2004), Regulation (EC) No 883/2004 of the European Parliament and of the Council of 29 April 2004 on the coordination of social security systems, *OJ* L166 30/4/2004 (1–123). http://eur-lex.europa.eu/LexUriServ/LexUriServ.do?uri=OJ:L:2004:166:0001:0123:en:PDF. [Accessed 2 December 2013].

European Union (2006), Directive 2006/123/EC of the European Parliament and of the Council of 12 December 2006 on services in the internal market, *OJ* L376 27/12/2006 (36–68). http://eur-lex.europa.eu/LexUriServ/LexUriServ.do?uri=OJ:L:2006:376:0036:0068:en:pdf. [Accessed 2 December 2013].

European Union (2010), Consolidated Version of the Treaty on the Functioning of the European Union, *OJ* C 326 30/3/2010 (47–200). http://eur-lex.europa.eu/LexUriServ/LexUriServ.do?uri=OJ:C:2010:083:0047:0200:en:PDF. [Accessed 2 December 2013].

European Union (2011), Directive 2011/24/EU of the European Parliament and of the Council of 9 March 2011 on the application of patients' rights in cross-border healthcare, *OJ* L88 4/4/2011 (45–65). http://eur-lex.europa.eu/LexUriServ/LexUriServ.do?uri=OJ:L:2011:088:0045:0065:en:PDF. [Accessed 2 December 2013].

Hervey, T. and McHale, J. (2004), *Health Law and the European Union*. Cambridge: Cambridge University Press.

IMS (2013) *Patient Apps for Improved Healthcare: From Novelty to Mainstream*. Report by the IMS Institute for Healthcare Informatics. http://www.imshealth.com/deployedfiles/imshealth/Global/Content/Corporate/IMS%20Health%20Institute/Reports/Patient_Apps/IIHI_Patient_Apps_Report.pdf. [Accessed 2 December 2013].

Mantovani, E., Quinn, P., Guihen, B., Habbig, A.-K. and De Hert, P. (2013), "eHealth to mHealth – a journey precariously dependent upon apps"?, *European Journal of ePractice* [online] http://www.epractice.eu/files/p5_2.pdf. [Accessed 2 December 2013].

Obermaier, A (2008), "The national judiciary – sword of European Court of Justice rulings: the example of the Kohll/Decker jurisprudence", *European Law Journal* 14(6): 735–752.

Papadopoulos, H., Sheth, V.B. and Wurst, M. (2013), "Comparison of US and EU regulatory approaches to mobile health apps: use cases of myVisionTrack and USEFIL", *European Journal of ePractice* [online] http://www.epractice.eu/files/p4_2.pdf. [Accessed 2 December 2013].

Rosenmöller M., McKee, M. and Baeten, R. (2006), *Patient mobility in the European Union: learning from experience*, European Observatory on Health Care Systems. http://www.euro.who.int/__data/assets/pdf_file/0005/98420/Patient_Mobility.pdf. [Accessed 2 December 2013].

van de Gronden, W., Szyszczak, E., Neergaard, U. and Krajewski, M. (eds) (2011), *Healthcare and EU Law*. The Hague, the Netherlands: T.M.C. Asser Press (Springer).

Weatherill, S. (2012), *Cases and Materials on EU Law*. 10th edn. Oxford: Oxford University Press.

Wismar, M., Palm, W., Figueras, J., Ernst, K. and van Ginneken, E. (eds) (2011), *Cross-border health care in the European Union: mapping and analysing practices and policies*. European Observatory on Health Systems and Policies. http://www.euro.who.int/__data/assets/pdf_file/0004/135994/e94875.pdf. [Accessed 2 December 2013].

World Health Organization (WHO) (2011), *mHealth: New horizons for health through mobile technologies: second global survey on eHealth*. Geneva: WHO Press. http://www.who.int/goe/publications/goe_mhealth_web.pdf. [Accessed 2 December 2013].

Part II

People – Professionals, Patients and Consumers

7

Physicians' Perspectives on eHealth

Birgit Beger and Michael Wilks

Setting the scene

Information Technology (IT) is now so integral to healthcare delivery that it has been suggested that the "e" in eHealth is redundant and should be dropped (Ebels, 2012). In the healthcare sector, both patients and physicians are facing a rapidly changing and challenging environment, due to the increased use of eHealth tools. General practitioners were the first to embrace office-based computers around 40 years ago; at that time the development of eHealth in primary care was bogged down by several issues. They included cost, the variety of systems available and the difficulties in migrating from paper-based records with a familiar format to electronic ones with different structures. Some of these problems persist. However, a bigger challenge today is the integration of data generated in one component of healthcare delivery into the wider healthcare IT system, so that, in terms of providing good patient care, a more seamless record can be shared across all three fields of primary, secondary and social care.

Outside of primary care, the development of eHealth has been decidedly patchy. Much of the problem has been either a lack of vision or an over-enthusiastic development of projects that then lose momentum or become unsustainable. An example of the latter is the United Kingdom (UK)'s Health Space project. Health Space was designed to allow limited access to a summary medical record; it also offered a personal health diary for recording information such as test results. It was, however, plagued by misunderstandings among the various groups tasked with its implementation, and suffered from issues of acceptability. This short-termism and lack of a wider vision for eHealth has disappointed European physicians, who are generally, if cautiously, committed to the idea that eHealth is an essential tool in the modernisation of the healthcare sector. Being evidence-based in their approach to care, doctors will welcome the use of eHealth solutions when these have demonstrable benefit for both patients and themselves.

Information is essential to good patient care. Information that is accurate, timely and up-to-date increases patient safety (Stroetmann et al., 2007). Information that updates physicians about good practice in treatment and medication ensures that they work according to an evidence base that is current and authoritative. Because physicians have always worked according to these kinds of principles, their enthusiasm for using technology that provides more rapid access to information and better linkage to a variety of databases can be assumed. However, it cannot be taken for granted without significant physician engagement in its development. Looking at present attitudes among medical practitioners, support for eHealth has been slow to develop; progress has been brought about largely by enthusiasts rather than by the medical profession as a whole. A lack of coherence and inadequate political support has delayed the creation of comprehensive systems that can gain wider support. Although this reluctance is likely to be modified, it is worth looking at the factors that discourage the uptake of health information technology by the medical profession.

This chapter describes the current relationship that the majority of physicians have with eHealth, how they are using it now and what emphasis they place on its future importance. It discusses barriers to their use of eHealth and their concerns about it before offering pointers towards reducing these barriers. It attempts a prediction of how eHealth will develop, and its fundamental effect on both the delivery of "health" (rather than "healthcare"), and the nature of a patient/doctor relationship. One of the authors is from the UK. Although examples are taken from that country, the experience of both authors, who are closely involved with the Standing Committee of European Doctors (CPME), which represents national medical associations across Europe, is that similar issues exist across the European Union (EU) at different levels and to differing degrees. CPME contributes the medical profession's point of view to the EU and European policy-making bodies through pro-active co-operation on a wide range of health and healthcare-related issues. It has a lively and active working group on eHealth, which helps to develop the organisation's position papers and contributions to eHealth projects (www.cpme.eu/cpme-working-groups-and-rapporteurs/ehealth/).

What are the barriers to eHealth development and deployment?

From the physician perspective, a number of barriers exist that inhibit the development and deployment of eHealth solutions. Removing them is critical to developing trust and acceptance. They can be summarised under the headings of legal, ethical and regulatory issues; data protection; standards and semantic and terminological interoperability; identification and authentication; finance and insurance; and, training and education.

Legal, ethical and regulatory issues

It is not always clear whether the sharing of health data by e-tools is fully covered by regional/national data protection legislation. Furthermore, it is even more unclear whether the professional insurance that covers health professionals includes coverage for liability in the case of adverse events arising from eHealth provision. This applies especially to the transfer of data across borders, where there is a lack of clarity concerning the responsibility for data handling, due to different security, storage and consent issues operating at state level (Chain of Trust, 2013, p. 19). These questions of professional liability for physicians remain to be resolved.

Creating a patient record requires the consent of the patient. For doctors, this ethically based approach is familiar, and is set out in professional codes of practice (Whitehouse and Duquenoy, 2010). In addition, laws on privacy and data protection serve to inhibit both inappropriate access and dissemination of sensitive data. That said, there is much work to be done to clarify the consent required for the transmission of sensitive information among IT systems (CPME, 2008). Although there may be processes that are familiar and acceptable under both the laws and regulations applicable within a single Member State, there is still legal uncertainty over the consent needed for cross-border transfer of data. To give one example: doctors taking consent from a patient for the transmission of a medical record from one country to another are unlikely to be fully familiar with the way in which that record is handled by the receiving country. It cannot therefore be said that the consent given by the patient is fully informed. An assumption may be made that a cross-border referral for treatment is made under a process of implied consent, but it is doubtful whether implied consent is an adequate process for information transfer. The European Commission's proposed Regulation on data protection (European Commission, 2012c) introduces greater clarity and harmonisation of the legal framework across the EU. However, the development of interoperable and secure systems of data processing and transfer between and within Member States is slow. Since it is of the utmost importance that patients have full information and legal certainty as to their rights, European physicians believe that patients must have given their explicit consent to the transfer and processing of their data when it has left the relative security of the particular country's healthcare IT system.

Data protection

Medical organisations have been generally supportive of eHealth developments, but often with reservations. Chief among their concerns has been the duty of physicians, as data controllers, to protect patient confidentiality. This duty is not just a legal requirement, but is also one demanded of them by their regulatory and licensing bodies. Confidentiality has been an integral part of medical deontological (ethical) tradition since the formulation and application of the Hippocratic Oath. In the 19th century, several European states further endorsed doctors' duty of secrecy through their penal codes (Maehle, 2003, p. 385). In line with the Commission's aim to enhance the rights of data subjects, the draft regulation of the European Parliament and of the Council on the protection of individuals with regard to the processing of personal data and on the free movement of such data (general data protection regulation) (European Commission, 2012c) introduces the "right to be forgotten"; a re-affirmation of the existing right under the current Directive to the deletion of personal data after the purpose for which it was processed has been fulfilled. On 21 October 2013, the European Parliament validated the Commission's approach and renamed this notion the "right to erasure". Although they understand the reasons behind a wish "to be forgotten", European physicians disagree with the proposed scope of such a right. In the treatment context, the "right to be forgotten or to erasure" should be balanced against the necessity for a physician to access a patient's electronic health record (EHR). Healthcare data should be stored, with appropriate security standards, in order to support patient safety in both present and future care and – in legal and liability terms – to determine that the medical treatments and decisions made by any European physician are given with the highest degree of legal certainty and accountability. In practice, a complete erasure of data cannot always be ensured; a request for this should certainly allow for a reasonable delay for the data controller to respond to the erasure request. Patients need to be informed of the risk to their care if certain, possibly crucial, information about them is not available to the treating physician. In light of the above concerns, the proposed exceptions with regard to the scope of the "right to be forgotten" to healthcare data should in fact be broadened. At the very least, it is suggested that a "flag" should be created in the health record of the patient to indicate that some information has been suppressed.

Standards and semantic and terminological interoperability

Standardisation has a variety of aspects. The standardisation of hardware or software is essential if medical records are to be transferred quickly and safely; consistency in coding between systems in primary and secondary care is essential; standardisation of data formats is also important. Beyond these aspects, healthcare IT systems will increasingly contain standardised care pathways and guidelines. These will come from such bodies as the UK's National Institute for Health and Care Excellence (NICE), which aims to advise on the most cost-effective and appropriate care. One result of greater consistency in the design of systems is that patients will be able to access more information about their conditions, a valuable addition to the information provided at a medical consultation, much of which is not retained by patients.

Standard data formats require expert input as well as user acceptance, and must be updated at regular intervals. A standard electronic patient summary is being developed at the European level. The intention is to create the minimum dataset required for a patient summary that can be transmitted across borders. Priority is being given to a dataset to be used in the context of unplanned cross-border care, since in these situations there is likely to be a deficit in the background clinical information available to the treating physician or surgeon. Such a dataset would be populated with information held in the patient's country-based record system. Synergy between the two healthcare systems would help support safer patient care. On 19 November 2013, the voluntary eHealth network of EU Member States, which had been created under Article 14 (2) of the cross-border directive 2011/24/EU (European Union, 2011), adopted guidelines on minimum/non-exhaustive patient summary dataset for electronic exchange. In line with these guidelines (eHealth Network, 2013), the basic information of a patient provides both *administrative* data, such as personal information, details of the healthcare provider in the home country and insurance information, and *clinical* data, such as information about allergies, vaccinations and recent surgical procedures. The network is co-chaired by the Commission and by Austria, as the chair representing the Member States. It brings together all 28 EU countries. In creating this "minimum dataset" it has become clear that, although there is convergence on the part of EU physicians on its content, there are substantial challenges to its creation.

Many countries have not yet progressed to the stage of holding a patient summary document. An opportunity exists here for the creation of an agreed cross-border dataset that may also inform the content of an electronic summary record (this could have a use both within a Member State as well as for purposes of cross-border transmission). Developing common standards and common terminology is key to achieving interoperability and requires the proactive engagement of all the main stakeholders involved in or impacted by the implementation of eHealth solutions (Chain of Trust, 2013, p. 28).

Semantic and/or terminological challenges are widespread (European Commission, 2012a). Semantic interoperability is defined as the "ability to interpret exchanged information achieved through shared terminologies" (Hoffmann and Podgurski, 2013, p. 58). Electronic systems rely on coding to describe as accurately as possible what health condition is being treated. In insurance-based health systems, such information will be shared with organisations responsible for reimbursement; in tax-based systems that operate an internal market, coding helps to identify the cost of a procedure or treatment, and can therefore be used to price a treatment for the purpose of commissioning care. On the prescription side, inconsistency of drug names and dosages bedevil the creation of safe prescribing databases, as does a lack of granularity in some coding systems, which identify conditions without adequate precision. Physicians welcome the publication by the European Commission of an eHealth Interoperability Framework (European Commission, 2013). The lack of interoperability in systems and services, such as electronic health records, patient summaries and emergency datasets, is a barrier to the further development of eHealth in Europe. Although interoperability would need to be achieved at local, regional and European levels, the mechanisms proposed within the framework should respect the principle of subsidiarity enshrined in Article 5 of the Treaty of the European Union. Following the conclusions of the eHealth Governance Initiative (eHGI) on semantic and technical interoperability (eHGI, 2012), the measures proposed with regard to semantics and terminology should not interfere with Member States' competences in eHealth. A principle that underlines the involvement of Member States in Article 14 (European Union, 2011) is that developments have to work with the differences between healthcare systems rather than to attempt to achieve EU-wide standards. Systems should therefore be built on information and communication technology infrastructures that already exist in the various Member States. As an organisation, the CPME believes that standardisation of information and harmonisation of definitions based on existing practices are important conditions for the greater interoperability of eHealth systems and services (CPME, 2013). This is not, however, to minimise the extent of the challenges to be faced in the future with regard to achieving harmonisation or unity in such diverse conditions.

Identification and authentication

Accurate identification, essential as a tool for authentication and authorisation of a healthcare professional, must at least be sufficient to reassure a patient that the practitioner is registered, licensed and free of disciplinary procedures. Hence, it relies on the existence of an effective and accessible dataset in which the necessary professional information is accurately held. A number of countries in Europe have such information. However, the information must be kept up-to-date, so as to be able to identify a physician with enough precision to determine his/her current specialty and status. Some countries hold very limited data. This may not represent a significant barrier to safety when care is given inside a specific country, since other checks on a physician's status will be available to the system and the patient, but it does matter when a patient is treated in another country by a physician whom s/he does not know. Competent authorities, such as medical regulatory bodies, do share information on registered practitioners, using the Internal Market Information system as a vehicle. The eHealth Network has been invited to advise Member States to develop this system to allow data exchanged under the operation of the Professional Qualifications Directive (European Union, 2005) to also be used to authenticate the identity of healthcare professionals.

Finance and insurance

The financing of eHealth systems varies substantially depending on whether the physicians concerned work within a national health system or an insurance-based health system. Some challenges are more pertinent to patients; others relate more to the physicians concerned. eHealth can yield obvious economic benefits for patients, as a result of a reduction in travel expenses related to ambulatory visits or for relatives caused by shorter or fewer hospital stays, and a lesser volume of the patients' own sick leave days. However, there are concerns that remain regarding the cost implications of the development of eHealth tools.

Proposals by the European Commission are to be welcomed to support research and innovation under the "Health, demographic change and well-being" element of Horizon 2020 (http://ec.europa.eu/research/horizon2020/index_en.cfm) – the title of the Commission's next major funding programme until 2020 – and in the framework of its European Innovation Partnership on Active and Health Ageing (http://ec.europa.eu/health/ageing/innovation/). In Europe, it is certainly necessary that all eHealth research and innovation programmes take into account cost implications, both for patients and physicians. eHealth technologies often require high development costs, and patients and physicians might not be in a position to support these. In addition, industry will benefit from the provision of development funds and a fast-track approval mechanism for new devices. Whatever the country's health system, there is a common need for coherent, integrated and comprehensive developments, in which policy and funding to support technology introduction work in step. In some Member States, such as the UK, a large percentage of physicians are either employed (in hospital care) or have an independent contractual relationship with the state system (primary care); for those clinicians who are directly employed, the costs of new IT systems will not affect them directly; it is the system that pays. However, in other Member States where most of the physicians are in "free practice" (they operate as independent professionals), the costs will need to be borne by them, by the sick funds operating in their countries, and through fees collected from patients. In either way, investment in eHealth is costly for patients, physicians and healthcare providers.

In times of financial crisis, when healthcare systems all over Europe are suffering from decreasing spending, cost implications are all the more important. Crucially, the need is for forms of investment that create a sustainability of systems and a political will that encourage incremental change to health and technology support based on a long-term plan. Such political will, and an ability to stop interfering with systems on a short-term basis, will do much to create trust in eHealth. With regard to the issue of insurance, there is currently a lack of adequate reimbursement regulations (this limitation might inhibit physicians from integrating eHealth into their practices). Much more attention needs to be given by insurers to reimbursing eHealth-based care, so as to incentivise its introduction. This will be of particular importance in the reimbursement for long-term integrated care, where developments in telehealth are driving new, and potentially cost-effective, care pathways. Sustainable, planned development relies on doctors' confidence that eHealth – as part of the overall care of the patient – is increasingly recognised as a reimbursable element of their practice.

Training and education

Education and training in eHealth are vital. Acceptance by physicians of eHealth solutions/services will be guaranteed not only if health professionals accept the benefits they bring to patient care, but also have confidence in using them. eHealth must therefore be included from the start in the health professionals' undergraduate and postgraduate curricula and in their continuous professional development programmes. Familiarity and confidence will be enhanced if healthcare managers develop clear strategies for a planned, integrated and incremental introduction of eHealth solutions; the participation of physicians must be included in the planning process in order to ensure a positive outcome. With regard to the eHealth Action Plan of 2012–2020 (European Commission, 2012b), the CPME emphasised the importance of setting up tailored and regular training at the workplace for health professionals, hence making eHealth part of continuous professional development (CPME, 2013). This workplace training introduction would help guarantee the acceptance of these new technologies by health professionals. Education, training and support should definitely address the use of technology. In general, the leveraging of the European Union's structural funds for the deployment at EU level of innovative eHealth tools and services foreseen in the proposed Action Plan is welcomed. These funds should also be used for projects intended to set up training activities for health professionals, including physicians.

How do physicians perceive these challenges?

There are at least four challenges for physicians as eHealth developments gather pace. They relate to the relative novelty of eHealth; the speed of innovation and the cost of adopting eHealth; the effects on the role of the doctor; and, specific concerns with regard to privacy issues (which were mentioned earlier, under data protection issues).

The newness of eHealth

New technology brings with it not only the need for individuals to adapt to change, but also for innovations to be embedded in clinical practice and organisational reconfiguration. As already stated, it also requires appropriate training so as to create both trust and familiarity.

Speed of innovation and cost of adopting eHealth

The pace and cost of change has been hard for many physicians: adjustment has been difficult. ePrescribing is widespread, and hospital-based specialists are familiar with remote reporting of X-rays, but other emerging technologies such as e-monitoring and telehealth require substantial system change, modification and investment. Incremental and sustainable development is the key to physician acceptance. eHealth developments build on innovation and technical development, and are always subject to economic and financial pressures. However, from a doctor's perspective they should meet the needs of the user in order to be successfully absorbed into regular practice. Healthcare and health professionals need to be intimately involved in the design of eHealth services. This includes participation in the evaluation of eHealth applications when they are purchased and in the assessment of their usability in daily practice.

Developments – in particular in sectors other than primary care – can be undermined by a lack of coherent planning or funding, and the introduction of systems that lack user support. In hospitals, systems often create multiple records and databases, and operate in silos. Many diseases require multi-team care, but the information needed to support care is poorly integrated. The delivery of long-term chronic care – an increasing demographic, social and budgetary challenge for all modern healthcare systems – should be based on the sharing of data between medical and social care organisations. At present, such a transfer between the two systems is uncommon. This leads to risks to patients, poor communication and "polypharmacy" (the giving of excessive or unnecessary prescriptions to patients).

However, stand-out successes of eHealth introduction include the development of teleradiology (for example, in the field of Picture Archiving and Communication System (PACS)) and telemedicine that allows access to specialist opinion by patients in remote geographic areas. The European Patients Smart Open Services (epSOS) project (www.epsos.eu) has successfully transferred basic patient summary information among Member States, and has provided a basis for cross-border ePrescribing that will inform a wider sharing of relevant data to support safer healthcare. Doctors make entries in written records on the basis of implied consent – making an assumption that patients will accept good record-keeping as being beneficial to their care. However, there is often more caution about recording data that may have widespread circulation without acquiring more specific consent. In 2012, the World Health Organization (WHO) claimed that the current European eHealth framework needs to be based on a more sustained foundation that includes the patients' point of view (WHO, 2012, p. 66).

Effects on the role of the doctor

The impact on the role of the doctor has two components. There is a fear that new technology will not free doctors to practise more medicine, but simply engage them in more data input. In addition, the concern that a fundamental change in the patient/doctor relationship, threatened by new technology and information flows, must not be underestimated. To deal with the first of these, if eHealth is implemented correctly, physicians will see some of their more routine daily activities facilitated. To develop trust and confidence, evidence is required that eHealth really does improve patient care without creating IT complexity. A good example of evidence of benefit is the reduction of acute admissions for heart failure obtained as a result of home monitoring of cardiovascular data. Such an example will generate confidence that a reduction in workload can be matched by an improvement in care outcomes. Priority should be given to developing IT systems to support care pathways where such gains will be seen. Cost benefits resulting from eHealth innovation lack evidence; providing such evidence, and introducing systems to exploit benefits, are of central importance.

Although the focus of this chapter is on physicians, the involvement in eHealth by patients must not be excluded. Physicians need to use technology to support (not replace) the patient/doctor relationship, while recognising that it will also deliver valuable information for patients outside the confines of the consultation. With regard to the role of the doctor, it cannot be denied that there will be apparent and substantial shifts in power towards patients. This will happen because of the importance of information. Patients with more information will have more ability to question the doctor's opinion and management, and will also have the opportunity to obtain a great deal of information outside the consultation environment. However, the acquisition of information will not necessarily be equated with the acquisition of knowledge. In future, the healthcare professional's role will include the mediation and filtering of a mass of information so as to get to the heart of the patient's special and individual circumstances. Done with skill and understanding, such a role should generate, rather than weaken, trust.

Privacy of patient data

Doctors have long been concerned about the privacy of patient data, a concern not helped today by human error in the sharing of data across sectors and fears of hacking. The 2013 Prism scandal involving the United States' National Security Agency's programme to access private user data from online email, search, video and communications networks shows how vulnerable IT solutions are (Ball et al., 2013; Greenwald and MacAskill, 2013). This gives new momentum to the revision of Directive 95/46/EC of the European Parliament and of the Council of 24 October 1995 on the protection of individuals with regard to the processing of personal data and on the free movement of such data (European Union, 1995). An inquiry committee was launched on this matter within the European Parliament's Civil Liberties, Justice and Home Affairs (LIBE) committee, by resolution 2013/2682 (RSP) (European Parliament, 2013).

Patient organisations, too, have expressed concern about a potential lack of security. However, it must be noted that patients do appear to accept a higher risk of inappropriate sharing of their data in the expectation that their care will be improved by more integrated data-sharing. An online survey undertaken by the Chain of Trust project "...revealed that patients are willing to compromise on certain aspects of their privacy if telehealth would prove to yield other benefits such as increased independence for elderly patients" (Chain of Trust, 2013, p. 20). The WHO (2012) also identified a potential lack of security concerning the use of electronic health records in contrast to paper-based health record files. This lack of safeguards exists because not all parties across the EU who are involved in accessing and processing health-related data are obliged to follow the same degree of legal or ethical behaviour.

Challenges to policy-makers

Trust and acceptability of health IT is therefore an issue that is inseparable from the requirement to deliver safe and effective development of eHealth communications among healthcare professionals. Much of the work on this has been developed at EU level, in relation to care given across EU Member State borders.

Most care in Europe is given not only inside a Member State, but also in a small, localised geographical area. Although cross-border healthcare represents a very small proportion of the contacts between patients and healthcare systems, the growth of citizen mobility around the Union and other impetuses will lead to an increase in collaboration between the healthcare systems of Member States. This collaboration will act as a significant driver for the alignment of a number of matters including systems, coding and similar legal and ethical processes across the EU.

The adoption of Directive 2011/24/EU of the European Parliament and of the Council of 9 March 2011 on the application of patients' rights in cross-border healthcare has now become a legislative anchor to eHealth, as Member States have agreed to co-operate in a voluntary network on cross-border issues in eHealth (European Union, 2011). Although currently at a low level, cross-border mobility of patients is already on the rise. Thus, it is becoming increasingly important that certain basic patient data – such as that related to allergies, medication and vaccination status – is available in an electronic and interoperable format, as proposed in the eHealth Network's

(2013) guidelines on a minimum/non-exhaustive patient summary dataset for electronic exchange.

A significant issue for policy-makers is to authenticate the identity (ID) of patients and healthcare professionals accurately. This is an essential step in authorising a physician to have access to a patient record. This challenge exists in many countries. Some European nations like Estonia or Finland operate on the basis of individuals having a universal ID that allows them access to a variety of services across unrelated sectors, such as tax and health. Other countries have an ID process that is specific to health. Yet others have a variety of identifiers that are used in their health systems.

The reasons for this range of approaches lie not only in the ways in which the various health systems throughout the EU operate; they also reflect various differences in public administration. As an example, there is a plurality of regulatory regimes and municipality of regulatory practices (Löfgren and Webster, 2009, p. 294) in the way that EU Member States implemented the EU Directive on data protection. Having said that, there is nonetheless an ambition to more strongly align public administration through e-government structures as outlined in the European Action Plan 2011–2015 (European Commission, 2010) as well as through the eHealth European Action Plan 2012–2020 (European Commission, 2012b).

Extending the benefits of eHealth

That eHealth brings benefits is undeniable. It has provided better access to healthcare in geographically remote or under-served areas such as parts of the UK (Scotland, for example), Norway and the Andalucían region of Spain. This success brings with it a problem that must be addressed. It remains to be seen how socio-economically weaker groups will be included in terms of access and use of eHealth tools, since computer literacy and the cost of technical set-up will be more difficult to achieve for some populations. It must be a governing principle that the benefits of eHealth can be shared among everyone independent of their socio-economic status; eHealth must not aggravate the disparity of these factors in terms of health outcomes. With regard to health inequalities, there is a much larger dimension. Evidence of the impact of socio-economic factors on the morbidity and mortality of different populations has been gathered on a regional and national basis (Wilkinson and Marmot, 2003). Identification of the added risk to different population groups of these "social determinants" will create powerful databases for how they can be addressed, allowing early intervention to reduce their impact on an individual's health as well as on the healthcare budget. Evidence of benefit exists, but at a level too local and disease-specific to drive developments on a national scale. This needs to change. The Chain of Trust survey has shown that eHealth is considered to contribute to the improvement of quality of care; eHealth is therefore a valid complement to conventional healthcare (Chain of Trust, 2013, p. 21). Patients feel enabled or empowered as a result of more interactive eHealth tools. Therefore, both patients and healthcare professionals think that eHealth has the potential to increase patients' adherence to treatment, care and lifestyle recommendations (Chain of Trust, 2013, p. 22). If eHealth is implemented correctly, physicians will see certain of their more routine daily activities facilitated, and communication with other colleagues improved. Duplication of tests and procedures will be avoided. If effective co-ordination and co-operation exist through interoperable systems, transfers of patient information within health systems can be ensured; patient safety and quality of care will be enhanced.

Patient groups, most notably the European Patients Forum, have been in the lead in encouraging health literacy. This is perhaps a reformulation of an earlier concept known as the "expert patient". Health literacy implies the acquisition of knowledge by patients sufficient to have an active involvement in the management of their condition. It indicates a considerable recalibration of the patient/doctor relationship, a change that the medical profession must accept. Technology and social media have created powerful, and often effective, patient fora in which there is enough knowledge to build a genuine alternative to the traditional doctor–patient model. What it may also create is such a plethora of information that the knowledge base becomes overwhelming. Whereas patients believe that the use of eHealth is conducive to increased patient empowerment, from the physician's point of view it seems that the web has created an infinite database for patients. What is missing is mediation between what information is relevant to the patient's own condition, and what is not. The doctor is in a good position to take on this role. If the relationship between patient and doctor is not redrawn in an alternate direction then there is likely to be a substantial shift towards patients relying on other sources of advice, most of them unregulated. Therefore, patients and physicians will have to re-work their relationship and enable the move to the new opportunities which IT offers for quality care. In supporting the treatment of long-term chronic care, patients feel more relaxed when their vital signs are monitored, combined with the possibility to alert health professionals in real time in the event that there are early indicators of deterioration. Further study is needed on the circumstances under which eHealth can support better healthcare, increase self-confidence, and promote awareness of symptoms and improved independence (Chain of Trust, 2013, p. 24).

Much debate takes place on the cost-benefits of eHealth. Such a debate has so many aspects that – in spite of the fact that up to now the developments in eHealth have mainly been driven by economic and technological interests – a conclusion on whether to develop technology in specific areas is probably impossible to justify on economic considerations alone. The European

Commission initiative on Telemedicine and Innovative ICT Tools for Chronic Disease Management states: "Europe is facing the challenge of delivering quality healthcare to all citizens, at an affordable cost. The increasing demand by citizens for best quality healthcare, the costs of managing chronic diseases and the need for prolonged medical care for ageing society are major factors behind this challenge" (European Commission, 2008). This initiative will stimulate technological development and thus create an eHealth market for European industry. Hence, it is most likely that the development of future eHealth applications will continue to be technological and market-driven. Healthcare for an ageing population and self-management of chronic diseases will in the near future become a huge market for healthcare delivery, and will probably be the main area for future applications of eHealth. Such a development must be guided by economic considerations of cost and benefit, however difficult these may be to rationalise, but must not be driven mainly by industry. This stance is important. It needs to ensure that patients obtain the best possible healthcare, and that both the medical profession and the technology underpinning this shift develop in a direction which supports this goal. What is needed is a balanced approach between cost and benefit considerations.

Future-gazing

The pace of technological change is bewildering, and naturally creates uncertainty as to how eHealth will both support and affect patient care, even in the very near future. Much of the concern about eHealth's development results from a certain resistance to change on the part of the medical profession, although in other areas, such as clinical practice, the profession is very good at adapting to changes in treatment. This willingness to adapt is based on both the acceptance of evidence that informs changes in healthcare, and also the professional requirement to offer patients optimum care based on up-to-date evidence. If it is correct to say that physicians are not fully ready to embrace eHealth, then it is also true that the acceleration of the rate of change in IT will present an ever greater challenge for those whose responsibility it is to introduce new technology. In fact, the resistance of the clinical profession may well be overstated. Younger doctors are usually enthusiastic about new technology. In other areas of their lives, both doctors and many patients are using social media and newer forms of communications. Such new knowledge and experience, when applied to healthcare, will argue for several changes. Examples include a much more personalised approach to care, and consequently a demand for more involvement by patients in their treatment and more responsibility taken by patients for monitoring outcomes. On its own, this change is not problematic, but it does need to be accompanied by a mind shift by patients and doctors alike, ideally at the same time and in the same direction. While patients and doctors may well react positively to the revolution taking place in health IT and in communication, society must also be confident that healthcare providers, insurers and governments will embrace these changes by creating sustainable, properly funded and secure data systems. Enthusiasm for eHealth among doctors and patients alike will be blunted if a coherent future is not articulated by these kinds of bodies.

In many ways, the development of eHealth has reached the foothills of what is still a long climb upwards towards a more integrated, relevant and sustainable IT system that supports healthcare delivery. Such an IT system should not govern healthcare delivery in the shape of a rigid scheme that infringes professional autonomy. Another critical consideration must be that currently any national health service is actually a national treatment service. The elements of a health budget that are devoted to prevention and to public health – important fields of eHealth deployment – are relatively small. eHealth needs to be harnessed in the support of public health, so that preventive programmes are underpinned by good data. Arguably, all of the currently configured and funded healthcare systems in Europe are unsustainable in the long term. However funded, the burden of dealing with demographic changes, and providing new technologies and more costly treatments, will outstrip the capacity of a healthcare service to meet these demands, whether the system is taxation- or insurance-based. The increase in long-term care of the elderly population is one factor, but life-style diseases, and the costs in investigation and treatment of conditions created by current screening measures, are others. Major changes need to be made to recognise, and react to, the enormous impact that the social determinants of health have and will increasingly have on future healthcare. The detailed identification of populations and individuals who are at an increased risk of chronic conditions can be made well before these conditions are diagnosed. This implies a much stronger focus on the causes of disease. Whether such an approach is cost-effective is for future generations of health economists to decide. However, if we can establish, at an individual citizen level, a risk that can be reduced by appropriate information and targeted screening, then such an approach must be encouraged. eHealth can offer major support to the identification of these factors, and can do so effectively from birth. It will help to identify and target people who are most at risk, well before they become patients. Screening, dietary advice and support can be targeted towards those who need it, helping to focus the use of resources more appropriately. Furthermore, developments like eHealth and work on virtual physiological humans – as outlined in other chapters of this book – are of course fascinating. There is much scope to improve the quality of healthcare for patients in the very near future through fast-paced innovation.

Conclusion

Physicians are predominantly positive as regards the aims that eHealth developments seek to provide. Key issues of professional practice must of course be addressed, such as data protection, professional confidentiality and concomitant improvements in the quality of care and patient safety. Doctors' daily work should, however, not be complicated by unusable or unsuitable IT systems.

Considerations of interoperability, patient safety, sustainability, professional acceptance, ease of use, legal and ethical certainty and security are the foundation stones of a health system – supported by eHealth – that will offer substantial benefits to healthcare, be it at a local, regional, national or European level. Healthcare management structures must provide appropriate training and education. The changing relationship between patients and their physicians must inevitably lead physicians to think deeply about how eHealth can strengthen what will become a different relationship between the two. The support of providers, insurers and governments is crucial to the incremental and sustainable introduction of eHealth, based on the principles set out in this chapter, which are so necessary if physicians are to be open and enthusiastic about eHealth's potential.

eHealth offers much: better integrated care, more reliable outcome data, the targeting of citizens who require early public health intervention, and the provision of information flows to doctors and patients that will ensure that up-to-date evidence on best practice is freely available.

The message from physicians is clear. If development in health IT continues to be undertaken piecemeal, without a clear strategy and a long-term view, the profession's support will be lukewarm. But work with doctors to design systems that they can use and that will over time be sensibly integrated into practice base these on good evidence of patient benefit, and doctors will work enthusiastically with health providers to test, develop and manage what will be farsighted changes to clinical practice and to their relationship with their patients.

Acknowledgement

The authors would like to acknowledge the work of the Chain of Trust project, co-financed by the European Commission, in which CPME was an active partner (www.chainoftrust.eu). They have drawn on a number of the project insights for some of the observations made in this chapter.

References

Ball, J., Borger J. and Greenwald, G. (2013, September 6), "Revealed: how US and UK spy agencies defeat internet privacy and security", *The Guardian*. http://www.theguardian.

com/world/2013/sep/05/nsa-gchq-encryption-codes-security. [Accessed 26 November 2013].

Chain of Trust (2013), *Chain of Trust: Understanding Patients' and Health Professionals' Perspective on Telehealth and Building Confidence and Acceptance*. Final project report. http://www.eu-patient.eu/Documents/Projects/ChainOfTrust/EPF-report-web.pdf. [Accessed 26 November 2013].

CPME (2008), E-Health – Consent and confidentiality. http://cpme.dyndns.org:591/adopted/2008/CPME_AD_Brd_251008_181_EN.pdf. [Accessed 26 November 2013]. For more information, please see: http://www.cpme.eu/data-protection/.

CPME (2013), CPME statement on "The eHealth Action Plan 2012–2020: innovative healthcare for the 21st century". http://cpme.dyndns.org:591/Adopted/2013/CPME_AD_Brd_27042013_017_Final_EN_eHealthActionPlan.pdf. [Accessed 26 November 2013].

Ebels, P. (2012, March 7), Putting the "e" in e-health. *EUobserver*. http://euobserver.com/e-health/115436. [Accessed 26 November 2013].

eHealth Governance Initiative (2012), Discussion paper on implications of the proposed general regulation on data protection for health and eHealth. http://www.ehgi.eu/Download/eHealth%20Network%20Paper%20-%20eHGI%20Discussion%20Paper%20Data%20Protection%20Regulation_FINAL%20adapted.pdf. [Accessed 26 November 2013].

eHealth Network (2013), Guidelines on minimum/non-exhaustive patient summary dataset for electronic exchange in accordance with the cross-border directive 2011/24/EU. http://ec.europa.eu/health/ehealth/docs/guidelines_patient_summary_en.pdf. [Accessed 26 November 2013].

European Commission (2008), Summary document on the European Commission initiative on telemedicine and innovative ICT tools for chronic disease management, 30 May 2008. http://ec.europa.eu/health/archive/ph_overview/health_forum/docs/ev_20080530_rd04_en.pdf. [Accessed 26 November 2013].

European Commission (2010), The European eGovernment Action Plan 2011–2015: harnessing ICT to promote smart, sustainable & innovative government, COM (2010) 743 final. http://eur-lex.europa.eu/LexUriServ/LexUriServ.do?uri=COM:2010:0743:FIN:EN:PDF. [Accessed 26 November 2013].

European Commission (2012a), Discussion paper on semantic and technical interoperability, 22 October 2012. http://ec.europa.eu/health/ehealth/docs/ev_20121107_wd02_en.pdf. [Accessed 26 November 2013].

European Commission (2012b), eHealth Action Plan 2012--2020 – Innovative healthcare for the 21st century. COM (2012)736 final. http://ec.europa.eu/digital-agenda/en/news/ehealth-action-plan-2012-2020-innovative-healthcare-21st-century, http://ec.europa.eu/information_society/newsroom/cf/dae/document.cfm?doc_id=1252. [Accessed 26 November 2013].

European Commission (2012c), Draft regulation of the European parliament and of the council on the protection of individuals with regard to the processing of personal data and on the free movement of such data (general data protection regulation). http://ec.europa.eu/justice/data-protection/document/review2012/com_2012_11_en.pdf. [Accessed 26 November 2013].

European Commission (2013), eHealth European interoperability framework study, http://ec.europa.eu/digital-agenda/en/news/ehealth-interoperability-framework-study. [Accessed 26 November 2013].

European Parliament (2013), Resolution of 4 July 2013 on the US National Security Agency surveillance programme, surveillance bodies in various Member States and their impact on EU citizens' privacy. http://www.europarl.europa.eu/sides/getDoc.do?type=TA&language=EN&reference=P7-TA-2013-322. [Accessed 26 November 2013].

European Union (1995), Directive 1995/46/EC of the European Parliament and of the council of 24 October 1995 on the protection of individuals with regard to the processing of personal data and on the free movement of such data, OJ L281 23/11/1995 (31–50). http://ec.europa.eu/justice/policies/privacy/docs/95-46-ce/dir1995-46_part1_en.pdf. [Accessed 26 November 2013].

European Union (2005), Directive 2005/36/EC of the European Parliament and of the council of 7 September 2005 on the recognition of professional qualifications, OJ L255 30/09/2005 (22–142). http://eur-lex.europa.eu/LexUriServ/LexUriServ.do?uri=OJ:L:2005:255:0022:0142:en:PDF. [Accessed 26 November 2013].

European Union (2011), Directive 2011/24/EU of the European Parliament and of the council of 9 March 2011 on the application of patients' rights in cross-border healthcare, OJ L088 04/04/2011 (45–65). http://eur-lex.europa.eu/LexUriServ/LexUriServ.do?uri=OJ:L:2011:088:0045:0065:en:PDF. [Accessed 26 November 2013].

Greenwald, G. and MacAskill, E. (2013, June 6), "NSA Prism program taps in to user data of Apple, Google and others", *The Guardian*. http://www.theguardian.com/world/2013/jun/06/us-tech-giants-nsa-data. [Accessed 26 November 2013].

Hoffman, S. and Podgurski, A. (2013), "Big bad data: law, public health, and biomedical databases", *Journal of Law, Medicine & Ethics*, Spring: 56–60.

Löfgren, K. and Webster, C.W.R. (2009), "Policy innovation, convergence and divergence: considering the policy transfer regulating privacy and data protection in three European countries", *Information Polity* 14 (4): 279–298.

Maehle, A.-H. (2003), "Protecting patient privacy or serving public interests? Challenges to medical confidentiality in imperial Germany", *Social History of Medicine* 16 (3): 383–401.

Stroetmann, V., Thierry, J.-P., Stroetmann, K. and Dobrev, A. (2007), *eHealth for Safety: Impact of ICT on Patient Safety and Risk Management*, Luxembourg: Office for Official Publications of the European Communities. http://www.ehealth-for-safety.org/news/documents/eHealth-safety-report-final.pdf. [Accessed 26 November 2013].

Whitehouse, D. and Duquenoy, P. (2010), "eHealth and ethics: theory, teaching, and practice", in Haftor, D. and Mirijamdotter, A. (eds) *Information and Communication Technologies, Society and Human Beings: Theory and Framework* (Festschrift in honour of Gunilla Bradley),Hershey, PA: IGI Global.

Wilkinson, R. and Marmot, M. (eds) (2003), *Social Determinants of Health: The Solid Facts*. 2nd edn. Copenhagen: WHO Regional Office for Europe. http://www.euro.who.int/__data/assets/pdf_file/0005/98438/e81384.pdf. [Accessed 26 November 2013].

World Health Organization (2012), *Legal Frameworks for eHealth: Based on the Findings of the Second Global Survey on eHealth*. (Global Observatory for eHealth Series, v. 5). Geneva, Switzerland: World Health Organization Press. http://whqlibdoc.who.int/publications/2012/9789241503143_eng.pdf. [Accessed 26 November 2013].

8

Nursing's Pivotal Role in eHealth: A Brief, Selective History

Nicholas R. Hardiker

Introduction

Florence Nightingale first drew attention to the problems associated with hospital record-keeping 150 years ago, thereby establishing a basis for contemporary health informatics. The advent of computers over the past half century or so provided new opportunities for nurses to engage with informatics. This chapter maps the evolution of nursing informatics over the past several decades, drawing on work around terminology and vocabularies. It charts nurses' involvement in informatics from their relatively humble beginnings to their pivotal role in many innovations in the field.

The "birth" of nursing informatics

Mirroring their important role as information brokers and co-ordinators of health and health care, nurses have been central to health informatics (eHealth) since its inception.

Florence Nightingale, a nurse who is widely credited as the founder of contemporary hospital epidemiology, was instrumental in establishing the basis for informatics as we know it today. For example, in *Notes on Hospitals*, published 150 years ago, she complained: "In attempting to arrive at the truth, I have applied everywhere for information, but in scarcely an instance have I been able to obtain hospital records fit for any purposes of comparison" (Nightingale, 1863). Nightingale also called for tables to provide "an (sic) uniform record of facts" covering, among other items, the total sick population, the number of cases and annual proportion of recoveries. Coincidentally, *Notes on Hospitals* was published around the same time as Charles Babbage was completing the design for his Difference Engine Number 2, which is widely considered to be a prototype for the first computer.

As far back as 1952, leaders in nursing have argued for a tighter focus on informatics: "The practice of extensive charting probably did no great harm a decade or so ago. There were plenty of nurses. The physician was not crowded with an office full of patients demanding of his time. Today, the nursing shortage being what it is, every effort should be made to utilize our nurses to the utmost and not take their time with clerical work of no immediate value" (Gorby, 1953). In the 1960s, very early into the practical application of computing, nursing was laying the foundations for a future informatics infrastructure. In 1962, the American Nurses Association included these relevant topic areas in its blueprint for research in nursing:

III Communication and Decision Making in Nursing – Research into the decision-making processes in nursing: communication, information theory and factors affecting decision-making.

A. Communication
   1. Processes
   2. Systems, including electronic monitoring devices
B. Accumulating, Storing and Retrieving Informatics Related to Patient-Care, Research and Professional Literature
C. Decision-Making
   1. The process of decision-making in nursing
   2. Factors influencing the process in various areas of nursing.

(ANA Committee on Research and Studies, 1962)

One of the most significant contributions to informatics from nurses has been work around standardised or controlled vocabularies. This work has been active for a number of years. Significant progress was made in the 1980s and early 1990s. There has very much been a need for systems that support the work of nurses in a multi-disciplinary service, and the representation of the contribution of that work in aggregated healthcare information.

At least four factors appear to have contributed to this enthusiasm:

- The imperative to manage resources more effectively;
- The emphasis on "evidence-based practice";
- The implementation of electronic patient records;
- A desire to ensure the visibility of nursing in healthcare systems.

The growth of nursing informatics

Nurses have been involved in health-related computer projects for several decades, and have been writing about their experiences for over 50 years. Much of this groundbreaking research still resonates today. For example, an early article (Sherman, 1965) entitled "Computer system clears up errors, lets nurses get back to nursing", in many respects mirrors contemporary imperatives to release time for nurses to provide direct patient care (NHS Institute for Innovation and Improvement, 2013a).

In 1975, Goodwin (now Ozbolt) and Edwards described the development and testing of a computer program to support the nursing process (a care-oriented modification of the scientific method) in the United States of America (USA) (Goodwin and Edwards, 1975). This is a functionality with which many researchers and developers are still struggling. To put this development into historical context, the work of Goodwin and Edwards was reported on two years before the nursing process was formally introduced to the United Kingdom, and six years before IBM launched its first personal computer.

But what is nursing informatics, and what is the role of nurses in informatics? One of the first published definitions for nursing informatics appeared in the proceedings of *MEDINFO 80*, the third World Congress of Medical Informatics, which was held in Tokyo in 1980: " ... the application of computer technology to all fields of nursing – nursing services, nurse education, and nursing research" (Scholes and Barber, 1980). Throughout the 1980s, a number of scholars reinforced this somewhat information technology-oriented view. For example, Hannah (Hannah, 1985) proposed the following definition: "The use of information technology in relation to any of the functions which are within the purview of nursing and which are carried out by nurses. Hence, any use of information technology by nurses in relation to the care of patients, or the educational preparation of individuals to practice in the discipline is considered nursing informatics."

At the end of the 1980s, however, Graves & Corcoran (Graves and Corcoran, 1989) looked beyond the mere application of information technology: "Nursing Informatics is a combination of computer science, information science and nursing science, designed to assist in the management and processing of nursing data, information and knowledge to support the practice of nursing and the delivery of nursing care." With this definition, the emphasis of nursing informatics moved away from applying information technology solely within the domain of nursing, to supporting nursing through much broader informatics.

There are three key features in the Graves and Corcoran definition that appear to characterise nursing informatics:

- Supporting health;
- Managing data, information and knowledge that is relevant to nursing;
- Using tools or techniques from a number of academic disciplines.

These features persist in more recent attempts to define nursing informatics. The current definition (originally adopted in 1998, but refined in 2009) by the Special Interest Group on Nursing Informatics of the International Medical

Informatics Association (IMIA-NI) (http://www.imia-medinfo.org/new2/node/151) stipulates: "Nursing informatics science and practice integrates nursing, its information and knowledge and their management with information and communication technologies to promote the health of people, families and communities worldwide."

Supporting informatics through various institutions and organisations

The fourth World Congress of Medical Informatics (*MEDINFO 83*) was an important event for nursing informatics as it provided the venue for the first meeting of IMIA-NI. IMIA-NI was established initially as Working Group 8 of the International Medical Informatics Association in order to serve the needs of people working in the field of nursing informatics. The need for a new working group had been identified in London in 1982 at a conference entitled "The Impact of Computers on Nursing". This first international conference on nursing informatics attracted 550 delegates – a number that is impressive even by today's standards – and demonstrated a significant groundswell of interest that persists to this day (Scholes et al., 2000).

The second international conference on nursing informatics, entitled "Building bridges to the future", was held in Calgary, Canada, in 1985. IMIA-NI assumed responsibility for organising this conference and continues to organise the ongoing International Congress in Nursing Informatics.

The original terms of reference for IMIA-NI have been expanded over their 30 years of existence into a set of goals and objectives. This is the organisation's mandate:

The focus of IMIA-NI is to foster collaboration among nurses and others who are interested in Nursing Informatics to facilitate development in the field. We aim to share knowledge, experience and ideas with nurses and healthcare providers worldwide about the practice of Nursing Informatics and the benefits of enhanced information management.

The Plan includes specific objectives:

- Explore the scope of Nursing Informatics and its implication for health policy and information handling activities associated with evidence based nursing practice, nursing management, nursing research, nursing education, standards and patient (or client) decision making and the various relationships with other health care informatics entities.
- Identify priorities or gaps and make recommendations for future developments in nursing informatics.
- Support the development of nursing informatics in member countries and promote nursing informatics worldwide.

- Promote linkages and collaborative activities with national and international nursing and healthcare informatics groups and nursing and health care organisations globally.
- Provide, promote and support informatics meetings, conferences and electronic communication forums to enable opportunities for the sharing of ideas, developments and knowledge.
- Participate in IMIA working group and special interest groups to present a nursing perspective.
- Develop recommendations, guidelines, tools and courses related to nursing informatics.
- Encourage the publication and dissemination of research and development materials in the field of nursing informatics.
- Support and work with patients, families, communities and societies to adopt and manage informatics approaches to healthcare.

(IMIA, 2013)

In short, IMIA-NI seeks to advance nursing informatics and to position nursing within the wider informatics community.

The General Assembly of IMIA-NI is made up of representatives from around the world who are nominated by national groups on nursing informatics. Examples include the British Computer Society Nursing Specialist Group and the American Medical Informatics Association Nursing Informatics Working Group.

A number of other organisations provide support for nursing informatics. For example, the Health Information Management Systems Society (HIMSS) maintains an online community that provides job listings, networking opportunities, salary guides and education for nursing informatics professionals (HIMSS, 2013). National groups also play a more local supporting role in their respective countries.

Doing informatics: A focus on clinical terminology

It would be difficult to find an area of health informatics that has not been influenced by nursing. For example, nurses have been central to developments from technical standards to automated decision support applications. However, one particular area in which nursing informatics has made a significant and visible contribution is in the field of clinical terminology.

A major driver for terminology work in nursing was the development of a Nursing Minimum Data Set (NMDS) throughout the 1980s in the USA (Werley et al., 1995). The NMDS is a high-level information model that provides a framework for the consistent collection of nursing-relevant data. Substantial terminology work had been carried out prior to the completion of this dataset. However, the work on the NMDS focused efforts and provided an impetus, particularly in the USA, for the more extensive development and refinement of structured terminologies for describing patient problems, nursing interventions and nursing-sensitive patient outcomes.

The enthusiasm for an NMDS has not waned over subsequent decades. In 1994, the American Nurses Association (ANA) Steering Committee on Databases to Support Clinical Nursing Practice recognised just four terminologies; today, the ANA acknowledges twelve terminologies and datasets. Examples of nursing-oriented terminologies recognised by the ANA are the Nursing Interventions Classification and Nursing Outcomes Classification (www.nursing.uiowa.edu/excellence/nursing_knowledge/clinical_effectiveness/index.htm); the Omaha System (www.omahasystem.org); NANDA International (www.nanda.org); the Clinical Care Classification (www.sabacare.com); and the Perioperative Nursing Data Set (www.aorn.org/Clinical_Practice/EHR_Periop_Framework/EHR_Perioperative_Framework.aspx). There are of course many more terminologies in use locally, regionally and nationally by nurses across the world.

In response to this proliferation of terminologies worldwide and the increasing need to provide comparable nursing data, in the 1990s a number of researchers concentrated on the need for a more rigorous approach to nursing terminology (for example, Henry and Mead, 1997; Hardiker and Rector, 1998). Their work in nursing concept representation continues to influence terminology work in nursing and beyond, and has provided a significant contribution to the development of reference terminologies such as SNOMED Clinical Terms and the International Classification for Nursing Practice. The first is a multi-disciplinary terminology administered by the International Health Terminology Standards Development Organisation (www.ihtsdo.org/snomed-ct), and the second is a nursing-focused initiative led by the International Council of Nurses (Coenen, 2003; www.icn.ch/pillarsprograms/international-classification-for-nursing-practice-icnpr).

In order to inform and support the development and integration of a nursing reference terminology, the Nursing Terminology Summit was established in 1999. It was an invitational international think-tank of terminology thought leaders that met annually for over a decade at Vanderbilt University, Nashville, USA (Ozbolt et al., 2001). The longevity of the summit was an indicator of its success; it provided a model of productive collaboration. This work has now been subsumed into the IMIA-NI Healthcare Standards Working Group.

This foundational terminology work also prompted efforts in international standardisation that built on work previously conducted in Europe (European Committee for Standardization, 2000). The standards initiative was jointly led by the International Council of Nurses and IMIA-NI (which demonstrated its supporting role in nursing informatics). It was conducted under the auspices of the International Organization for Standardization (ISO). The result was an international standard, entitled "Integration of a Reference Terminology Model for Nursing". This standard defines the desirable characteristics of statements that describe nursing diagnoses and nursing actions (International Organization for Standardization, 2003).

The ISO 18104 standard (ISO 18104:2003) was the first international technical standard for nursing; it was also the first international standard to come out of the terminology working group of the ISO's Health Informatics technical committee (ISO/TC215). This was a significant achievement. It positioned nursing informatics as a major player within the wider field of health informatics. The standard is currently under revision, and has the new title of "Categorical structures for representation of nursing diagnoses and nursing actions in terminological systems".

Nursing continues to be a trailblazer in the standardisation field. For example, in 2005 the International Council of Nurses, which is based in Geneva, Switzerland, launched Version 1 of its International Classification for Nursing Practice. Prior to its launch, the International Classification for Nursing Practice Strategic Advisory Group had recommended the provision of a formal foundation to the terminology, based on the Web Ontology Language, in order to support its development and maintenance and to ensure consistency. The Web Ontology Language (known as OWL) has been used in all subsequent versions and releases. The latest revision of the World Health Organization's International Classification of Diseases (ICD-11) is also now, for the first time, using OWL to support its development (www.who.int/classifications/icd/revision/en/index.html).

Advancing informatics and broadening its reach

Florence Nightingale wrote in *Notes on Nursing,* an earlier, sister publication to *Notes on Hospitals*:

> If you find it helps you to note down such things on a bit of paper, in pencil, by all means do so. I think it more often lames than strengthens the memory and observation. But if you cannot get the habit of observation one way or other, you had better give up the being a nurse, for it is not your calling, however kind and anxious you may be. (Nightingale 1860)

Nursing has clearly moved on. Although the pace of adoption of information and communication technology (ICT) in healthcare has been slower than in many sectors, nurses across the world are increasingly realising its inevitability and its implications for nursing practice and patient care.

Many countries across the world, such as Australia and Canada, now have national information and communication strategies for healthcare. National regulators, such as the United Kingdom's Nursing and Midwifery Council (http://www.nmc-uk.org) are now rolling out standards for nurses' education that require informatics as core curriculum content. These standards also include a list of basic competencies for practice. These include the use of ICTs; the maintenance of accurate, clear electronic records (along with paper records); the security and confidentiality of information; and the use of data and information to improve the health of individuals, communities and populations, and to support decision-making.

The curricular concentration on these issues is hardly surprising, since allegations against nurses in fitness for practice hearings, in the United Kingdom at least, often feature informatics-related concerns such as a failure to maintain adequate records, incorrect administration of drugs, access to pornography sites and inappropriate use of social networking sites.

The lack of access to appropriate technology in the workplace – as one of several factors – is seen to negatively affect the ability of specialist nurse practitioners to carry out their role: "Lack of office space, clerical support, communication technology, and educational opportunities are common role barriers, and inattention to these basic resources marginalises the purpose and legitimacy of APN roles" (Bryant-Lukosius et al., 2004).

However, a lack of access to ICT is not the only issue. In addition, this phenomenon is not confined to specialist nurses. Like other health professions, at all levels of nursing, job descriptions and even contracts of employment increasingly include aspects of informatics, from collecting data to generating reports via electronic systems. There are good reasons for this. There is evidence to support the application of informatics in healthcare, from greater adherence to guidelines through decision support systems, to enhanced surveillance and monitoring and reduction in medication errors (Chaudhry et al., 2006). However, evidence to support the application of informatics to nursing itself remains sparse (Urquhart et al., 2009). More research is needed to genuinely demonstrate to funders and other stakeholders the benefits that are already accruing in practice. For example:

> Healthcare staff no longer need to return to their office or waste hours trying to track down patient information. This means greater productivity and a much better patient experience. (NHS Institute for Innovation and Improvement, 2013b)

There is little doubt that nursing informatics should be considered a discipline or a specific field of study. There are now numerous Masters-level training programmes across the world that either focus on nursing informatics or that include at least a large component of nursing informatics. Two examples of such courses are offered at the University of Colorado and the University of Phoenix in the USA. Similar Doctoral-level programmes are increasing in number, and are now available in the USA at, for example, the universities of Maryland and Minnesota.

More questionable is whether nursing informatics should be considered as a profession in its own right. To draw a parallel with nursing, the professionalisation of nursing was built on a number of key foundations. They included the following three levels:

- marketable specialised knowledge (affording also a degree of autonomy);
- standards of practice (with controlled entry into the profession);
- regulation by an occupational organisation associated with disciplinary powers (Schober and Hinchliff, 1985).

These building blocks are now in place in many countries, and consequently, nursing is regarded as a profession in those countries.

Nursing informatics also comprises a unique body of knowledge. It is related to, but distinct from, nursing, information science and ICT, as organisations that are seeking to recruit nursing informatics specialists across the world will testify. Standards of practice and organisational regulation, however, are less mature in nursing informatics, even though ICT in a health context clearly has the potential to harm. For example, in closed-loop medication systems, drug dispensing is fully automated with no human checks. Various initiatives are in place, such as the Informatics Nursing Certification by the American Nurses Credentialing Center in the USA, which demonstrate that those who are certified meet nationally recognised standards in nursing informatics. Initiatives such as these would suggest that a move towards the further professionalisation of nursing informatics is inevitable, although there is still some way to go.

Conclusion

Nursing informatics has come a long way since its birth. Its identity as a discipline is now clear, it has a robust support system and an expanding and marketable knowledge base and it continues to make important contributions to the wider health informatics and informatics agendas. There is little doubt that nursing informatics has the ability to help nurses, their colleagues and, not least, their patients. Yet it is worth acknowledging that nursing informatics also has the ability to do harm. The need for consistent standards of practice and organisational regulation must now be considered essential.

There is widespread agreement that nursing informatics is not about technology. Nor is nursing informatics seeking to turn nurses into technicians.

However, if the benefits of nursing informatics are to be realised, it is important that nurses at all levels not only engage in the agenda, but also embrace its potential. In the short term, this will involve the development of new skills and more importantly, new knowledge, not least so that individual nurses can fulfil their professional obligations in an increasingly technological world. In the medium and long term, the experience of using ICT in nursing practice will provide unimaginable opportunities to transform nursing practice and to improve health across the world.

Acknowledgements

This chapter draws its inspiration in part from a previous publication (Hardiker and Park, 2005).

References

ANA Committee on Research and Studies (1962), "ANA blueprint for research in nursing", *American Journal of Nursing* 62 (8): 69–71. Available at: http://journals.lww.com/ajnonline/Abstract/1962/08000/ANA_Blueprint_for_Research_in_Nursing.16.aspx.

Bryant-Lukosius, D., DiCenso, A., Browne, G. and Pinelli, J. (2004), "Advanced practice nursing roles: development, implementation and evaluation", *Journal of Advanced Nursing* 48 (5): 519–529.

Chaudhry, B., Wang, J., Wu, S., et al. (2006), "Systematic review: impact of health information technology on quality, efficiency, and costs of medical care", *Annals of Internal Medicine* 144: 742–752.

Coenen, A. (2003), "Building a unified nursing language: The ICNP", *International Nursing Review* 50 (2): 65–66.

European Committee for Standardization (2000), *CEN ENV Health Informatics – Systems of Concepts to Support Nursing*. Brussels: CEN.

Goodwin, J.O. and Edwards, B.S. (1975), "Developing a computer program to assist the nursing process: phase I – from systems analysis to an expandable program", *Nursing Research* 24 (4): 299–305.

Gorby, J.H. and Johnson, L.W. (1953), "Nurses' notes cost money – so why not simplify them and economise?", *Modern Hospital* 81 (4): 54–56.

Graves, J.R. and Corcoran, S. (1989), "The study of Nursing Informatics", *IMAGE: Journal of Nursing Scholarship* 21 (4): 227–231.

Hannah, K. (1985), "Current trends in nursing informatics: implications for curriculum planning", in Hannah, K.J., Guillemin, E.J. and Conklin, D.K. (eds) *Nursing Uses of Computers and Information Science*. Amsterdam: Elsevier Science Publishing, Inc., 181–187.

Hardiker, N. and Park, H.A. (2005), "Nursing informatics: a personal review of the past, the present and the future", *Journal of Korean Society of Medical Informatics* 11 (2): 119–124.

Hardiker, N. and Rector, A. (1998), "Modelling nursing terminology using the GRAIL representation language", *Journal of the American Medical Informatics Association* 5 (1): 120–128.

Henry, S.B. and Mead, C.N. (1997), "Nursing classification systems: necessary but not sufficient for representing 'what nurses do' for inclusion in computer-based patient record systems", *Journal of the American Medical Informatics Association* 4 (3): 222–232.

HIMSS (2013), Nursing Informatics Community http://himss.files.cms-plus.com/HIMSSorg/Content/files/NursingInformaticsCommunity.pdf [Accessed: 16 September 2013].

IMIA (2013), http://www.imia-medinfo.org/new2/node/151 [Accessed: 16 September 2013].

International Organisation for Standardisation (2003), *International Standard ISO 18104:2003 Health Informatics – Integration of a Reference Terminology Model for Nursing.* Geneva, Switzerland: International Organisation for Standardisation.

Nightingale, F. (1860), *Notes on Nursing.* New York: D. Appleton and Company.

Nightingale, F. (1863), *Notes on Hospitals.* 3rd Edition. London: Longman, Green, Longman, Roberts, and Green.

NHS Institute for Innovation and Improvement (2013a), Releasing Time to Care: The Productive Ward http://www.institute.nhs.uk/quality_and_value/productivity_series/productive_ward.html [Accessed: 16 September 2013].

NHS Institute for Innovation and Improvement (2013b). Redesigning District Nurses Services http:// www.institute.nhs.uk/nhs_live/case_studies/redesigning_district_nurses_services.html[Accessed: 16 September 2013].

Ozbolt, J., Androwich, I., Bakken, S., Button, P., Hardiker, N., Mead, C., Warren, J. and Zingo, C. (2001), "The nursing terminology summit: collaboration for progress", in Patel, V., Rogers, R. and Haux, R. (eds) *MEDINFO 2001.* Amsterdam: IOS Press, 236–240.

Schober, J. E. and Hinchliff, S. M. (1995), *Towards Advanced Nursing Practice: Key Concepts for Health Care.* London: Arnold.

Scholes, M. and Barber, B. (1980), "Towards nursing informatics", in Lindberg, D. and Kaihara, S. (eds) *MEDINFO 80.* Proceedings of the 3rd World Congress on Medical Informatics. Amsterdam: North-Holland, pp. 70–73.

Scholes, M., Tallberg, M. and Pluyter-Wenting, E. (2000), *International Nursing Informatics: A History of the First Forty Years 1960–2000.* Swindon: The British Computer Society.

Sherman, R. (1965), "Computer system clears up errors, lets nurses get back to nursing", *Hospital Topics* 43 (10): 44–46.

Urquhart, C., Curell, R., Grant, M.J. and Hardiker, N.R. (2009), "Nursing record systems: effects on nursing practice and healthcare outcomes (Review)", *Cochrane Database of Systematic Reviews* (1): 1–68.

Werley, H., Ryan, P. and Zorn, C. (1995), "The Nursing Minimum Data Set (NMDS): A framework for the organization of nursing language", in Lang, N. (ed.) *An Emerging Framework: Data System Advances for Clinical Nursing Practice.* Washington, DC: American Nurses Association Publishing. Chapter 2.

9
The Emerging Role of the Health Informatician as a Key Player on eHealth

Jean Roberts

Introduction

This chapter looks at a wide range of aspects of the deployment and application of information technology (IT) across the health domain. It considers the role of specialist informatics and IT professionals, the health informatics skills and competencies required by other clinical and health and management personnel, and the emerging involvement of citizens in this area. It concentrates on the human resource issues relating to eHealth and, more broadly, health informatics. The workforce is a crucial element in the equation of producing effective information support to clinical specialists and health managers operationally, in education and research, and in both strategic and tactical planning. The health informatics workforce spans fields such as public and private care delivery, policy and planning, product and service provision and academia. Over time, informatics professionals have had to face different challenges, many of which are considered in this chapter. Much of the basis for the text in this chapter is the work and experiences of the United Kingdom (UK) Council for Health Informatics Professions (UKCHIP, www.ukchip.org) which is the regulatory body for health informaticians working in and for health services across the UK. Other countries are adopting and adapting the standards of generic and specialised informatics and professionalism used by UKCHIP. Many examples of eHealth in this chapter are drawn from the UK situation; comparisons with activities in other countries are also made although not exhaustively.

Defining the health informatics professional brand

It is becoming increasingly necessary to define health informatics[1] as a brand and as a profession. A first point to note is the importance of using the term "health informatics professional" rather than making a delineation between a health informatics practitioner and a health professional. The importance of this distinction lies in recognising that practitioners and professionals are selected from the same job role roster, albeit at differing levels.

The key criteria of professionals, set out by Lord Benson (House of Lords, 1992), is that they meet standards of competence, professional behaviour and ethical rules and work for the benefit of the public. Given that all healthcare practice now requires information and a capability to analyse and reference that information, health informatics professionals, including eHealth practitioners, stand "at the shoulder" of all clinicians and managers. Like those clinical and managerial individuals, health informatics practitioners must act in a professional manner and be recognised as professionals. The concept of the health informatics professional is however still developing, as noted by Hersh (Hersh, 2010) in his work reviewing the health information technology workforce, in which he argued for "more research to better characterise the workforce of those who develop, implement and evaluate HIT systems [which will] better inform the development of optimal competencies and curricula for their most effective training and education".

Characteristics of the health informatics workforce

Health informatics professionals operate in a wide variety of contexts, and face numerous challenges locally, nationally and globally.

Many countries worldwide are recognised members of the global organisation, the International Medical Informatics Association (IMIA, www.imia.org), but the situation regarding workforce recognition and profiling in a large number of countries is not clear. However, both the European Union (EU) and the United States (US) demonstrate a formal interest in several workforce issues including workforce flexibility, recognition and mobility through formal communications, such as the EU–US transatlantic eHealth/Health IT Roadmap (USHHS-EC (2013)) and the EU–US Memorandum of Understanding on Cooperation surrounding health-related Information Communication and Technologies (USHHS-EC (2010)).

National and EU-level policy commitments address a wide number of individuals, including health informatics specialists, clinicians, health managers and other end-users who require selective skills in health informatics to carry out their daily work. They include "Strategies for development of a skilled health IT workforce and of eH/HI proficiencies in the health professional workforce such that clinicians can fully utilise the technology's potential to enhance their professional experience and performance" (USHHS-EC (2010)). Yet the health informatics community "salami" is sliced in different ways by different bodies. There is variety in the diverse categorisations of careers and skills described. For example, the UK National Health Service Health Informatics Career Framework (www.hicf.org) (Figure 9.1) is designed as a set of detailed job role descriptors. It is based on some guiding "stepping stones" that reflect opportunities for workforce migration and personal development.

The UKCHIP has developed a set of standards across four quadrants (Figure 9.2), covering general and specialist competences in both informatics and professionalism. The detailed content can be seen on www.ukchip.org .

There are a number of ways to categorise the health informatics community: it can contain a range of personnel who have health informatics skills and competencies. It is proposed to classify job roles into two distinct categories: those

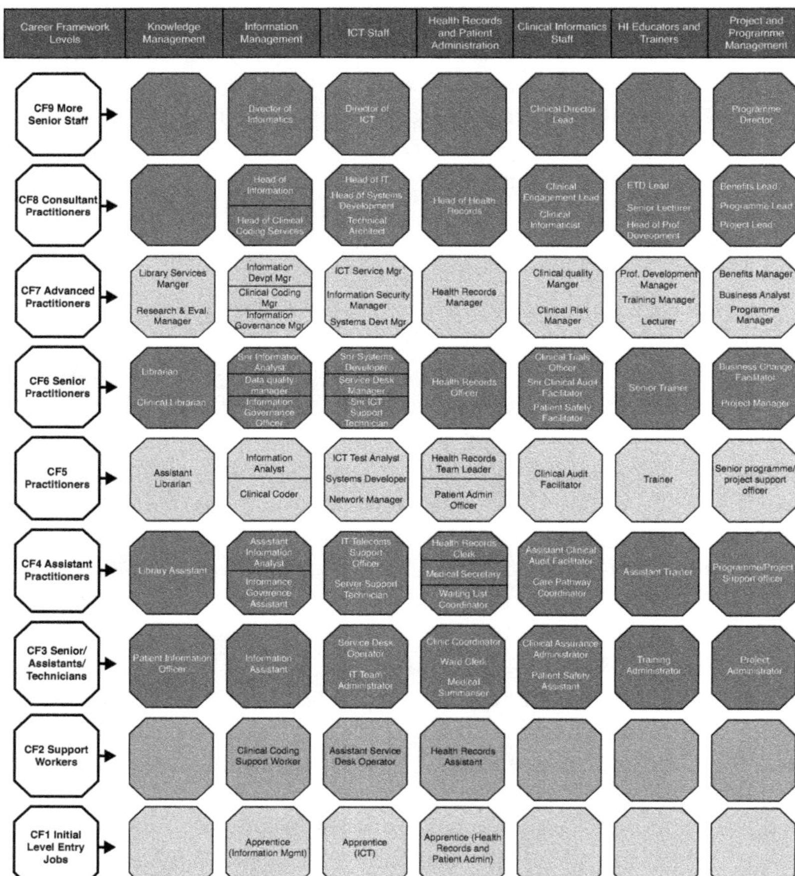

Figure 9.1 NHS Health Informatics Career Framework, Stepping Stones (permission NHS Wales)

Figure 9.2 Structured Standards Schema, UK Council for Health Informatics Professions (permission UKCHIP)

who work "in the system" (who are end-users) and those who work "on the system" (who are, for example, designers, developers and educators).

Hence, individuals can be defined either as domain-sensitive health informatics professionals or as experts from a related field who have "embedded" competences. A team of people active in health informatics can be described by their collective competences. A human resource planner or manager can define the skills required to carry out a particular project by a group or groups of individuals. That person-level information can then be aggregated so as to build a profile of what support current health informatics provides, for example, to the care services. This process offers a picture of how third parties can provide input to the mixed economy of health services, if and when the outsourcing of specific services becomes a higher priority.

Health informatics performance outcomes – however delivered – could be benchmarked and evaluated. Realistic gap analysis and modelling of future health informatics workforce demands for specific projects, staff succession planning or service restructuring (due to reorganisations or strategic changes) may all be needed. Some national health services providers or chains of private health providers are carrying out these types of analysis already.

By using consistent definitions of skills and competences, various risks could be reduced. The risks include that the conclusions reached by such workforce projections may be variable due to differential definitions, and data inconsistency may result from a lack of monitoring of workforce mobility.

To add complexity, members of the health informatics workforce may change their jobs many times over a career lifespan. They may move through the health domain from operational health delivery organisations, to academia, commercial consultancies and solution providers, as well as among these organisations. This may make a clear and distinct career profile hard to maintain for a health informatician. Unless commonly recognised definitions and standards are used, giving explicit career guidance to individuals could be challenging and recording their career progress could be unclear.

Alongside the health informatics professional, other healthcare professionals acquire health informatics' skills through the specific requirements of their profession. These skills are then embedded alongside selected skills belonging to the health informatics professional. Increasingly such skills and competences are also being identified in individual citizens who wish to become more involved in their own care and have access to their electronic health records.

A significant population of expert end-users is being created who are involved in, and can be recognised for, their embedded competence in health informatics. Typically, these experts are operational health professionals – clinicians, health managers and allied health professionals or health science professionals. These end-users are needed both to validate design specifications and to test the solutions developed to ensure that they are "fit for purpose". Their competence should be defined using the same standards as those of health informatics professionals in order to enable effective dialogue and avoid misinterpretation of the requirements of any application solution.

Future challenges for the health informatics workforce context

Given the increasingly public role of health informatics professionals, changes are to be expected in their workforce context. A number of challenges are emerging in terms of the health informatics workforce. At least five drivers are immediately obvious. These drivers include health informatics professionals' extended direct interaction with members of the public; some "right-sourcing" of health information processing; an explosion of the myth that health data belong to doctors; support for the use of secondary data; and an increase in the use of mHealth.

Extended direct interaction with members of the public – Health informatics professionals may soon begin to interact in a more intensive way with the general public. An informatics-literate public whose members can access extensive domain-specific information will create expectations regarding at least two health issues. These include, first, a capacity to investigate the efficacy of proposed treatments and, second, an international anticipation of certain practices, which may be unachievable and remain unfulfilled in particular countries or cultures without a full range of technologies in place. Health informatics professionals may therefore be asked to explain in lay terms why a technological situation or a clinical case is not applicable in a specific hospital or facility. On the technical side, this could involve, for example, not being able to access one's own personal health record electronically or to receive an SMS message as a reminder of an outpatient appointment; on the clinical side, it could be an explanation for why a certain drug regime or an operating theatre procedure identified on the Internet is not feasible locally.

Right-sourcing (offshoring or outsourcing) of health information processing – The processing of health information may increasingly be outsourced and delivered by third-party organisations. Today, many services that are not thought to be at the core of healthcare delivery are under pressure. They are considered ripe for offshoring (or "right-sourcing", as Sparrow (2004) termed it). In my own response to the generalities of offshoring, I stated that "We cannot stop the process of globalisation but intend to take our place within it, both ensuring our people are recognised for their expertise and experiences and that anyone working in our domain respects its singularities" (Roberts, 2006). Health informatics professionals have to be able to seriously evaluate the business cases for information processing in support of health delivery and their being undertaken in a variety of ways: for example, recognition that healthcare either can or cannot be delivered at a distance, or by third parties, or without taking the context into consideration.

Exploding the myth that patient data belong to the doctor – In general terms it is correct to say that patient data belong to the patient, in the sense that patients have the right to control who has access to their data and for what purposes. In most situations and jurisdictions, they will also have some legal ownership rights. However, some clinicians are still of the opinion that data about patients belong to doctors themselves and that they can determine what is done with that data unilaterally. They may therefore request health informatics professionals to process the data without having obtained the consent of the patient and without the support of any previous evidence base or professional practice. Health informatics professionals have to feel that they can refuse diplomatically the task requested of them if this kind of situation occurs.

Supporting secondary use of data – An example of secondary use of data might include exploration of the re-use of health record contents (for example, in an anonymous format for financial return, probably by third-party researchers). If health informatics staff members are not committed to a professional code of conduct, this could result in their supporting inappropriate use of the information collected for other purposes and for which the subject's consent had not been given. Having a professional code would support health informatics professionals in refusing to carry out actions that are not professional or are unethical. The UK is currently developing processes that will enable agreement on managing health data for secondary analysis at clinical cohort and population levels in a manner that is trusted by the public. This is being undertaken to address at least three concerns: that data are being used without explicit consent for analyses which are being conducted in an improper manner, or data manipulations or deductions are being applied that are not ethically sound, or datasets are being combined in ways that are inconsistent or unsuitable for the analysis requested.

mHealth as a concept – Mobile technologies are becoming ubiquitous. mHealth enables health information to be transmitted across wireless networks. mHealth is already grasped and understood by many citizens. This move is accelerating the fact that expanding numbers of members of the public are becoming more engaged in their own care. Health informatics professionals will increasingly be involved in producing shareable and more robust versions of the mobile applications ("apps") available and in transmitting, validating and collating information from these types of solutions into patients' medical histories.

More and more, health informatics professionals will be required to emerge from behind their desks. They will form part of the "front office" health team that interacts directly with the public. Thus, they will need to understand the legal, ethical and health contexts in which they work. They will be seen as a direct asset for the hospital or other facility in which they work in terms of operational management and strategic planning. They will "sit at the right hand" of the management team. They may proactively present the analysis of performance, highlight opportunities that result from various emerging technologies and point out any epidemiological population movement that has a potential impact on the surrounding health space.

Professional growth and evolution of health informatics

Health informatics development has not yet taken all the steps seen in Figure 9.3, which is based on the UK context (Roberts, 2005). This diagram shows the main phases of development in health informatics in broad terms as they have taken place in the UK. The steps may have occurred in different sequences in other countries. In fact, some steps may have been more exaggerated or others ignored – such is the diverse progression of the health informatics discipline internationally!

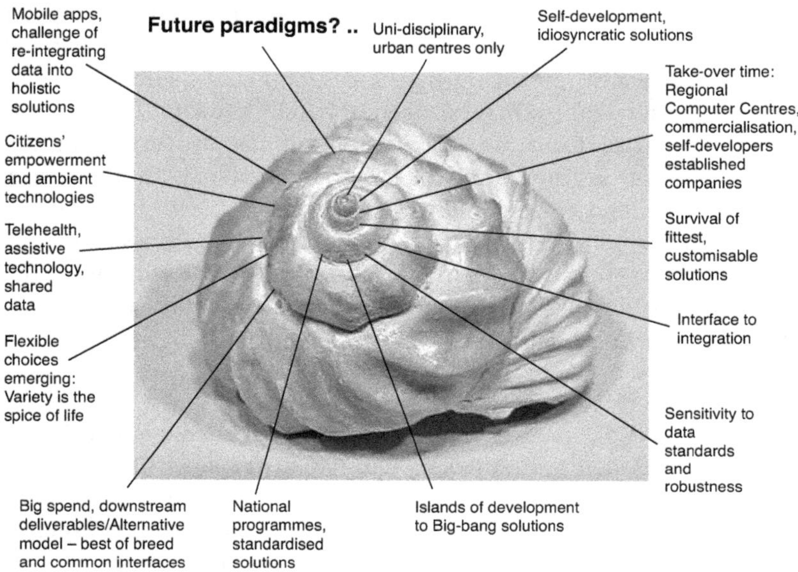

Figure 9.3 Schematic development phases of health informatics over time in England

At each of the points in the progression in health informatics, the origins, roles and competences of the health informatics professionals will have changed by expansion, specialisation or some other variation. They will have had to cope with changes in technologies, organisational developments and national or regional action plans and programmes.

Most countries in the west have full Internet access. This permits professionals to explore a comprehensive body of knowledge about health informatics and its deployment in the fields of research, efficient clinical interventions and care support. Health services are a 24/7 operation: patients may present themselves to their doctors with complex clinical challenges that require multi-professional responses, sometimes across sectorial or national boundaries and after consideration of the global evidence base. Clinical and management professionals need to be able to validate and verify findings on a just-in-time basis, either by using embedded health informatics competences themselves or by involving health informatics professionals in support of their decision-making. Making informed decisions on behalf of their patients has a down-stream impact on strategic initiatives to make the organisational system in which they work safer and more targeted to better, high-quality patient outcomes. Informed decisions can also bring about a more viable business proposition for that organisation.

Bringing about these futures will require health informatics competences to be available at many levels within organisations and in collaboration with individual health informatics specialists, clinicians, administrators and managers. The data required may be taken from multiple sources on a real-time or asynchronous basis. Collating information from care delivery organisations, coupled with that from voluntary agencies, social welfare bodies, fitness management practices and citizens themselves as end-users will take some years to achieve. People's concerns about data compatibility, cross-over impacts between the interventions of organisations with different objectives and the contentiousness of correlating this with data about exercise, eating and other lifestyle factors, have all to be faced.

Entry and career progression

> Traditionally people have entered health informatics from either the health sector or the technology industries. These career paths are still very common and moves can be made at any time during your progression. Many skills are transferable and with the addition of continued professional development and learning you can progress up the tree as far as you choose.
>
> (extract from Health Informatics Careers Rough Guide, BCS Health 2004)

Health informatics can be taken up at any point along a career spectrum: from entry to specialist senior levels. Embedded health informatics competences can be gained as an adjunct or as an integral part of initial training and development. This flexibility, however, creates a challenge for the professionalisation of health informatics. Current health informatics professionals may include personnel with a range of different career backgrounds and entry points:

- Medical professionals who developed their own health informatics solutions and gradually specialised in health informatics;
- Other clinical professionals who moved up into senior operational roles in the management of the health informatics services in their hospital, clinic or related organisation;
- Technology-grounded individuals who came into the health domain to operate or implement health informatics solutions, using their generic knowledge of hardware, project management competence or software skills, which they then applied in the health informatics sector;
- Experts in particular areas which need domain-sensitivity, such as ethics, legal or business analysis functions.

Regardless of an individual's point of entry to the career, continuing professional development is common to achieving success in health informatics.

Members of UKCHIP are required to submit a continuing professional development plan every year on re-registration to the association in order to indicate that they have made efforts to keep informed of domain changes. Examples of the kinds of evidence that they can provide include producing papers and presentations to inform the community of new ways of working or health informatics deployment, distilling the implications of a scientific paper, producing help or guidance for a department on new systems functionality, or writing articles describing the implications of an emerging technology for local newsletters.

Ultimate personal goals as a health informatician

There is no doubt that 21st century healthcare will continue to require health informatics professionals who have the skills to help the healthcare profession as a whole to:

- Audit existing clinical performance and guide the introduction of new interventions;
- Assess emerging health technologies and the efficacy of their application;
- Manage the performance of operational health facilities (such as hospitals and clinics) and staff;
- Offer input to strategic health planning, organisational effectiveness on a day-to-day basis and when infrastructures and policy changes occur;
- Inform research into emerging developments, new therapies and initiatives to improve efficiency and effectiveness and thereby increase efficacy, quality and patient satisfaction;
- Understand social circumstances, aspirations and lifestyle factors as contributors to achieving better health.

Challenging and stimulating horizons

Recognising, planning for and taking part in future developments are all actions to retain the position of health informatics to support clinical and health management changes over time. This section of the chapter makes observations on where the next challenging factors may arise and what can be done to mitigate risk and maximise the potential from these.

Grid and cloud computing – While the grid is currently predominantly used by researchers, cloud computing is being considered for use either directly by health service providers, or via third-party IT or informatics services organisations, in a similar manner to remote hosting or facilities management contracts. Using third parties gives the care provider the opportunity to concentrate on its primary purpose of health and wellness. Informed choice of locations and appropriate clinicians for necessary interventions will become the norm: it will be based on complex business analyses of performance statistics and ratings.

The health informatics support for such distributed services will require health informatics professionals to become even more aware of the structural and policy cultures in all the jurisdictions in which they work in order to maintain compliance with their professional code of conduct. They will increasingly need to be able to explain the efficacy of technologies in the context of healthcare. The choices of technology-based devices that are readily available are rapidly expanding. Therefore, health informatics professionals will be challenged to integrate eclectic devices or to describe or defend why such interconnections may not be viable, secure or appropriate.

Ambient assisted living – Increasing the utilisation and types of devices for data monitoring that raise alerts and capture data could be claimed to have the potential to reduce the need for health informatics professionals in the domain of ambient and assistive living. However, a number of substantial issues will need to be addressed on an ongoing basis by health informatics professionals. Assistive technology deployment will increase as health and social care services move to provide people with more independence, choice and control, and deliver even better care to people with long-term conditions. These types of patients are now much more involved in their own care and are becoming expert patients with extensive knowledge of their condition. These technologies enable them to take some responsibility for their condition management. Working with their health/social care providers, they can safely be given greater control over their lives. Self-management programmes can be designed specifically to reduce the severity of their symptoms and improve their own confidence, resourcefulness and self-efficacy.

Online communities of "e-patients" increasingly share evidence and information about specific conditions, and offer each other mutual reassurance. The sample apps described later in this chapter are real examples. In October 2002, Ron Merrell, Head of the Medical Informatics and Technology Applications Consortium at Virginia Commonwealth University in the USA, observed that "... In the new world order, the ePatient will be in an electronic care continuum with global medical knowledge" (NHS, 2012). This scenario is becoming a reality in more circumstances over time.

Health-related apps – Health apps are online health and care tools from many sources, all of which are increasingly accessible from mobile devices or personal computers. They enable people to use "good" information to make choices about their health and care. As more apps are used, informed members of the public will gain ready access to large amounts of health-related information. Demands to engage with health professionals will increase regarding key lifestyle activities, health choices and treatment options. Smart phone apps are becoming well utilised in student courses, for both study refreshers and to log workplace practice experiences. Health informatics professionals will bridge between end-users and providers to ensure that the devices and apps are appropriate, robust and meet ethical and socio-technical requirements.

Using health technologies innovatively has no predictable end point. Technology is however only one element in the equation of "effective, efficient and efficacious" care and treatment. In the mid-term, clinical decision-making will still require a trusted clinical professional to be able to respond rapidly to unexpected circumstances that could have life or death consequences. As Kwankam (2012) says "evidence of benefit is important in e-health adoption ... but 'pull' forces are needed in many countries if e-health is to be transformed from a passion of a select few individuals to a mainstream activity that effects the entire health system." Health informaticians will be crucial to the innovation process in order to ensure that all developments are robust, safe for patients, reflect good clinical practice and, where necessary, are consistent with all relevant related information sources and the appropriate legislative/regulatory context.

The place of the professional health informatics workforce: A summary

Technological deployment in the health space will never stand still as long as technology continues to develop. It was previously claimed that health use of technology lagged significantly behind that of commercial industry. However, continental research programmes, large-scale national initiatives taking place worldwide and capitalisation of ubiquitous devices in public use must now have closed the gap somewhat. Care delivery continues to be stretched due to an ageing society and raised patient expectations; so the demand for ever-increasing health information quality and quantity goes on. Technology is not an end itself, it has to be designed, developed and deployed with sensitivity for the health and care domains.

The practicalities of general workforce mobility require data to be available securely, as, when and where needed by authorised, authenticated health professionals and other invited persons. Preferably, this includes a holistic picture of an individual's clinical history, family traits and population trends. As Landman et al. (2010) state: "to interact appropriately within digital environments and maintain your reputation, remember the following: monitor your personal reputation; understand the privacy settings of the websites you use; remember your audience (invited and uninvited); be aware of the permanence of online content and maintain professional boundaries."

Setting up a website that has apparent legitimacy of content and credibility is now so easy that offering indicators of its plausibility, quality and authoritative sourcing are becoming ever more necessary.

Health informaticians, who act professionally, are now crucial to many technological and organisational domains in the health and care fields such as ensuring sound interfacing and interoperability, creating robust solutions and maintaining necessary quality of data content and functionality. They are ever more responsible for achieving "fitness for purpose" for applications and outputs in conjunction with articulate end-users and commissioners of services.

Note

1. The terms used for the emerging activity of health informatics have varied over time and place in terms of both the application solutions and the people who designed, developed, delivered and taught others about them. Here the term "health informatics" is used to include all these concepts and several others: patient information requirements, the content of a global evidence base, the development of technical infrastructures and structures and the cultural priorities and professionalism of those working in the field. This approach has received substantial support from an ongoing poll undertaken by the UKCHIP group on LinkedIn. Similarly, those who work in and across the health domain in informatics are termed "health informaticians" rather than eHealth practitioners or IT professionals. Hence, the top-level expression of health informatics, as an all-encompassing term, is used throughout this chapter. Health informatics is the term used by the UK Council for Health Informatics Professions, and is intended to be inclusive of all the constituencies within the community it voluntarily regulates (see www.ukchip.org).

Bibliography

BCS (2004), *Health Informatics Careers Rough Guide.*

George, C., Whitehouse, D. and Duquenoy, P. (eds) (2012), *eHealth: Legal, Ethical and Governance Challenges*. Heidelberg: Springer-Verlag.

House of Lords (1992), *Hansard, HL Deb.* (1991–92) 538, cols. 1208–10 (08 July 1992). http://hansard.millbanksystems.com/lords/1992/jul/08/the-professions#column_1208 [Accessed 26 November 2013].

Hersh, W. (2010), "The health information technology workforce: estimations of demands and a framework for requirements", *Applied Clinical Informatics* 1 (2): 197–212. doi:10.4338/ACI-2009-11-R-0011.

Kwankam, S.Y. (2012), "Successful partnerships for international collaboration in e-Health: the need for organised national infrastructures", *Bulletin of World Health Organisation* 90: 395–397. doi: 10.2471/BLT.12.103770.

Landman, M.P., Shelton, J., Kauffmann, R.M. and Dattilo, J.B. (2010), "Guidelines for maintaining a professional compass in the era of social networking", *Journal of Surgical Education* Nov–Dec; 67 (6): 381–386. doi:10.1016/j.jsurg.2010.07.006.

NHS (2012), *Learning to Manage Health Information: A Theme for Clinical Education* http://www.eiceresources.org/images/learningtomanage_12.pdf [Accessed 26 November 2013].

Roberts, J. (2006, May), *Reflections on Right-Sourcing in the Health Domain, Commentary on Health Implications: Playing to UK Strengths* [online]. www.bcs.org/content/conWebDoc/3930[Accessed 26 November 2013].

Roberts, J. (2005), *The Contribution Made to the Support of Healthcare Delivery and Management by Health Informatics at a Local and National Level Over a Period of Thirty Years*, Ph.D. thesis (University of Teesside).

Sparrow, E.A. (2004), *A Guide to Global Outsourcing: Offshore Outsourcing and Other Global Delivery Models*. Swindon: British Computer Society.

USHHS-EC (2013), *Transatlantic eHealth/health IT Cooperation Roadmap* (March revision) http://ec.europa.eu/information_society/newsroom/cf/dae/document.cfm?doc_id=1787 [Accessed 26 November 2013].

USHHS-EC (2010), *Memorandum of Understanding between The United States Department of Health and Human Services and The European Commission on Cooperation Surrounding Health Related Information and Communication Technologies* http://www.healthit.gov/sites/default/files/HHS_EC_MOU_CooperationHealthInfo_and_ComTechSigned.pdf [Accessed 26 November 2013].

10
eHealth for Patient-Driven Healthcare

Diane Whitehouse and Magda Rosenmöller

Introduction

Leading patient advocates are sending the message that "[h]elping empower patients and patient organisations benefits not only their own wellbeing but has been shown to improve the wellbeing of the community as a whole." (www.eu-patient.eu/Initatives-Policy/)

Today, the balance of responsibility in patients taking care of their own health is changing. eHealth offers a way to facilitate this transition. In terms of patient-driven healthcare, supported by eHealth, it is important to keep abreast of various developments: the kinds of improvements that patients can benefit from while using eHealth; how eHealth can enhance patients' healthcare; how information technology (IT) can help patients to achieve the full potential offered by a number of exciting innovations; and how, with the help of patients, better solutions can be found to the challenges inherent in health systems.

This chapter therefore explores how eHealth is being used by Europe's patients. It offers details of a number of initiatives, which have taken place or are underway, under the umbrella of two non-governmental organisations. From the policy viewpoint, the chapter looks at how recent European policy documents focus on the needs of patients through a series of eHealth-related activities up to the year 2020 (European Commission, 2012a; 2012b; European Union, 2012). Looking beyond this point, it examines how organisations and companies are offering innovative products and services to meet current and future healthcare demands. It also asks what further insights into the future of human beings' health can be gained by considering the implications of a number of converging technologies. Finally, this chapter can be read usefully in conjunction with three papers in the same section of this book that relate to the needs of patients and consumers: those on physicians' perspectives on eHealth (the chapter by Birgit Beger and Michael Wilks); on the use of the

Internet (the chapter by Célia Boyer and Mayoni Ranasinghe); and on social networks (the chapter by Denise Silber).

Patients – involvement in health and care

For a decade or more, European organisations have been increasingly pro-active in advocating more dynamic roles for patients. Here, the roles of just two of those organisations are examined.

The European Patients Forum (www.eu-patient.eu) was founded ten years ago, and brought together a whole series of patient initiatives. Health advocacy is at the heart of the forum's work, and this non-governmental organisation works actively with the European Union's institutions to promote a patient-centred philosophy and agenda. By monitoring all the emerging European policy developments, it keeps its members – which include a wide range of national and condition-specific organisations – informed about the latest news on policy initiatives. Besides its involvement in the policy area, the forum organises a considerable number of events – workshops and conferences. It also leads, and is engaged in, various European projects. These projects are not necessarily associated with eHealth. The forum has coordinated a handful of projects – called the *Chain of Trust, EMPATHY, EUPATI,* and *Value+* – and has participated in a dozen more. Two are particularly interesting in relation to eHealth: *Value+* and the *Chain of Trust.* First, Value+ (www.eu-patient.eu/Initiatives-Policy/Projects/ValuePlus/) focused on promoting patients' involvement in European Union-supported health-related projects. It ran between 2008 and 2010. Through an extensive literature review and the organisation of a series of focus groups and surveys, Value+ looked into the meaningful involvement of patients in projects in general and, in particular, in eHealth-related projects. As a result, it was able to produce a handbook, toolkit and policy-related recommendations. These documents advised on how larger numbers of patients might be better involved in health-related initiatives, including eHealth, not only in terms of their quantity or volume but also with regard to the quality of the learning and insights which could emerge (European Patients Forum, 2009; 2010). Second, the *Chain of Trust* project (www.chainoftrust.eu) ended in early 2013 (see the chapter in this volume by Beger and Wilks for more details). From the perspective of the main end-users of telehealth services across the Union, it assessed whether, and how, their views have evolved since the initial deployment of telehealth, and what barriers remain to building confidence in, and acceptance of, increasingly different but innovative types of services.

The European Health Telematics Association (EHTEL) is a pan-European multi-stakeholder forum. It provides a leadership and networking platform for European corporate, institutional and individual actors dedicated to improving healthcare delivery through eHealth. Founded 15 years ago in 1999, EHTEL serves and convenes a growing membership of more than 50 organisations. Although its members represent a variety of viewpoints, they are united in their interest in making eHealth work and enlarging the eHealth constituency in the European Union. EHTEL therefore facilitates the sharing of experiences about eHealth with colleagues and representatives across Europe and beyond.

One of the multitude of backgrounds and interests of EHTEL's stakeholders is that of patients. Hence, EHTEL has established a Patient and Citizens Task Force: this is a unique discussion group within the European eHealth community. It is composed of both individuals who are patients in their own right and who are representatives of different patient groups. The task force has produced a series of position papers: for example, on eHealth care at home, eHealth and patient safety and electronic health records (EHTEL, 2006a; 2006b; 2006c). EHTEL too coordinates and participates in European co-financed projects that have a strong eHealth and patient profile. EHTEL's large network of stakeholders can make a substantial contribution to these initiatives in terms of representing the views of patients alongside other actors: these include health professionals, healthcare providers, company executives and personnel working in eHealth competence centres and the field of telemedicine more generally.

In a workshop held in December 2013, EHTEL organised a public discussion on the role of patients in eHealth (http://www.ehtel.org/activities/ehtel-symposium/sustainable-partnerships-for-well-being-and-eHealth). The workshop brought together experiences from two projects focused on people with chronic diseases, patient empowerment and the self-management of health through the effective use of electronic patient records. One project is PALANTE (www.palante-project.eu) and the other is SUSTAINS (www.sustainsproject.eu). What follows is a description of the interventions into a panel debate at the workshop. Issues discussed included dilemmas about the holding and sharing of patient data as well as patients' expectations that their health data will be shared at the level of the local general practitioner in an enclosed environment that they understand well. The views expressed show that there are many challenges with regard to saying precisely where one's medical record is (physically) located. In order for patients to give their authorisation for the sharing of these data, they need to know who is using them and for what purposes. Personal data are moving out of, and away from, the localised medical team into distributed storage in the cloud, where they may also become available for research purposes. At least for the present time, a doctor, nurse and patient share some degree of physical proximity and some knowledge of each other. Once patients' personal data are held in storage, however, they "somehow just become a digital map of 1s and 0s". Thus, such data may not be treated with quite the same level of respect as it would be in a local setting. As David Garwood, an active member of the EHTEL Patient and Citizen Task Force, noted "... as patients we need to understand this process, and have information on it." In the eHealth field, the need for both clear information for patients as well as from patients is increasingly recognised.

Policy – implications for patients

The historically passive role of patients in healthcare is already changing. The central role of patients in eHealth has been underlined formally by the European Commission, in two related publications: what is known as the eHealth Action Plan (European Commission, 2012a) and the eHealth Task Force report on *Redesigning Health in Europe for 2020* (European Union, 2012). Both documents have interesting implications for European patients.

The task force report (European Union, 2012) considers new realities, such as a world in which household gadgets are all connected and provide information to a person's online wellbeing journal or where patients, together with their healthcare providers, can review their full medical records online and discuss different, personalised, options for care. Both of these scenarios were the products of the work of a small expert group, called the eHealth Task Force, which worked on collating dramatic, indeed somewhat alarming, statistics. The data collected include the overall volume of government spending on healthcare throughout the European Union; the proportion of the disease burden played by chronic conditions and information on the two-thirds of people who experience two or more chronic conditions by the time they reach retirement age.

The task force makes a plea for a radical re-design of health in which it signals that technology can play a substantial role. It states clearly the importance of three influences on healthcare: first, patients/the population as "change is [now] driven by public demand for something new and better"; second, a supportive legal framework; and, third, growth in the market. The report identifies five interrelated levers for change that build on each other: they include personal data; the liberation of data; connectivity; revolutionising health; and including everyone/everything in enhancing health. It underlines the importance of the role of individuals, citizens in general and specifically patients. The ensuing five recommendations support these levers for change, and seek to create the conditions for eHealth to transform healthcare. These recommendations propose formulating a new legal basis for health data in Europe; creating a beacon group of Member States and regions committed to open data; focusing on health literacy; making use of powerful data; and ensuring a re-orientation of European policies and funding.

Unsurprisingly, therefore, this emphasis on the collection, exchange and analysis of health data comes to the fore in a second policy document, the European Commission's eHealth Action Plan (European Commission, 2012a). In the action plan, the focus of eHealth is very much on "the interaction between **patients** and health-service providers, institution-to-institution transmission of data, or peer-to-peer communication between **patients** and/or health professionals" (authors' emphasis).

At least for the purposes of its launch, the 2012 eHealth Action Plan was portrayed as an instrument geared to enhancing the healthcare experience of Europe's patients. The goal of the plan was stated as being "to improve healthcare for the benefit of patients, [and] give patients more control of their care and bring down costs". This appears to be a transposition of the classic trio of ambitions set out almost a decade earlier to improve the access to, the quality of and the economics (efficiency and effectiveness) of healthcare services (European Commission, 2004).

Access to healthcare is today understood as patient empowerment, control and even the self-management of health. Two European Commission Commissioners made similar statements in this regard: "The new [2012] European eHealth Action Plan sets out how we can bring digital benefits to healthcare, and lift the barriers to smarter, safer, patient-centred health services", announced Neelie Kroes, Commission Vice-President for the Digital Agenda. Tonio Borg, Commissioner for Health and Consumer Policy, then stipulated that "eHealth solutions can deliver high quality, patient-centric, healthcare to our citizens. eHealth brings healthcare closer to people and improves health systems' efficiency. Today's Action Plan will help turn the eHealth potential into better care for our citizens."

At the press launch of the action plan, patients were portrayed as being absolutely in the driver's seat. The 2012 action plan itself is, however, in reality less explicit about the benefits to be obtained by patients from this shift towards eHealth. As is usual for European policy documents, its emphasis is equally, if not more, on the economy and the need for industrial growth. The plan describes the threats posed by the increasing cost of European healthcare as a measure of gross domestic product, and it outlines how 2007 expectations for expansion of the eHealth market were inhibited by the socio-economic crisis. It identifies seven barriers to the deployment of eHealth. Examples of these barriers include a lack of awareness of, and lack of confidence in, eHealth solutions among patients, citizens and healthcare professionals. Thus, there is a need for greater trust in eHealth: a topic that has been increasingly identified by a number of discussion groups and decision-makers, including patients themselves, and that is looked at also in this volume's chapter on the physicians' perspective on eHealth (see Beger and Wilks). The plan lays out a series of ways of overcoming these barriers. It sets out four objectives, all of which include raising awareness and confidence-building:

- achieving wider interoperability of eHealth services;
- supporting research, development and innovation in eHealth and wellbeing to address the lack of availability of user-friendly tools and services;

- facilitating uptake and ensuring wider deployment;
- promoting policy dialogue and international cooperation on eHealth at global level.

Each objective is, in turn, sub-divided into a number of concrete actions. Of course, several different aspects of eHealth covered in the plan are associated with patients. They relate to patient-centric technologies for cost-effective healthcare; health literacy; the role of patient summaries – that is, simple and concise subsets of electronic health records or electronic patient records; a review of data protection regulations so as to create greater patient trust in the storage and management of electronic health data (particularly "the integration of user-generated data with official medical data"); and a clarification of the status of mHealth and associated medical devices and applications. Even more practical actions could be undertaken on the policy level to make patient-centeredness a real advantage for European citizens.

Current and future opportunities

Although policy development is advancing – and implementation occasionally drags its feet – many practical shifts in direction around health, and especially eHealth, for individuals and patients are taking place. They include a focus on individual responsibility and self-management of health, health literacy, use of technologies, and – in the longer-term future – convergence of technologies and movement towards the implementation of the concept of transhumanism, thereby enhancing human beings' intellectual, physical and psychological competences.

Today, many practical experiences exist of active patient involvement in their care. Three examples follow: the three perspectives described are those of a company, a health provider and patients.

Some companies make patient involvement in their healthcare their competitive advantage. A case in point is Flowlab (www.flowlab.biz). A Spanish telemedicine accelerator for health providers, Flowlab aims to make a difference in enabling chronic patients to self-manage their pathologies and bring them an improved quality of life. The company brings healthcare to the side of patients, anywhere that they might be, and in the most simple and fun manner possible. It leverages the most advanced technology to make barriers disappear, especially in terms of heightening accessibility, understanding and usability. To design these services, Flowlab needed to gain deep insights into patients' desires: hence, it undertook anthropological and ethnographic studies with a set of patients, learned directly from the end-users and enabled joint team–patient learning throughout the development process. A profound understanding of patients' attitudes, fears, hopes and difficulties, and what their illness or condition means to them, was gained by the system's designers and developers. This awareness and analysis meant that Flowlab could design applications that really fit patients' needs, and increase patients' involvement and responsibility taking for their own health.

In other settings, patient empowerment is part of the organisation's strategy. The United States' Veterans Administration (www.va.gov) is trying to change its approach from a disease-centred to a patient-centred one. It does so, not by starting from a specific disease but with what really matters to patients (www.va.gov/health/newsfeatures/20120827a.asp). For Tracy Gaudet of the Veterans Administration, IT is the way to hardwire this shift, from personal health record to a whole person health record, so as to " ... design[ing] a personalised health plan to meet patients' goals". Commitment, training, trust and support are important elements of the Veterans Administration culture and community, which will make it an interesting initiative to follow.

Much is also done by patients themselves: for example, educating patients in their new role by using the Internet and other IT tools to improve patients' literacy. Examples include patient universities, such as www.universidadpacientes.org and www.patienten-universitaet.de.

The convergence of technologies and people will also have an important impact on patients' experiences of their wellbeing. Both individual responsibility and community commitment for people's health have profound roles to play in health improvements. To portray patients as being in command of their health is a highly attractive prospect. Mobile telephones, in particular, seem to be such an easy technology to use, and the applications available on them – including health apps – can cost pennies or cents. Together, this combination of devices and software renders the ability to monitor the effects of diet, exercise or sleep via mobile health increasingly easy and immediate. This seductive image of health self-management is especially appealing to people of particular classes and educational backgrounds who may be the early users of such technologies. Indeed, many people want to take as much responsibility for their health, welfare and well-being as they possibly can and improve it as far as they are able, using eHealth to support them. Yet, as lobby groups and academics have pointed out, a minimum of what is referred to as health literacy is needed in order to influence one's own health – the capacity to know what are the implications of certain lifestyle choices with regard to diet, consumption, pleasures and physical activities (European Health Literacy Survey, 2012; Kickbusch et al., 2013). Many patients lack these competences, not simply in Europe. Ultimately, though, "Strengthening health literacy has been shown to build individual and community resilience, help address health inequities and improve health and well-being" (Kickbusch et al., 2013).

Management of the self – and its support through eHealth – is, however, not the only part of the health equation: environmental influences and the genetic template must also be considered. The environment in which a person resides – and the air he or she breathes – is more or less either clean or polluted (European Commission, 2013). Life expectancy can vary as much across a single city, such as Glasgow in Scotland, as it can across the entire European Union from west to east or north to south. A person therefore has – or has not – the luck to be born and then reside in a particular part of a town or city or in a specific country. The employment choices that are available to people are of vital influence on their health: jobs can have both immediate and long-term effects, particularly in industries that demand hard labour or involve the handling of dangerous materials. In addition, a person is born with a completely individual set of genes, although the history and development of those genes date back many generations – as can be seen in fascinating areas of research on genetics, epigenetics and biogerontology by, for example, the Lepperdinger Group (www.uibk.ac.at/iba/lepperdinger/). These genetic aspects could have important implications for the way in which patients, pharmaceuticals and technology interact. Actual health outcomes are the result of a combination of all of these complex genetic, lifestyle, employment, educational and environmental factors.

As people at large become increasingly familiar with the often easy-to-use technologies that offer them support in their daily lives, it can be expected that patients too will become more open to taking technology use on board. Prime among these technologies today are mobile phones and, indeed, smart phones. Such technologies offer clear opportunities that enable patients to deal with their own physical health and mental health conditions, and their treatments.

Provided that there are perceivable improvements in the quality of life, and doubts about data privacy and protection are assuaged, patients are increasingly likely to become enthusiastic adopters of eHealth. They may act as a strong driving force for the use of a variety of eHealth-related devices. In the future, these smaller, and easy-to-use, eHealth technologies may become ever more miniaturised, intimate and come closer to people's bodies and minds.

As shown in the International Federation for Information Processing *Converging Technologies: Brain, Body, and Being* conference, held in Slovenia in 2010, futurists see the convergence of devices and equipment as a distinct trend in science and technology (IFIP WG9.2, 2010). Several important technologies and fields of science are merging: principal examples include bio-technologies, cognitive sciences and nanotechnologies. Different media are also coming together: for example, creative media, cloud computing, the Internet, mobile telephony and social networks. Although some technologies may drop out of sight, disruptive technologies may emerge with little foresight – yet they may be crucial in changing health systems and the role of patients (Christensen et al., 2009).

In general, however, trends and developments often take longer to materialise than are first expected. It is therefore particularly important to be conscious of how an emerging notion, such as transhumanism, may ultimately develop. How will the enhancement or advancement of human beings expand, and what is the role that technologies will play in this progress? The field is one which is gaining momentum, and generating considerable enthusiasm as well as resistance and a desire to regain control (see, for example, De Grey with Rae, 2007; Garreau, 2005; Hughes, 2004; Kurzweil, 2006).

From the standpoints of social awareness, societal awareness and ethics, it is important to take several actions. It is crucial to assess where this joining-up of technology and society is bringing humankind, to emphasise in what direction human beings would like to head in the future and what pro-active actions they should prioritise, and to determine how to take responsibility – alongside people and patient – for these future priorities, particularly in terms of health, care and welfare.

Concluding reflections

This short chapter offers a rapid overview of the relationship between patients and eHealth, and improved healthcare. It explores the modification in expectations that is taking place with regard to patients taking greater responsibility for their health status. General initiatives, European co-financed projects and European and international policy developments are all coming together to enhance the health and care of human beings. By 2020, the ambition is to increase the healthy lifespan of the Union's citizens by two years (European Commission, 2012b, p. 3). To help with this initiative, it is clearly important to remain alert to contemporary technology developments in the field of eHealth. Looking some 30 years beyond that time-horizon – as far forward as 2050 – the implications of tomorrow's emerging technologies for people at large (http://ec.europa.eu/digital-agenda/en/digital-futures), and patients specifically, also need exploration.

Acknowledgements

We would like to especially thank Nicola Bedlington of the European Patients Forum and David Garwood of EHTEL for their intellectual and emotional support towards the early development of this chapter even though, ultimately, they did not contribute more fully to it. The opinions expressed here, and any possible errors of interpretation, are therefore entirely those of the authors.

References

Christensen, C.M., Grossman, J.H. and Hwang, J. (2009), *The Innovator's Prescription: A Disruptive Solution for Health Care.* New York: McGraw-Hill.

De Grey, A.D.N.J. with Rae, M. (2007), *Ending Aging: The Rejuvenation Breakthroughs That Could Reverse Human Ageing in Our Lifetime.* New York: St. Martin's Press.

EHTEL (2006a), *eHealth Care in the Home. A Position Paper.* Brussels: EHTEL European Health Telematics Association, Patients' and Citizens Task Force.

EHTEL (2006b), *eHealth and Patient Safety. A Position Paper.* Brussels: EHTEL European Health Telematics Association, Patients' and Citizens Task Force.

EHTEL (2006c), *The Electronic Health Record. A Position Paper.* Brussels: EHTEL European Health Telematics Association, Patients' and Citizens Task Force.

European Commission (2004), *e-Health – Making Healthcare Better for European Citizens: An Action Plan for a European e-Health area,* COM (2004) 356 final. http://eur-lex.europa.eu/LexUriServ/LexUriServ.do?uri=COM:2004:0356:FIN:EN:PDF [Accessed 18 December 2013].

European Commission (2012a), *eHealth Action Plan 2012–2020 – Innovative healthcare for the 21st century,* COM (2012) 736 final.http://ec.europa.eu/health/ehealth/docs/com_2012_736_en.pdf [Accessed 18 December 2013].

European Commission (2012b), Taking forward the Strategic Implementation Plan of the European Innovation Partnership on Active and Healthy Ageing. COM(2012) 83 final.http://ec.europa.eu/health/ageing/docs/com_2012_83_en.pdf [Accessed 18 December 2013].

European Commission (2013), A Clean Air Programme for Europe. COM(2013) 918 final. http://ec.europa.eu/environment/air/pdf/clean_air/Communication%20Clean%20Air%20Programme.pdf [Accessed 18 December 2013].

European Health Literacy Survey (HLS-EU) (2012), http://www.maastrichtuniversity.nl/web/Institutes/FHML/CAPHRI/DepartmentsCAPHRI/InternationalHealth/ResearchINTHEALTH/Projects/HealthLiteracyHLSEU.htm[Accessed 18 December 2013].

European Patients Forum (2009), *The Value+ Handbook. For Project Co-ordinators, Leaders and Promoters on Meaningful Patient Involvement.* Brussels: European Patients Forum. http://www.eu-patient.eu/Documents/Projects/Valueplus/doc_epf_handbook.pdf [Accessed 18 December 2013].

European Patients Forum (2010), *The Value+ Toolkit. For Patient Organisations on Meaningful Patient Involvement. Patients Adding Value to Policy, Projects and Services.* Brussels: European Patients Forum.http://www.eu-patient.eu/Documents/Projects/Value+%20Toolkit.pdf [Accessed 18 December 2013].

European Union (2012), *eHealth Task Force Report – Redesigning Health in Europe for 2020.* http://www.e-health-com.eu/fileadmin/user_upload/dateien/Downloads/redesigning_health-eu-for2020-ehtf-report2012_01.pdf [Accessed 18 December 2013]. Brussels, European Commission.

Garreau, J. (2005), *Radical Evolution. The Promise and Peril of enhancing Our Minds, Our Bodies – and What It Means to Be Human.* New York: Broadway Books.

Hughes, J. (2004), *Citizen Cyborg: Why Democratic Societies Must Respond to the Redesigned Human of the Future.* New York: Basic Books.

International Federation for Information Processing Working Group 9.2 (IFIP WG9.2) (2010), Converging Technologies: body, brain, and being, Working Conference in Maribor, Slovenia. 17 and 18 May 2010. http://www.itas.kit.edu/downloads/ta-kalender_20100518_cfp_converging_technologies_ifip_wg9.pdf [Accessed 18 December 2013].

Kickbusch, I., Pelikan, J.M., Apfel, F. and Tsouros, A.D. (eds) (2013), *Health Literacy. The Solid Facts*, World Health Organization. Copenhagen: WHO Regional Office for Europe.

Kurzweil, R. (2006), *The Singularity Is Near: When Humans Transcend Biology*. London: Penguin Books.

11
Dynamic Quality Control for a Changing Internet

Célia Boyer and Mayoni Ranasinghe

Introduction

As technologies develop and expand, they tend to need accompanying organisations, regulations and codes of conduct to ensure optimally high-quality services. Over the past four decades, there have been enormous developments in the use of information technology, particularly in terms of the Internet and the World Wide Web. These changes have affected health information and healthcare substantially, and patients are benefitting considerably as a result. This chapter therefore explores not only this recent history, but also a number of contemporary changes that are about to affect the field of health even more, including mHealth, serious gaming and information standardisation. It then examines how the growth of the Internet has been closely associated with the establishment of the Health on the Net Foundation (HON) and its code. As the future of the Internet becomes more complex, so too HON is changing in different ways; this chapter outlines these exciting organisational and technical developments.

The evolution of the Internet and its link with health information

The history of the Internet dates back more than 40 years, when in 1969 the United States (US) military funded a research network called the Advanced Research Projects Agency Network (ARPANET). In November 1990, the English computer scientist Tim Berners-Lee – with the help of Belgian computer scientist, Robert Cailliau – published a proposal to build a "Hypertext Project" in which information would be published in a hypertext format on the Internet. The Internet became even more popular once Marc Andreessen, a computer science student from the University of Illinois, together with a fellow student, wrote a computer program for a user-friendly browser called Mosaic that included graphics and could function on most computers.

In just one decade, between 1998 and 2008, the number of webpages published on the net grew by almost a trillion. To accommodate this massive increase, the number of Internet hosts also experienced exponential growth. Today, there are 440 million computers directly linked to the Internet while millions more have access through private accessing schemes. There would of course be no supply without demand; in 1995, there were only 16 million Internet users; in 2008 there were an estimated 1.5 billion people using the net (Duffy Marsan, 2009).

The Internet explosion brought about another significant turn: access to health information. Estimates of health information seeking behaviour consistently showed high growth (Lacroix et al., 1994). In fact, as soon as people started to have access to the Internet, they used it to access health information. By 1997, almost half of all Internet users had looked for health information (Brown, 1997). Those people who had previously only been able to obtain health information through their doctor now had free unrestricted access to it. Thus, patients began to be empowered. This was indeed the beginning of a revolution!

Since then, the health-related Internet experience has moved on in leaps and bounds. What was once a fascinating experience that offered access to limitless information through a computer in the comfort of the home has become a regular everyday occurrence. It is now perfectly normal to be able to access the Internet and find answers to health-related questions in a matter of minutes, without having any kind of interaction with the family physician.

There are at least four technical developments that are taking place around the Internet. As the Internet and the Web develop, they converge and merge with other technologies. They also raise new challenges. Here, we take the opportunity to explore developments in Web 2.0, mobile health, health-related serious gaming and information standardisation – each of which has a link with health-related Internet use by patients. All these developments are explored with a view as to why they matter for health and eHealth.

Web 2.0: The growth in collective intelligence

Just as any successful book can be revised to produce a second, third or more editions, the World Wide Web – an interlinked set of hypertext documents that uses the Internet – has also undergone revisions to improve the Internet experience. One such revision was the start of two-way Web information flow that used blogs and forums. The Web 2.0 – the second major version of the Web – has allowed Internet users to take part in collective discussions by directly contributing to the work of other users, information publishers and subject experts.

One significant change has been the ever-increasing popularity of blogs, both in terms of their number and readership. These figures concentrate on the

US. In January 2004, fewer than 20 million Americans were reported to be blog readers. Just two years later, this figure had tripled to over 55 million. Over a similar 24-month period, the number of blogs published on the Internet had also increased, from blogs created by over 5 million Americans in January 2004 to just under 20 million in January 2006 (Rainie, 2006, p.13).

The healthcare domain changed dramatically with the advent of Web 2.0. More and more "e-patients" – patients who obtain information about their medical conditions through electronic media such as the Internet – participated and interacted in health information communications, forming a kind of collective intelligence. According to a study conducted by the Pew Research Center in 2009, 20 per cent of all Internet users who looked for health information online had also actively contributed to the online health content in the following four ways (Pew Internet and American Life Project, 2013):

- Posted comments, queries or information on a health blog, forum, listserv or other group discussion site;
- Posted a review about a medical professional on a review site;
- Posted a review of a hospital on a review site;
- Shared photos, videos or audio files about health issues.

Thus, the arrival of Web 2.0 greatly empowered patients. They now not only have the ability to access unlimited amounts of health information, but also to offer their contributions and opinions and to take a more active role in accessing health information.

Additionally, Web 2.0 provided a big step forward for patients with chronic conditions, especially in terms of the emotional and psychological support that could be offered as more and more disease-specific support organisations were "born" on the Internet, or existing ones went online. The Web forum platform enabled patients to share their experiences with others, find and give empathy and gain strength from like-minded people.

Another booming trend, social networking, has also found its niche in the healthcare domain. On Facebook, people create pages to raise money for loved ones who are experiencing serious health conditions, healthcare associations are formed and "liked" and health pages are created to promote awareness of specific conditions or diseases. For example, PatientsLikeMe (www.patientslikeme.com) is a social networking site dedicated to healthcare, with patients as its intended audience. It enables patients with a specific condition to track and share their medication, discuss their experiences with other people who have the same condition and form strong bonds with other people of like minds. This innovative website enables patients to be empowered and to create positive and proactive attitudes towards their condition. In doing so, they gain and give emotional support from and to others.

Web 2.0 has without doubt pushed the frontier of eHealth forward significantly. However, the advent of Web 2.0 is not recent news: it has existed for a decade or so, and there are now other ways to gain access to health information. Nowadays, patients can not only tentatively diagnose their own conditions through a symptom checker, such as those on the National Health Service (NHS, 2013) or the Mayo Clinic (2013) websites, but they can also provide all their own medical findings and receive a full diagnosis from a health professional. HealthTap (www.healthtap.com) is one of the very few websites that offers free expert healthcare advice to the general public. In addition, other experts in the same field can rate the response of a particular expert: this enables patients to select what is the best response for them.

In summary, the World Wide Web has helped to change the patient–doctor interface in a dramatic manner. In the industrial age, the personal doctor was perhaps a patient's only source of healthcare, through his or her provision of treatment, referral to specialist doctors and health education offered through health information. In the information age, this relationship still exists and remains very much a part of the existing healthcare model, but other developments have taken place, resulting in a much more empowered patient. Today's patients are able to access health information through RSS feeds from their favourite websites as soon as new information is published. They can rate and review their healthcare provider, discuss health-related matters with other informed patients and even obtain expert healthcare information from doctors other than their own.

Mobile health

Having now entered the second decade of the 21st century, there are even further advancements in information seeking and gathering, and one example of this is mobile health (mHealth). Whereas previously people used personal computers or, at best, laptops to access the Internet, today more and more Internet users are using their smart phones or tablets to obtain the same information. For example, the latest survey performed by the Pew Internet and American Life Project in May 2013 shows that 91 per cent of adults in the US own a mobile phone whereas 56 per cent of adults own a smart phone; 31 per cent of the mobile phone owners and 52 per cent of the smart phone owners have used their phone to look up health or medical information; 19 per cent of the smart phone owners state that they have downloaded an app specifically to track or manage a health-related event (Pew Internet and American Life project, 2013).

Mobile health is indeed the next step towards the autonomous patient – a person who is more involved and better informed about his or her healthcare than even those who use only the Internet for their health-related activities.

For example, a recent study from PricewaterhouseCoopers (PwC, 2012) showed that, on the one hand, 59 per cent of mHealth users have already stated that, for them, it has replaced visits to their healthcare professional, although 42 per cent of doctors feel that it actually makes patients too independent.

mHealth grants patients easier access to care and control of their own health. They can track a health event (such as diet, exercise and weight) while on the go, receive reminders for taking medication or attending a doctor's appointment, all in order to take better charge of their own health. One such mobile app, called the WellDoc® DiabetesManager® System is an award-winning tool, which uses mobile phones and the Internet to enable healthcare professionals to extend real-time healthcare beyond the bricks and mortar of a doctor's office (www.welldoc.com).

Based on blood glucose data, this app provides real-time evidence-based behavioural coaching for people with type 2 diabetes. However, this is only one part of this app; the other part is a cloud-based expert analytic system that conducts longitudinal analysis and which provides help to physicians with their future decision-making (Figure 11.1). Initial randomised controlled trials have demonstrated significant reductions in the levels of glycated haemoglobin levels (the average of the blood glucose levels over one to three months, which acts as an indication of a patient's blood glucose control) in test subjects who used this diabetes management software. Additionally, both the healthcare professional and patient satisfaction levels were clinically and statistically significant (Quinn et al., 2008).

Though this type of app is currently revolutionary, it will only be a matter of time before similar software has been developed for most of the chronic

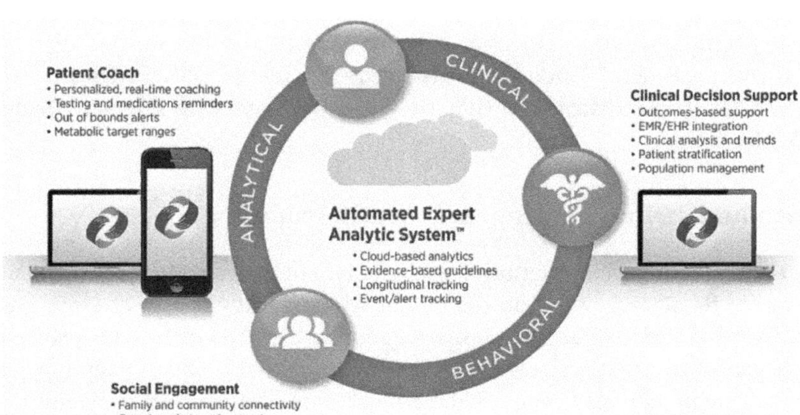

Figure 11.1 An automated expert analytic system

Source: http://www.welldoc.com/Products-and-Services/Our-Products.aspx © WellDoc.

endemic diseases, and it might soon be a regular occurrence for physicians to prescribe not only medications for their patients, but also health apps. However, the issue of proper regulation again comes into play here. After several discussions, the US Food and Drug Administration (FDA) has now created guidelines on how mHealth apps would be regulated (FDA, 2013). Yet not all mobile health apps will come under FDA scrutiny; rather a select sub-set of apps will fall under their selected definitions.

So what about the plethora of mobile apps that are currently being released daily? How will ordinary people know what apps are "good" and what is "bad"? Just as the growth of the Internet demanded guidelines and regulation, so it appears mHealth apps also do. With proper guidelines in place, and with the participation of regulatory bodies, mHealth will likely come to be an indispensable tool in the very near future of healthcare.

One development has been the release of multiple mHealth apps by various pharmaceutical companies. The Dose of Digital wiki, for example, illustrates the range of firms involved and the diversity of available applications (Dose of Digital, 2013). Many of these apps are related to their products and provide detailed information about the use of one or more medication.

An example is the Glucagon app developed by the pharmaceutical firm Eli Lilly (2013), which provides important information about the company's Glucagon injection product, a virtual injection practice tool, injection tutorial and information about where the patient can obtain the product along with expiry dates. Given that the information that patients are able to recall after leaving a doctor's office is relatively small, such an app would be a big benefit to patient care. However, where there is "good" there is also likely to be "bad", and this is no different in the domain of medical apps. In 2011, an app called AcneApp was found to be making false claims about being able to treat acne by using light emitted by the app. This, along with another similar apps, were forced by the Federal Trade Commission (FTC) in the US to withdraw their claims after it was discovered that they did not have any scientific backing (FTC, 2011).

Health and serious gaming, and use of avatars

Other significant developments have taken place in the gaming industry, usually known for its play-oriented products, but whose profile is also changing with the advent of serious gaming. Serious games are a type of learning software, which uses multimedia resources: under the guise of a game, they have specific real-life objectives that could be educational, therapeutic, preventative or other – serious gaming essentially means learning while having fun. Serious games can be applied to many health-related settings, among them psychological. One such serious game is Nevermind (www.nevermindgame.com),

Figure 11.2 Nevermind's twisted labyrinths
Source: http://sgschallenge.com/wordpress/2013/06/13/sgsc-2012-finalist-nevermind-nominated-for-most-innovative-at-games-for-change/ © Nevermind Game.

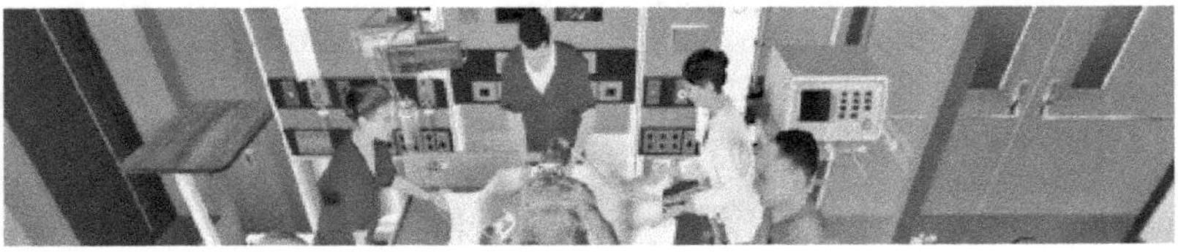

Figure 11.3 Health professionals portrayed in a virtual learning tool
Source: http://www.breakawaygames.com/serious-games/solutions/healthcare/ © BreakAway, Ltd.

an adventure horror game where the player has to solve various puzzles and find his or her way through a set of twisted labyrinths. If the player is able to stay calm during these terrifying experiences, the game becomes progressively easier; if the player gives into the fear, it gets harder. The objective of the game is to teach players to gain better control of their internal responses to stressful situations so that they are able to do the same in the real world.

Serious games not only benefit patients, but also healthcare providers. For example, *Pulse!!* is a virtual learning tool intended to train healthcare professionals in clinical skills without the risk of harming actual patients (Breakaway, n.d.).

Another recent development in the healthcare domain has been the use of avatars for healthcare. Detailed 2-D images of the human anatomy are used by a doctor to explain a particular problem, while patients use it to show their doctor where a specific problem is. One such tool is Healthcorpus (www.healthcorpus.

com), which enables readers to see a virtual human body with a 3D view of all the regions of the body. It allows patients to better understand the workings of the body and, in so doing, understand their own condition. Healthcorpus was developed by the Swiss software company Nhumi Technologies (www.nhumi.com). While the application is still only in its beta version, it already appears to provide a definite step towards better patient understanding, improved doctor–patient communication and overall higher quality healthcare.

Information standardisation

Having unlimited access to health information clearly has obvious advantages, but the one major drawback is a lack of uniformity in the quality of this information gathered by patients, which is crucial. For example, one study demonstrated that even physicians acquiesce to clinically inappropriate requests from patients, which are generated by inaccurate online health information, due to their fear of damaging the physician–patient relationship or because of a lack of time to do otherwise (Murray et al., 2003). Other studies from the early 2000s indicated that the public at large uses general search engines mainly to access health information by entering short, frequently misspelled, terms (McCray and Tse, 2003). Though information quality is reported to be important to consumers, their observed behaviour does not completely reflect this. Online health information seekers have been shown to access findings mostly only from the first webpage and not to pay much attention to other indicators of credibility (Morahan-Martin, 2004; HON, 2011b). Accessing only trustworthy information is a common challenge across the spectrum of all types of Internet users, who range from inexperienced to very seasoned. Even Internet-savvy users have been shown to have difficulty in differentiating accurate from inaccurate online health information (Ayonrinde, 1998; Sacchetti et al., 1999).

Providing health information regulation helps to educate members of the public and bring about awareness in them regarding the need for the quality and trustworthiness of online health information. From an information provider's point of view, information regulation and standardisation is very advantageous, especially for those sites which are small and do not have a medical editorial board, and so might otherwise be deemed less credible. A regulatory set of guidelines for online health information provides credibility while at the same time empowering webmasters: it does so through the overall improvement of their websites in terms of presentation, user-friendly interface and content management.

A survey conducted by the Health on the Net Foundation has shown that webmasters feel that the three most common outcomes of having their website HONcode certified are an increase in credibility, better management of the website and better presentation of the content on their website (HON, 2011b).

The future of the Internet

Today is far from the end of the development road for the Internet; the future holds endless possibilities for further innovations and developments for the net as a whole as well as for eHealth. For instance, patients will become more connected through continuous monitoring systems and completely connected networks. See the Scenario (in the associated box).

Box 11.1 Scenario – Monitoring blood pressure: the example of John

Imagine a scenario where a man, let us call him John, has a chronic condition such as hypertension. John is in his house, which is a patient-centred medical home that has full home monitoring. John is not aware that his blood pressure has risen, but when he goes to eat a snack, as he opens the fridge door, the pulse monitor built into the fridge door measures his higher blood pressure. His heart rate and pulse regularity are also detected, and all these data are used to determine if the event is an emergency. If it is (for example, if a heart attack appears to be imminent), an alarm is transmitted to the nearest emergency hospital. Immediate instructions are given to John to mitigate the impending problem until an ambulance arrives. However, if this is not an emergency, John's data are compared with other data obtained in the preceding hours (such as when John last touched a light switch or tap, or flushed the toilet). A pattern of rising blood pressure is detected, and in addition, John's "smart pill dispenser" provides information regarding his medication. It can keep him and others, such as a carer or a health professional, informed about whether he has taken his medication today. All these data are then transmitted to his local hospital where they are interpreted along with his previous data.

A similar pattern in John's rising blood pressure is discovered, always at a specific time of the day. John's doctor is sent the trends detected by the various devices around his home, saving him the trouble of finding the data himself. John's healthcare provider looks at the trends and decides the developments are not serious, and therefore books an appointment with the doctor for the following week. This appointment is immediately transmitted to John's smart home, which records the date and time of the appointment. At set times before the appointment, John is reminded of the time, and at the time of the session, John goes to his smart monitor where his doctor is waiting online to conduct the consultation. John's pressure, pulse, ECG and all other necessary vital signs are measured. His doctor asks John the necessary questions and gathers that the only change in medication that is needed is a slight increase in his dosage. The doctor writes out an e-prescription, which is transmitted to the pharmacy closest to John, who has only to pick up the medicine. If John forgets to go to the pharmacy, his smart pill dispenser – which detects that the new medication has not been collected yet – reminds him of this. Once the prescriptions are collected, the pill dispenser checks automatically that the dosage and times are correct and any reminders are set accordingly for John. Throughout all of these procedures, strict security and privacy guidelines are followed by all the devices that are collecting and dispensing information.

This sort of streamlined, seamless healthcare will unquestionably be possible in the not-so-distant future, and in fact, such smart monitoring has already begun. One example is Propellerhealth (www.propellerhealth.com), an organisation that provides smart monitoring for people with asthma. It uses a device, which fits over an inhaler to detect the number of times it is used, where it is used and at what time. These data are then transmitted to doctors, patients and public health specialists who are then able to manage the disease in real time. Another initiative is Cardionet (www.cardionet.com), which allows physicians to diagnose and treat patients with heart arrhythmias using an integrated technology, which detects heartbeat by heartbeat ECG monitoring in real time. This is a truly exciting future that lies ahead for healthcare in the information age: the possibilities appear endless.

The beginnings of HON

The Health On the Net Foundation (www.healthonnet.org) is an organisation that provides quality standardisation of online health information. HON's service is entirely voluntary: webmasters submit their health websites for review according to a quality code of conduct called the HONcode, and are guided by HON reviewers to achieve the result of a trustworthy website, which is allowed to display the HONcode logo as testament to its credibility: it is referred to as a HONcode seal. For the past 17 years, HON has offered this service completely free of charge. However, a completely free service is not sustainable and thus, underwent some changes at the beginning of 2014. HONcode certification of new websites remains completely free, after which the annual re-evaluation and re-certification is carried out as part of a paid membership.

HON came into being just as the Internet was starting to thrive. In the mid-1990s, the growing number of health websites, with varying levels of quality and trustworthiness, that were not uniform and were characterised by a complete lack of regulation, became a topic of great importance to a group of concerned health and IT professionals. A vote was undertaken to create a permanent body to "promote the effective and reliable use of the new technologies for telemedicine in healthcare around the world", during a telemedicine conference held in 1995 and attended by the leading telemedicine experts of the time (HON, 2013a). The proposal was approved unanimously. As a result, the HON Foundation was launched, and was functioning actively six months later. Seventeen years later, HON's code (HON, 2013b), referred to as the HONcode, remains a well-known code of conduct among users of the health Internet, and is the longest-standing initiative of its kind. Although similar regulatory standards have been launched over the years, the majority have not been sustained.

Figure 11.4 HONcode quality seal

The HONcode

The HONcode, developed by HON, is the earliest code of conduct used to regulate online health information. Since it was first written in July 1996, there have been several other codes developed. Although many of these accreditation schemes have since been abandoned, the HONcode is still going strong.

There appear to be several reasons for the code's success. One of the biggest probable success factors of the HONcode has been that since inception, it has remained free and even now, the HON membership takes into account the revenue of websites. It can be used in particular to promote trustworthy online health information in developing countries where an online presence is relatively limited. From the public's point of view, revenue-sensitive nature of the HONcode membership fee means that all quality health information will be available for access by users regardless of its backing (in other words, whether it is sponsored by a large transnational company, such as the large pharmaceutical corporations, or a small website created by an individual). Having this option available greatly widens the quality of the health information pool available to members of the public: it enables small, specialist websites to gain the credibility to challenge the notion that only large websites provide quality health information.

Additionally, in terms of success, the HONcode principles are available in 35 languages on the HON website, while detailed instructions for applicants are available in eight languages. This openness and transparency further increases the code's accessibility to information providers and consumers alike.

Its eight quality principles are the cornerstone of the HONcode's code of conduct. At the beginning of the code, there were six principles. Six months later, a revision was published that added principles relating to the transparency of the funding sources and of any advertising. The simplicity of these principles (as well as the manageable number of guidelines) has allowed webmasters to adhere to the HONcode while ensuring quality control of their websites.

Box 11.2 The HONcode: principles

Principle 1	**Authority:** Give qualifications of authors
Principle 2	**Complementarity:** Information to support, not replace
Principle 3	**Confidentiality:** Respect the privacy of site users
Principle 4	**Attribution:** Cite the sources and dates of medical information
Principle 5	**Justifiability:** Justification of claims/balanced and objective claims
Principle 6	**Transparency:** Accessibility, provide valid contact details
Principle 7	**Financial disclosure:** Provide details of funding
Principle 8	**Advertising:** Clearly distinguish advertising from editorial content

As is well known, the Internet is particularly dynamic. With the huge changes that have taken place in the net over the years, any quality accreditation scheme would have had to accommodate, or model itself on, this degree of flexibility, and the HONcode is no different. Although the eight basic principles of the HONcode are unchanged, it has responded to the ever-changing nature of the Internet by adapting its principles to better suit the dynamic scenario that is the continuously evolving Internet.

Internet regulation in low-income countries has had even bigger benefits for them than for their high-income counterparts. Guidelines and well-supported standards, such as HON's, provide much needed recognition to the existing small pool of local online health information, and it empowers webmasters to provide better quality information. Although there are only a few HONcode certified websites in such low-income countries like Guatemala, Mali or Pakistan, this is the beginning of an increasing awareness among the public in these kinds of countries regarding the requirement for quality online health information. Additionally, the HONcode provides recognition to webmasters in developing countries – this is especially significant in geographic regions where there are minimal local health information resources.

The HONcode has positive effects for both health information providers and consumers. It informs, educates and empowers the public, and recognises the efforts taken by health information webmasters while holding them accountable to their readers.

A case study of a Web 2.0 application of the HONcode

Over the past few years, the emergence of Web 2.0 has enabled two-way discussions among Internet users. The result has been a growth in health blogs and forums, with examples including well-read blogs such as Kevin Pho's (www.KevinMD.com) or KidneyNotes.com (www.kidneynotes.com), multi-topic forums such as eHealth Forum (www.ehealthforum.com), or targeted forums such as the Anxiety Forum (www.anxietyforum.net). Even a decade ago, it was estimated that one in four health Internet users join an online support group, with one study finding that users rated support groups as more helpful than physicians, including for their emotional support, convenience, cost-effectiveness and information offered (Cline and Haynes, 2001). Patients who participate in online support groups are considered to be more empowered than patients who do not, in terms of their degree of empathy and recognition, sharing of experiences, the help that they offer to others and their building of friendships (van Uden-Kraan et al., 2008).

However, the drawbacks of the interactive Web are also significant, and include new forms of exposure to non-credible information through data provided either for advertising or other commercial purposes, or simply through inaccurate information being offered to other users by otherwise well-meaning users. The HONcode Web 2.0 Guidelines (HON, 2011a) were introduced as a result, in 2008. The main differences between the regular HONcode principles and the HONcode Web 2.0 principles include such issues as the moderation of forums and blogs, regulations for posting (references for health information in posts and posting of advertisements), and consistent, complete transparency and honesty on the part of both information providers and consumers. These five-year-old 2.0 guidelines have been used to resolve numerous issues related to violation of the HONcode certification.

Citizen surveillance or HONcode 2.0

HON is a dynamic organisation that adapts itself to the ever-changing nature of the Internet. A recent development has been the sudden growth on the

Internet of websites providing reviews and ratings. Almost anyone who uses the Internet will have come across such websites as ratemyprofessor.com, yelp.com, tripadvisor.com or has used the rating feature on amazon.com. Similar developments are also taking place in the healthcare environment. A study from 2010 identified 33 physician-rating websites, which allowed patients to rate physicians in the US (Lagu et al., 2010). There are several such websites that are HONcode certified, and experience with these sites shows that rating is a useful and informative tool for consumers to learn about a service or product before committing themselves to buying or using it. This "people-helping-people" model is an excellent concept to apply to HON itself.

Providing tools for Internet users to rate HONcode certified websites will have several advantages. Currently, HONcode employees review HONcode certified websites, but with the advent of a HON rating platform, HON will benefit from the help of all concerned online citizens acting as extra pairs of eyes and ears. Rating will be carried out according to selected guidelines from the HONcode code of conduct. Other optional features which will provide added value include the ability for raters to add a comment about the website. The actual reviews will also be rateable. This is similar to other rating websites, where every review has a "was this review helpful" question attached to it, with the option for the user to then click "yes" or "no".

Just as the viewpoint of the public is important, so too is feedback from healthcare providers, hence another proposed tool for the future HON model would involve physicians, with doctors also able to rate health websites, although the guidelines that they use will be somewhat different from those used by the general public. Physicians' guidelines will focus mostly on targeted credibility factors, such as the presence of references in health information, the currency of the information and who the authors of the health articles are. The guidelines for the general public will encompass more generalised views, such as accessibility of the site, the comprehensibility of the health information and the usefulness of the site. These two new approaches of feedback from both the public and healthcare providers will provide another dimension to the ratings received. Users' expectations about ratings will differ, depending on whether the rater is a general health information consumer or a health practitioner. The plans are still only in the pipeline, but at HON the hope is to implement the advances in the near future.

Access to quality and trustworthy health information

HON recognises that access to quality health information for everyone is an important step towards equality of health. To facilitate users' access to trustworthy online health information, a project called Khreshmoi (www.khresmoi.eu) has been co-funded by the European Commission. Khresmoi stands for Knowledge Helper for Medical and Other Information users. Over its four years of existence, it aims to create a user-friendly environment in which various groups of users (the public, physicians and radiologists) can search for and access curated online health content. Khreshmoi uses advanced technologies and various selected resources to provide people with a trusted environment where to find local health information, and international sources with translation services. Khreshmoi combines both sources of texts (such as online journals, books and trusted websites) and images. Khreshmoi for everyone (everyone.khresmoi.eu) is a search engine for online health information intended specifically for members of the public.

Conclusions

The World Wide Web is a truly wondrous achievement. Almost single-handedly, it has heralded the coming of the information age, and has now become an integral part of daily life in the developed world and, to a lesser extent, the developing world. For example, a study carried out a decade ago in India already showed that 70 per cent of Internet consumers said that their healthcare decisions were influenced by something they read on the Internet (Akerkar and Bichile, 2004).

The Internet revolution has had a very significant effect on the healthcare domain; great advances are being made in terms of the prevention, diagnosing and treatment of various medical conditions. Probably the greatest stride has been in terms of patient empowerment and patient education, where unlimited health information resources are now available to anyone with access to a computer or a mobile phone. The changes that the Internet has brought about over the course of the past two decades are too numerous to list, but individual examples remain fascinating.

Nevertheless, there are still significant drawbacks to the Web, often affecting the most vulnerable people in society, and still many inequities and uncertainties to be rectified. The Internet continues to be heavily under-used in areas that could greatly benefit from it, with health applications and health information as two elements particularly in need of improvement. Confidentiality, privacy and security are also aspects of the Internet that need to be enhanced.

The future of healthcare in this digitalised arena is something that a few decades ago would have seemed to belong to a science fiction novel; now, it is becoming very much part of the real world. For example, some of the more advanced uses of informational networks in healthcare include swallowable and wearable sensors that will provide real-time feedback on a person's reaction to a particular medication, and smart bandages that send electrical charges to areas of chronic pain. Sensory devices attached to people's bodies will provide ongoing feedback so that patient monitoring will take place from inside patients' homes, without any need for them to meet physically with the treating physician (Larrea-Puemape, 2013).

There are ever more innovations under development, and if these emerging technologies are used within set guidelines, the possibilities to improve healthcare appear quite endless. The challenge remains, however, to maintain high-quality standards and guidelines for usage, so as to ensure that uniformly credible, evidence-based tools (technologies) are available across the spectrum of healthcare stakeholders, from the patient to the healthcare giver. These issues have to be addressed as further Web development occurs. Organisations like HON are ready to take on these challenges as they arise, in order to provide equitable and trustworthy online health information for general health information consumers.

References

Akerkar, S.M. and Bichile, L.S. (2004), "Health information on the internet: patient empowerment or patient deceit?", *Indian Journal of Medical Sciences* 58 (8): 321–326.

Ayonrinde, O. (1998), "Patients in cyberspace: information or confusion?", *Postgraduate Medical Journal* 74.874: 449–450. doi:10.1136/pgmj.74.874.449.

Breakaway (n.d.), *Pulse!!: Virtual Clinical Learning Lab for Health Care Training*. Hunt Valley MA: Breakaway Limited. http://www.breakawaygames.com/serious-games/solutions/healthcare/, s.v."Pulse" [Accessed 7 October 2013].

Brown, M.S. (1997), Consumer health and medical information on the Internet: supply and demand. FIND-SVP.

Cline R.J. and Haynes K.M. (2001), "Consumer health information seeking on the internet: the state of the art", *Health Education Research* 16 (6): 671–692. doi:10.1093/her/16.6.671.

Dose of Digital (2013), Mobile App Wiki. http://www.doseofdigital.com/healthcare-pharma-mobile-app-wiki/ [Accessed 7 October 2013].

Duffy Marsan, C. (2009, February 9), The Evolution of the Internet, *Network World* [online] http://www.networkworld.com/slideshows/2009/020909-evolution-internet.html#slide4 [Accessed 7 October 2013].

Eli Lilly (2013), Glucagon App http://www.glucagonapp.com/Pages/index.aspx [Accessed 7 October 2013].

FDA (US Food and Drug Administration) (2013), *Mobile Medical Applications* http://www.fda.gov/MedicalDevices/ProductsandMedicalProcedures/ConnectedHealth/MobileMedicalApplications/default.htm [Accessed 7 October 2013].

FTC (Federal Trade Commission) (2011), "'Acne Cure' Mobile App Marketers Will Drop Baseless Claims Under FTC Settlements" (8 September 2011) http://www.ftc.gov/opa/2011/09/acnecure.shtm [Accessed 7 October 2013].

HON (Health On the Net Foundation) (2011a), Certification for collaborative Websites/Websites with Web 2.0 elements [25 February 2011] http://www.hon.ch/cgi-bin/HONcode/guidelines_comments_en.pl [Accessed 7 October 2013].

HON (2011b), Survey results: satisfaction on HONcode certification after 1 year [29 November 2011] http://www.hon.ch/HONcode/Surveys/Results1Year.html [Accessed 7 October 2013].

HON (2013a), Our beginnings [5 June 2013] http://www.hon.ch/Global/ [Accessed 7 October 2013].

HON (2013b), The commitment to reliable health and medical information on the internet [13 June 2013] http://www.hon.ch/HONcode/Webmasters/Visitor/visitor.html [Accessed 7 October 2013].

Health Games Research (n.d.) *Pulse!!* The Virtual Clinical Working Lab http://www.healthgamesresearch.org/games/pulse-the-virtual-clinical-learning-lab [Accessed 7 October 2013].

Healthcorpus (n.d.), Healthcorpus http://healthcorpus.com/ [Accessed 7 October 2013].

Lacroix, E.-M, Backus, J.E.B. and Lyon, B.J. (1994), "Service providers and users discover the Internet", *Bulletin of the Medical Library Association* 82 (4): 412–418. PMCID: PMC225967.

Larrea-Puemape, D. (2013, August 21), "Mobile minute: how wearable tech is changing healthcare", *Business 2 Community* [online]. http://www.business2community.com/tech-gadgets/mobile-minute-how-wearable-tech-is-changing-healthcare-0591060 [Accessed 7 October 2013].

Lagu, T., Hannon, N.S., Rothberg, M.B. and Lindenauer, P.K. (2010), "Patients' evaluations of health care providers in the era of social networking: an analysis of physician-rating websites", *Journal of General Internal Medicine* 25 (9): 942–946. doi: 10.1007/s11606-010-1383-0. PMCID: PMC2917672.

McCray, A.T. and Tse, T. (2003), "Understanding search failures in consumer health information systems", *AMIA Annual Symposium Proceedings* 2003: 430–434. PMCID: PMC1479930.

Morahan-Martin, J.M. (2004), "How Internet users find, evaluate, and use online health information: a cross-cultural review", *CyberPsychology & Behavior* 7 (5): 497–510. doi: 10.1089/cpb.2004.7.497.

Mayo Clinic (2013), Symptoms [13 July 2013] http://www.mayoclinic.com/health/symptoms/SymptomIndex[Accessed 7 October 2013].

Murray, E., Lo, B., Pollack, L., Donelan, K., Catania, J., Lee, K., Zapert, K. and Turner, R. (2003), "The impact of health information on the Internet on health care and the physician–patient relationship: national U.S. survey among 1.050 U.S. physicians", *Journal of Medical Internet Research* 5 (3): e17. doi:10.2196/jmir.5.3.e17.

NHS (National Health Service) (2013), Symptom checkers [28 August 2013] http://www.nhs.uk/NHSdirect/pages/symptoms.aspx [Accessed 7 October 2013].

Nevermind. (n.d.), Nevermind. http://nevermindgame.com/NM_2.0/Nevermind.html>.

Pew Internet and American Life Project (16 September 2013), <http://www.pewinternet.org/Presentations/2006/Blogs-and-health-care.aspx>.

Propeller Health (n.d.), Our Solution http://propellerhealth.com/solutions/ [Accessed 7 October 2013].

PwC (PricewaterhouseCoopers) (2012), *Emerging mHealth: Paths for Growth.* http://www.pwc.com/en_GX/gx/healthcare/mhealth/assets/pwc-emerging-mhealth-full.pdf [Accessed 7 October 2013].

Rainie, L. (2006, March 21), Blogs and Healthcare, *Pew Internet*, http://www.pewinternet.org/~/media//Files/Presentations/2006/2006%20-%203.21.06%20Children's%20Hospitals%20(final).ppt.ppt [Accessed 7 October 2013].

Quinn, C.C., Sysko Clough, S., Minor, J.M., Lender, D., Okafor, M.C. and Gruber-Baldini, A. (2008), "WellDoc(TM) mobile diabetes management randomized controlled trial: change in clinical and behavioural outcomes and patient and physician satisfaction", *Diabetes Technology and Therapeutics* 10 (3): 160–168. doi:10.1089/dia.2008.0283.

Sacchetti, P., Zvara, P. and Plante, M.K. (1999), "The internet and patient education – resources and their reliability: focus on a select urologic topic", *Urology* 53 (6): 1117–1120. PMID: 10367838.

van Uden-Kraan, C.F., Drossaert, C.H.C., Taal, E., Shaw, B.R., Seydel, E.R., and van de Laar, M.A.F.J. (2008), "Empowering processes and outcomes of participation in online support groups for patients with breast cancer, arthritis, or fibromyalgia", *Qualitative Health Research* 18 (3): 405–417. doi:10.1177/1049732307313429.

12
Social Networks for Health: A Personal Snapshot

Denise Silber

Introduction

The idea of using computers to improve healthcare began to be discussed in the 1950s. The electronic medical record, hospital information systems and telemedicine have been pursued for some decades now. eHealth, a term in use since 1997, describes the use of digital services throughout healthcare. However, healthcare systems whose information exchange is fully computerised remain the exception. Healthcare social media is giving new life to eHealth with the introduction of opportunities for individual initiative, user-generated content and the exchange of experience through a wide variety of online communities and applications. Some of these are grassroots initiatives on Twitter and Facebook. Others are developed on individual websites and mobile platforms. These services are typically intended either for health professionals or for patients and consumers, and too rarely enable collaboration between professionals and patients. The ideal scenario would be to have fully integrated programmes that connect diagnostic and learning tools, clinical data and user experiences to bring about the best interest of patients everywhere.

Introduction to an ideal world

How would healthcare be improved, if new technologies could ensure that relevant, transparent health data would find itself in the right place at the right time? In an ideal world, consumers would have knowledge of all their options, with support from other people as needed, and they would be properly informed and motivated to take the best care of themselves. They would be treated by the best available, up-to-date professionals, regardless of distance. Surgical and prescription error would be largely non-existent. Preventive health measures would be better known, understood and put into practice. Although this ideal state of healthcare is still some time away, I believe that social media platforms can contribute considerably towards helping us reach that ideal. But before I explain the role of social media in healthcare, it is important to understand how we reached this point in the development of the digital side of healthcare.

Computers and healthcare over the generations

In the 1950s as the modern computer was being invented, a few pioneering healthcare professionals around the world began to recognise its potential to make medicine more efficient. They helped found what would become the field of Medical Informatics or Health Information Technology (IT). Over the next two decades, this new field began to introduce innovations such as Electronic Medical Records, Hospital Information Systems, Telemedicine and Telemonitoring (http://en.wikipedia.org/wiki/Medical_informatics). However, multiple factors prevented these concepts from becoming the everyday tools that they deserve to be. Changing an ongoing healthcare organisation without delaying care was – and still is – a challenge. Health professionals were not trained in the basics of informatics and they resisted the introduction of the computer in their consultations. Individual hospital departments and individual hospitals created their own software and either could not or would not participate in programmes beyond their original borders. As a result, multiple electronic record systems came into being and were incompatible. While the purpose of information systems was to help improve co-ordination among healthcare stakeholders, the lack of co-ordination at the outset made it difficult and costly to get the process started.

The World Wide Web, introduced in the early 1990s, brought a new era in information technology, expanding it beyond the hands of the computer specialist. The web made it possible for the "average" computer user to search through massive amounts of information that had previously been reserved to people connected to university libraries. People with similar concerns and interests could find one another through forums and mailing lists. Anyone could present his or her own data, needs and products to the world with a simple web page, through either self-taught html programming or the services of a webmaster. As concerns health and medicine, given this new access to information, the public at large could in theory begin to learn about and impact the way medicine was practised. The creation of the term "eHealth", in the late 1990s, with a new generation of related start-ups, research programmes and organisations, gave new life and hope to medical informatics through web-based activities. More and more people realised that the greater introduction of information technology would improve the quality of healthcare. Yet large-scale adoption of computer-based tools within the clinical process remained the exception. Citizens did not then (nor do they sufficiently now) press decision-makers for the computerisation of health systems.

Now the opportunity to improve healthcare thanks to new technologies is getting yet another chance, with the advent of the second generation of the web, or Web 2.0, and Social Media platforms. New forms of communication and exchange, and new tools and services, are appearing more rapidly than ever before. Healthcare social media tools have greater potential to reach the end-user than "traditional" eHealth initiatives, thanks to the power of social media to connect interested people. Today, around the world, in every language, there are healthcare social media tools such as online communities and mobile applications, offering an extensive variety of possibilities.

Nonetheless, that world that we have been grasping for, a world that optimises existing health and medical innovation thanks to appropriate use of new technologies, is still a work in progress.

My adventures with eHealth: From Europe to the United States (US) and back

My story with eHealth began in 1994 on a trip to Boston (US). As an American living in Paris, I was running the healthcare communications consultancy I had founded in my adopted city. At a Harvard Business School alumni meeting of my class in Boston, I listened to classmate Dan Bricklin, whom the Dean had invited as a speaker. A computer geek from childhood on, Dan, the father of the first spreadsheet, VisiCalc, presented the World Wide Web, the new key to information and learning for the years to come. I went back to Paris and signed up immediately for my first Internet subscription, turned on that noisy modem, and began to do my own searching on Infoseek!, Altavista and other now forgotten Google predecessors. Although fewer than 10 per cent of people were online at the time, even in the US, which was leading the Internet revolution, I was amazed at the professional contacts I established on the web in the coming months, not only in my country of origin, but also in South Africa, Australia and elsewhere in Europe with people at leading health institutions, researchers, patient activists and physicians.

Determined to do my share to introduce what was then called "the medical Internet" to France, my company launched its own website, including one of the earliest French and English lists of suggested health links, and began to create medical web sites for others. I became part of an international movement of Internet health evangelisers. I joined the Medical Web Masters mailing list group and, later, the Internet Healthcare Coalition to explore issues regarding the "quality of health information on the web". We were all driven by the potential progress we hoped that the Internet would bring to patients and professionals everywhere – progress based on improving access to the right information and the right people through the Internet. I moved to the US to work on one of the earliest second-opinion start-ups for international patients and doctors. Working on the subject of second opinions, I was exposed to the difficulties of introducing change. I learnt that while computer-assisted diagnosis had good results in improving accuracy of diagnoses, professionals did not support it. I saw as well that, while some patients were participating in the improvement of their own care, "patient empowerment" was not very welcome. At conferences to explain the use of the Internet in healthcare, evangelisers got shot down by healthcare professionals who did not recognise the positive role of the pro-active patient. And as scaling up these new services was a challenge, many start-ups were unable to reach a critical mass.

In 2000, I returned to France and was consulting in digital health when the Internet bubble burst in the US. In 2003, I was given the opportunity to write a report for the European Commission's first high-level conference on eHealth. The late Professor Jean-Claude Healy, then head of the European Commission Directorate-General Information Society eHealth unit and a visionary, to whom this book is dedicated, knew that eHealth desperately needed more recognition and visibility. He declared that a European awards process would celebrate the best eHealth applications. The resulting report, *The Case for eHealth* (Silber, 2003) would place European eHealth achievements in perspective, telling people where we were and where we were headed. The European Commission had defined eHealth as *the application of information and communications technologies (ICT) across the whole range of functions that affect healthcare, from diagnosis to follow-up* (Silber, 2003). The Holy Grail of eHealth was the Electronic Health Record that would allow the sharing of medical records between providers and patients. It would be at the centre of a computerised health system with a continuous exchange of relevant information. However, the computerised health system was, with some rare exceptions, not to be. The most wired health systems tended to occur in organisations where care management and budgetary decisions were in one set of hands. None of those systems seemed to include more than a few million patients. Even those integrated care organisations that had the means to develop extensive information systems were mostly built around the flow of information among health professionals, and not from or to the patient. Had patient involvement been the first priority of those systems, they would not have left the gaping hole into which the web and its subsequent social networks plunged. Thus, the web has been the stage for initiatives by individuals and organisations rather than by health systems.

Nonetheless, by 2003, *the Case for eHealth* was able to report on some initiatives in Europe that had reached significant size. Many are still active today (they are listed here in alphabetical order):

- CISMeF, a French portal for quality medical information resources created at the Rouen University Hospital;

- Health On the Net, in Geneva, Switzerland, with its eight quality criteria, and 3,000 certified sites at the time;
- NHS Direct, in England, with its medical information portal and associated call centre, for residents of the UK;
- Orphanet, a European multilingual online encyclopaedia for rare diseases, supported by Inserm, the French research institution, which is now the official curator of rare diseases for the World Health Organization;
- Sundhed – at the time, a Danish pharmacists' portal for the renewal of prescriptions – and today, the Danish national portal;
- WebSurg, a multilingual distance education program for surgeons created by the founder of the European Institute of Telesurgery in Strasbourg, France, Dr Marescaux. On 7 September 2001, he operated, from Manhattan, on a patient in France through a telesurgery known as Operation Lindbergh (http://en.wikipedia.org/wiki/Lindbergh_operation).

At the first European eHealth conference in 2003, it was too soon to speak of Web 2.0, a term which had not yet been coined. And none of the above sites enabled user-to-user communication. But in the years immediately after the conference, the World Wide Web moved deeply into its second generation, which is characterised by the importance of online social networks. Online social networks became the prime source of traffic (http://mostpopularwebsites.net/) and time spent on the Internet. More and more sites began to link to social networks through content sharing options. An increasing share of mobile device time was spent on social media. I became one of the early supporters of Web 2.0 and social media in Europe and initiated the first international conference in Europe on healthcare social media. Doctors 2.0 & You, established in Paris annually since 2011 (http://www.doctors20.com/press-releases-2011/), pursues the purpose of increasing awareness of healthcare social media for all healthcare stakeholders. Case studies are presented in the same forum by patients, professionals, hospitals, government, industry, and of course technology companies, in an attempt to break down traditional healthcare isolation. During the two-day 2013 edition, the conference hashtag #doctors20 generated 8,000 tweets in 12 languages (http://www.symplur.com/healthcare-hashtags/doctors20/). Thanks to the topical content posted all year long, the website registers traffic from over 100 countries. Curating the conference content is an ideal vantage point for observing what is happening in the field globally. Many of the social networks for health cited in this text have been presented at Doctors 2.0 & You conferences.

Defining the social media universe

A social network is a container or platform for user-generated content. *Wikipedia, itself one of the earliest and most important social networks, provides*

Table 12.1 Key social media platforms in chronological order

Year	Name	Description
2001	Wikipedia	User-generated encyclopaedia
2003	LinkedIn	Community for all professions
2004	Facebook	Community of "friends" sharing their TimeLine
	Flickr	Sharing of photos
2005	YouTube	Video-sharing platform
2006	Twitter	Microblogging
	Slideshare	Sharing of presentations
2010	Pinterest	Scrapbooking
	Instagram	Sharing photos with filters
2011	Google+	Sharing with selected circles of contacts

a more formal definition. A "social network" is an online service or platform that facilitates social relations among people who share interests, activities, and connections. A social network service consists of a representation of each user (often a profile or account), his/her social links or contacts, and additional services (http://en.wikipedia.org/wiki/Social_networking_service).

Social networks succeed when users develop enough contacts and personal content on a specific platform to make leaving too "costly". As each network offers a particular approach or service, Internet users tend to belong to more than one network. Table 12.1 contains a list of well-known platforms that have generated communities around an activity, a description of what they do and when they were launched.

Games are merging with social media. Although no one serious game is as universally used as the above social networks, social media is increasingly interconnecting with gamification. Serious games enable players to learn about important subjects in a fun way. Playing for rewards, whether game points or actual services and products, incentivises players to return to the application and makes for a regular flow of traffic on it. Simulation is a form of serious game which is applicable to many sectors, including health.

Social networks for health

Social networks for health and wellness refer to the use of either all-purpose social networks based on health-related subjects or to a specialised health-related social network. Specialised health social networks typically use general social networks to engage with users and promote their web site.

There are three user scenarios for healthcare social media: professional social networks; networks reserved for consumers and patients and networks that link both professionals and consumers.

Whatever the usage scenario, with all social networks, healthcare social networks share the fact that they are reliant on "user-generated content". On Facebook, there are groups limited to professionals, others are limited to patients and there are also mixed communities for patients and health professionals that are typically intended to afford patients the possibility of engaging in a dialogue with professionals.

How important are social networks for health? We often read about the quantity of health and medical information that the web makes available. However, if the Internet has become indispensable to most users, it is not just because of access to articles and information. It is also very much for the opportunity to discuss with and ask questions of people experiencing a similar situation. Whether as consumers or professionals, the greatest number of minutes per day is spent on the collaborative Web 2.0 and social media platforms and applications that have developed over the past decade (http://www.linkedin.com/today/post/article/20130709145114-2967511-global-social-media-networks-set-to-overtake-facebook). Given their size, these social media platforms not only have access to more users than individual health initiatives, they also host more health content than dedicated online health initiatives:

- YouTube has the most health videos and health video channels;
- Facebook has thousands of invisible and visible patient and professional community groups;
- Wikipedia has the most medical articles on medical conditions and medicines;
- iTunes has the most medical podcasts.

Most specialised healthcare social networks create a presence on general social media networks in order to promote their existence. Facebook lends itself to many health-related activities because of the sheer numbers of people who use it, the frequency of use by each member and the presence of images. These activities include seeking out patients with rare or not-so-rare diseases; managing disease support groups and connecting healthcare professionals. Individual diagnoses have been made by visitors seeing a photo of someone whose disease was not previously identified (http://allfacebook.com/facebook-diagnosis-saves-boys-life_b50685). As photos are dated on social networks, the evolution of someone's appearance over time can assist in evaluating the person's condition. A Stanford professor, Jennifer Aaker, used social media to launch a campaign to promote bone marrow donations and recruited 100,000 donors in the South Asian community of the US (http://www.youtube.com/watch?v=N1Mjjk32t00).

Specialised health social networks are typically virtual communities for patients, caregivers, researchers and practising professionals. Communities may provide multiple services in order to encourage frequent use of the community.

These include:

- participating in a community to share information and support;
- creating an online health record;
- accessing reviews of hospitals, professionals, drugs;
- contacting a professional to make an appointment, ask a question by email or communicate via a video;
- comparing costs of health-related services and products.

Services for professionals include communities where they can:

- discuss and consult with peers;
- share data;
- access drug and other databases;
- play serious games and do simulations for educational purposes.

Of course, online relationships in healthcare bring their own set of challenges:

- Online patient and professional communities more often live side-by-side than interactively;
- The particular constraints on healthcare limit social media "freedom";
    - Provider organisations and professionals must avoid being perceived as using the web to advertise
    - Secure web environments require investment
    - Regulatory constraints limit communication options for private industry
    - Public health, governmental agencies and not-for-profit organisations are often understaffed in terms of their communication roles.
- Acceptable and successful business models are difficult to define;
- Patients and professionals do not always respect privacy guidelines.

The digital health online space is nonetheless attracting a greater share of venture capital than healthcare in general (http://www.informationweek.com/healthcare/mobile-wireless/venture-capitalists-keep-digital-health/240157685).

Many international examples of specialised healthcare social media are available for viewing either as a mobile site or via a mobile application. There are an ever larger number of them, and they range widely over both consumer services and professional services (Boxes 12.1 and 12.2 list a number in alphabetical order).

Box 12.1 International social media consumer services

3GDoctor (https://www.3gdoctor.com) enables patients in England and Ireland to enter their personal health record online and consult with a specialist of their choice, via a mobile video application.

CancerContribution (http://www.cancercontribution.fr) is a social network platform created in 2011 by CancerCampus, a French organisation of cancer institutions around Institut Gustave Roussy. CancerContribution's mission is to further "health democracy", thanks to a public web platform for discussion and voting on ways to improve the condition of cancer patients.

The Children's Hospital of Barcelona, Spain, HSJD (http://www.hsjdbcn.org/portal/en/institut-pediatric/inicio) is an extensive user of social media to communicate with professionals and patients. It had nearly 2 million views on YouTube in February 2013.

Endogoddess (https://itunes.apple.com/us/app/endogoddess/id464431379?mt=8) from the US, created by physician Jennifer Dyers, and MySugr (https://mysugr.com/) from Vienna, created by patient, Fredrik Debong, are other examples of the use of serious game techniques in healthcare, in this case, for diabetes. Patients are motivated to return to the app through gaming principles.

IBG Star is an iPhone accessory and a mobile application that enables patients with diabetes to have an all-in-one place to follow their condition and communicate their data. Users comment on the application on iTunes (https://itunes.apple.com/us/app/ibgstar-diabetes-manager/id506018173?mt=8).

In 2007, an American patient and online editor, Amy Tenderich, wrote an open letter to the then CEO of Apple, Steve Jobs, suggesting that the iPhone should include a number of new design ideas for patients. A few years later, Sanofi, the Paris-based global pharmaceutical company, introduced this integrated application internationally.

NHS Choices (http://www.nhs.uk), the largest UK health web site, provides information and automated translation, and allows users to compare hospitals and professionals. The accompanying NHS Direct mobile application has beaten British records for downloads. NHS Choices manages at least nine Facebook, Twitter and YouTube accounts. The NHSChoices YouTube channel (http://www.youtube.com/user/NHSChoices) had 13 million+ views as of Spring, 2013. NHSChoices (https://twitter.com/NHSChoices) alone had 83,000+ Twitter followers in July 2013, a high figure for a European health Twitter account although it was less than 2 per cent of the total NHS users. The NHS also manages hundreds of other Twitter accounts. In 2009, during the swine flu epidemic, the NHS saw an uptake in its activity on Twitter and created @nhsflu. The NHS London-based trusts ran a social media Christmas campaign in 2011 to divert users from the emergency phone call system, whose waiting times increased during the end of year rush. The UK Department of Health runs a weekly tweet-up targeting NHS professional under the hashtag #nhssm. NHS Direct web portal closed on March 26th, 2014, after 15 years of service, for contractual reasons related to the management of the related phone services.

PatientsLikeMe (http://www.patientslikeme.com), established in 2003 in the US, was one of the earliest sites to enable English-language users from any location to access other patients with similar characteristics and to generate comparative data graphs. A study evaluating the results of lithium, based on data from the amyotrophic lateral sclerosis community, was published in 2008 (https://www.patientslikeme.com/press/20110425/27-patientslikeme-social-network-refutes-published-clinical-trialbr-bri-nature-biotechnology-paper-details-breakthrough-in-real-world-outcomes-measurement-i-).

Renaloo (http://www.renaloo.com) is a French association for kidney patients that began as the founder's blog in 2002, became a full website and then an online community. The site protects patient identity for those patients who use a pseudonym. Renaloo involved physicians and patients together in an 18-month campaign to modify clinical practice in France for kidney patients. This campaign generated 8,000 questionnaire responses by French kidney patients, an impressive score.

The **REShape & Innovation Centre** of the Radboud University Medical Centre (in the Netherlands) founded by Lucien Engelen, manages various social media services. AED4.us (http://www.aed4.us/) is a website and smartphone application that visualises the geolocation of defibrillators in the Netherlands. Locations are submitted by users. AYA4 – All You Have Asked For (http://www.radboudreshapecenter.com/portfolio_2/1/) – is a community for young cancer patients. My Radboud at Home explores how to improve communication between a patient and specialists in the paediatric oncology department.

Syrum (http://www.syrum-game.com/), a serious game, present on Facebook and developed in Europe by Boehringer-Ingelheim, has the purpose of teaching players how to build a pharmaceutical company.

Treato (http://www.treato.com), founded in Israel, gathers social media statements on patients' experience with medicines from around the world, and uses them to provide a rating of each drug.

Twitter hashtags are playing an important role in diabetes communication. #GBDOC #DEDOC #FRDOC are, respectively, diabetes online communities of Great Britain, Germany and France, using both Twitter and Facebook to communicate with interested persons with diabetes, through live Tweetchats and comments on Facebook.

UCB, the Belgian company, was the first pharmaceutical company to facilitate the creation of a PatientsLikeMe community. Carenity (http://www.carenity.com) offers a similar community-type service in France.

Various consumer- rating services exist in Europe, for drugs, doctors, hospitals and health insurance schemes. **Meamedica** (http://www.mijnmedicijn.nl), founded in the Netherlands by a pharmacist, provides a multilingual user platform for posting patient drug reviews. **Patient Opinion** (https://www.patientopinion.org.uk) is a not-for-profit patient feedback service, founded in 2005 by a National Health Service (NHS) physician who wanted to give patients a channel for expressing their suggestions to NHS hospitals. Patients contribute their opinion, and subscribing hospitals receive feedback. International sites such as **Doctoralia** (http://www.doctoralia.es), headquartered in Spain, and **Keldoc** (http://www.keldoc.com) from France combine user reviews with the possibility for the patient to set up an appointment with a professional.

The majority of physicians connect online with other physicians in social media environments, whether in private Facebook groups managed by a doctor, or in dedicated websites whose concept was originally created by a physician. Online physician communities tend to be operated as portals with multiple services, but sharing a common benefit for doctors: the possibility of exchanging medical questions with identified peers in a secure environment (Box 12.2).

Box 12.2 International social media professional services

Among the oldest physician communities, **DocCheck** (http://www.doccheck.com/), created in Germany in 1996 by a dentist, began as a way for physicians to obtain a unique password for access to secure sites. Today it operates internationally.

Doctors.Net (http://www.doctors.net.uk/), another pioneer, established in the UK in 1998 by a former NHS physician, counts on nearly 200,000 physicians.

Diagnosia (http://www.diagnosia.com), an international physician community, created in 2010 in Austria, specialises in the discussion by physicians about medicines.

DXY (http://en.wikipedia.org/wiki/DXY.cn), a healthcare professional site in China founded in 2006, has 3.2 million members, 2 million of whom are practising physicians. **Sermo physicians' community** was created in the US in 2006 and was acquired in 2012 by WorldOne, a company with a global strategy.

Serious games, often combined with simulation techniques for medicine or surgery, are gaining recognition. Some are accredited by medical schools for continuing medical education points. For example, **insuOnline** (https://www.ncbi.nlm.nih.gov/m/pubmed/23612462/?i=6&from=/23723719/related) from Brazil is performing research about the efficacy of its serious game on diabetes management for primary care physicians (http://www.ncbi.nlm.nih.gov/pmc/articles/PMC3628160/).

Finally, there are thousands of applications for physicians designed to assist with diagnosis, dosage of medicines and evaluating images and sounds. They provide opportunities for physicians to discuss the image or case. In addition, mobile applications can of course be reviewed and commented on.

Future perspectives

This chapter began by presenting the history of health IT and the fact that large-scale programmes from governments and institutions remain rare after decades of efforts. This can be contrasted, however, with the frequent introduction of healthcare social media tools and the potential exposure of larger numbers of users to them through social media platforms. These tools aim to fill the gaps in the existing healthcare systems. Surely the solution remains somewhere in the connection between these two worlds so that diagnostic and learning tools, clinical data and user experience can all work together in the best interest of patients everywhere. Jean-Claude Healy would have been an active social networker, encouraging public health organisations to adopt Web 2.0 techniques and platforms and promoting collaborative research and evaluation of social media. Let us all keep his eHealth dreams moving forward!

Reference

Silber (2003), The case for eHealth, EIPA, http://www.epractice.eu/files/download/awards/D10_Award1_ResearchReport.pdf.

Part III

Practice – New Ways of Working and Other Challenges

13

The Role of eHealth in Supporting Care Coordination

Nick Goodwin and Albert Alonso

Introduction

All western industrialised nations face important new challenges in meeting the long-term health and social care needs of their populations. Over the past two decades, an important demographic and epidemiological transition has taken place. Age-related and long-term chronic illnesses have replaced communicable diseases as the biggest challenge that health systems must now address. More than half of the growing number of people aged over 65 in Europe are living with more than three chronic conditions, and about one-fifth have five or more concurrent health problems (Anderson and Horvath, 2004). This shift means that the economic burden of age-related chronic illness represents between 75–80 per cent of healthcare expenditure, a figure that is also expected to rise as society ages (Nolte and McKee, 2008). Current health and care systems, however, appear to be ill equipped to meet the challenge as they have developed systemic and institutional structures that focus on cure rather than care. As a result, and particularly in an era of economic uncertainty, most countries and regions have begun the search for new and more integrated care models – supported by technological innovation – that place the emphasis on preventing ill health, supporting self-care and delivering care closer to people's homes.

This chapter focuses first on the nature and importance of integrated care to the future of health systems before then moving on to consider the enabling role of eHealth (and the range of technologies available) in making integrated care possible.

What is integrated care and why is it important?

Integrated care is a widely used concept in different health systems across Europe and worldwide, yet the meaning of the term varies. This reflects the multi-dimensional nature of a concept that has been applied from several disciplinary and professional perspectives and is associated with diverse objectives (Nolte and McKee, 2008). Nonetheless, integrated care is a simple idea – combining parts so that they form a whole (in other words, are integrated) in order to optimise care co-ordination and treatment around people's needs (Goodwin, 2013).

The hypothesis central to integrated care is that it should contribute to meeting the "triple aim" goals in health systems of: improving the patient's care experience (in other words, satisfaction, confidence and trust); improving the health of people and populations (such as morbidity, mortality and quality of life) and improving the cost-effectiveness of care systems (Berwick et al., 2008). Hence, integrated care initiatives have tended to focus on improving continuity and co-ordination of care to patients and carers. This includes supporting people to self-care and take greater control over their care and treatment options; enabling better communication between clinical and non-clinical professionals and improving collaboration and networking across the various components of care service delivery (Ouwens et al., 2005). It is for these reasons, therefore, that eHealth strategies that support information exchange among professionals – and between professionals and patients – are hallmarks of the more effective approaches to managing people with long-term chronic illness (Hofmarcher et al., 2007; Bodenheimer, 2008; Ham, 2010). Moreover, new technologies can help drive innovations in how and where care is delivered, supporting the ability to deliver care in the home environment.

Understanding integrated care

Though integrated care can mean different things to different people, the common logic behind the approach is to make better use of the existing financial and human resources by co-ordinating care more effectively around the needs of people. However, the process of achieving integrated care is complex with implications on how care systems operate at every level: organisational; managerial; professional and at the service level. Different local and national contexts are hugely influential in determining how a care system might best support integrated care, and understanding "what works" within these dynamics can be challenging.

Over the years, a number of different taxonomies of integrated care have been advanced to understand how integrated care might be achieved. Typically, these have included (Nolte and McKee, 2008): *types* of integration (for example, organisational, professional, functional); *breadth* of integration (such as vertical, horizontal, virtual); *degree* of integration (in other words, across the continuum: linkage, co-ordination to full integration); and *processes* of integration (cultural and social as well as structural and systemic). However, relatively few attempts have been made to understand the full complexity of integrated care initiatives. Moreover, it is clear that no single "best practice" model exists and that better care co-ordination for people is the result of a complex inter-play of activities undertaken on multiple levels (for example, systemic, organisational, professional) (McDonald et al., 2007).

Despite such complexity, a number of different models have been developed to guide understanding of the design of integrated care initiatives and set out core components and principles that should be met. The most influential of these has been the Chronic Care Model (CCM), which was developed in recognition of the failure of health systems in meeting the needs of people with chronic illnesses (as historically, they were largely built on acute, episodic models of care rather than on care focusing on more longitudinal, preventative, community-based and integrated approaches) (Wagner et al., 1999; Wagner et al., 2001; Pruitt et al., 2002). The CCM aims to provide a comprehensive framework for the organisation of healthcare in order to improve outcomes for people with chronic conditions.

According to the CCM, better patient outcomes are associated with the presence of six interrelated components: supported self-management; clinical decision support systems; delivery system redesign; clinical information systems; the availability of community resources and a supportive health system to enable this to happen. The key to the success of the CCM has been productive, two-way communication among the members of a multi-disciplinary team both managing patients and supporting them to better manage their own care (Coleman et al., 2009). Implicit in this relationship is the role of information and communication technologies (ICT) to support such capability.

Other conceptual frameworks related to integrated care include Integrated Health Networks, which take into account the internal processes required for provider organisations to achieve their integrated care objectives (Vazquez et al., 2009). Co-ordination, continuity and access of care are core components of the framework. Similarly, Integrated Health Service Delivery Networks, a strategy developed by the Pan American Health Organization in 2011, provides a road map for integrated care development at a national level in the Americas (Montenegro et al., 2011). Seen as an evolving and continuous process of development over time, the model describes the need to create certain system attributes so that integrated care can become a reality. This includes domains such as models of care; governance and strategy; organisation and management and financial allocations and incentives.

This work highlights how achieving integrated care requires an understanding of complex inter-relationships. Indeed, the concept of the *complex adaptive system* has been used in the context of integrated care to describe the often non-linear and fundamentally unpredictable outcomes that can result from the way in which physicians, patients and other actors in the healthcare system interact (Edgren and Barnard, 2012). Work by Valentijn et al. (2013) has mapped how these inter-relationships among the different dimensions of integrated care operate on the macro- (system integration), meso- (organisational,

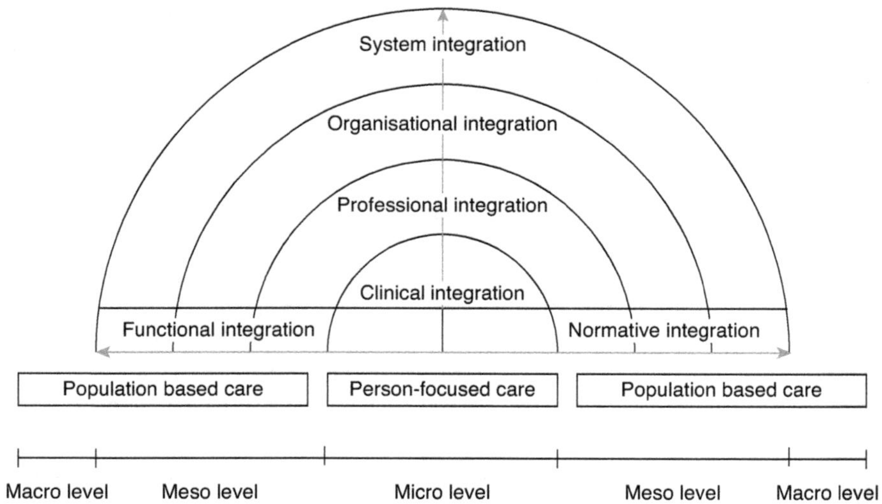

Figure 13.1 The levels of integrated care

professional) and micro-levels (clinical, service and personal integration) (Valentijn et al., 2013) (see Figure 13.1).

Nonetheless, some essential elements are of key importance. *Functional integration* (in other words, ICT and eHealth) is necessary to ensure connectivity across the care continuum. Functional integration acts with a dual purpose: forming the "glue" through which complex care systems are held together and providing the "grease" that enables these systems to inter-connect effectively and flexibly.

The role of eHealth in integrated care

eHealth is an overarching term for a range of ICT that seek to assist and enhance the management of health and lifestyle (Billings et al., 2013). The implementation of eHealth solutions has increased considerably in recent years as the political and strategic importance of developing new health technologies has been recognised (Carretero et al., 2012). In Europe, eHealth has been promoted as an innovative solution for both chronic care and ageing and for a more sustainable model of care (COM, 2007; COM, 2010). Indeed, evidence worldwide demonstrates that eHealth strategies can lead to better care outcomes at reduced cost where these are implemented effectively (Clark and Goodwin, 2010). As Box 13.1 shows, the range of eHealth technologies associated with this agenda are many and varied.

Box 13.1 eHealth technologies that support integrated care

Ambient assisted living (AAL) – a bundle of technologies used to enhance the quality of life for older people living in the home environment.

Assistive (adaptive) technology – any system or device that allows individuals to perform tasks that they would otherwise be unable to perform (such as accessible keyboards, speech recognition software, text telephones).

Decision-support systems – computer-based information systems that support care professionals and providers in making effective planning and treatment decisions (for example, for predicting at-risk patients and/or making care treatment decisions across care pathways).

Electronic health records – systematic collections of the health records of patients and populations that can be shared across different health and social care settings.

Gerontechnology – techniques and products based on knowledge of the ageing process that attempt to match technological applications to health, housing, mobility, communication, leisure and work.

Telecare – a service that uses a combination of alarms, sensors and other equipment (for example, fall sensors and pendant alarms) to help people live independently (usually in their own homes) by monitoring their activity and connecting them to care services in times of need.

Smart home technology – a collective term for home-based information technology (IT) services that increase safety and help support independent living (for example, fall monitors, automatic lighting and environmental control systems).

Telehealth – the remote exchange of physiological data between a patient and medical or nursing staff to assist in diagnosis, monitoring and supported self-care (for example, home units or mobile phone applications to measure and monitor blood pressure and other vital signs for clinical review at a remote location).

Telemedicine – the remote delivery of healthcare treatment services through the use of alerts, images, audio, video or other types of data used to make a clinical diagnosis and facilitate treatment.

Sources: (Graafmans and Brouwers, 1989; Clark and Goodwin, 2010; Billings et al., 2013).

Electronic health records

An electronic health record (EHR) is defined as a systematic collection of electronic health information about an individual patient or whole populations (Gunter and Terry, 2005). The purpose of EHRs is to develop a database of people's healthcare records that can be shared across different health and social care settings. EHRs are a key capability to support integrated care as they potentially allow for an entire patient history to be viewed by different care agencies. This enables much more effective trends in care needs and use to be determined, offering the potential for more targeted and integrated approaches to meet these needs.

The ability to bring datasets together into a single electronic patient record has often been cited as a prerequisite for effective integrated care in practice (for example, Bodenheimer, 2008; Ham, 2010). However, creating EHRs is often problematic – not just because of the technical difficulties in combining data across different recording systems, many of which do not contain "patient identifiers" essential to the process – but because of legal issues related to data governance that restricts the sharing of sensitive personal information about patients. Nonetheless, most Western countries are seeking to create such systems. For example:

- In Australia, the *Personally Controlled Electronic Care Record (PCECR)* is a major ongoing national initiative being developed through territorial, state and federal governments;
- In Canada, in Quebec, the PRISMA initiative has sought to create integrated care records as a key way to make more effective decisions about patient care, specifically for those with long-term medical conditions;
- In Estonia, a national EHR system has been created that registers virtually all residents' medical histories from birth to death;
- In the Netherlands, a national strategy initiated in 2013 has sought to integrate data from general practitioners, pharmacists and hospitals into a national EHR;
- In the United States of America (US), many care systems have developed sophisticated EHRs. These include the *HealthConnect* system of Kaiser Permanente and the *VistA* system of the Veteran's Health Administration.

Inter-professional communication

The ability of the members of integrated care teams to maintain good inter-professional communication is at the very core of the success of integrated care practices. According to an updated Cochrane Review, interventions aiming at improving inter-professional communication can have a positive impact on healthcare processes and outcomes even if the authors were not able to be precise about the key elements that define such successful communication (Zwarenstein et al., 2009).

Two recent papers shed some light on these key elements. Nancarrow and colleagues list up to ten characteristics that should be considered by teams aiming at improving their communication skills (Nancarrow et al., 2013): positive leadership and management attributes; communication strategies and structures; personal rewards, training and development; appropriate resources and procedures; appropriate skill mix; supportive team climate; individual characteristics that support interdisciplinary team work; clarity of vision; quality and outcomes of care and respecting and understanding roles. These mostly organisational components are complemented by the work of Stans and colleagues who investigated the barriers and facilitators that influence inter-professional practice using the domains of CCM as a framework (Stans et al., 2013). The authors found that most of the problems with regard to inter-professional communication were due to the lack of structure in the care process combined with a lack of a shared view on the goals to be achieved. Accordingly, as a remedial action they suggested the creation of a clear process mapping and the incorporation of tools to facilitate its use, arguing that each professional should know "who should do what, when and how".

Many of these ten elements are included in integrated care programmes. However, it is important to highlight the role that eHealth can play in efficiently supporting some of these aspects of integrated care. This is notably the case of process mapping and the clarification of roles and tasks allocated to professionals. ICT solutions exist to describe care processes, define care teams, schedule tasks and run process execution. Additionally, these solutions are often enriched by a set of complementary tools, most of which have been developed out of the field of Computer Supported Collaborative Work. Thus, eHealth is slowly becoming an indispensable ally in integrated care.

Decision support systems

The potential of eHealth systems to represent knowledge and clinical reasoning is a very interesting characteristic when the structuring and standardisation of the process of care is crucial for the success of care co-ordination models (Ali et al., 2011).

Accordingly, the introduction of Decision Support Systems (DSS) in clinical work is considered a priority in Europe. However, in spite of some successes, like the PHTS Telemedizin diabetes programme in Germany (Kubitschke et al., 2010), most authors prefer to be cautious. The importance of the context of use – how and when professionals use such systems – in terms of the overall success of eHealth seems to be a component that has been insufficiently investigated (Anchala et al., 2012; Divall et al., 2013). Also, introduction of DSS has not always been accompanied by the required support, and there is not adequate evidence of its benefits, thus creating doubts and hesitation regarding its use among professionals (Mitchell et al., 2009). Not surprisingly, as in many other areas of integrated care, the organisational aspects of DSS are of fundamental importance. Unless properly addressed, the potential of these systems to effectively support co-ordination of care delivery can be thwarted (Goud et al., 2010).

Case-finding tools for predictive risk assessment

Successful approaches to integrated care often rely on the ability to find "at risk" individuals within local communities. Without appropriate care and support, such individuals may become the next unplanned emergency hospital admission or need institutionalised care. This is known as case-finding. There are a number of tools and techniques that can be used for case-finding. The most accurate are predictive models that use statistical algorithms to predict an individual's level of future risk of admission (Billings et al., 2006; Georghiou et al., 2011). In practice, most programmes use a combination of a predictive model and clinical judgement to target which people would benefit most from either a primary or community care-based service. The most powerful predictive models require good quality data (for example, access to an individual's previous hospital admission records; records of health status and care usage held in primary care practices; and data from social care, pharmacies and other care providers, where available). Predictive models can also be built that not only identify at-risk individuals but also systematically assess how effective preventive care interventions are likely to be (Lewis, 2010). By enabling health systems to focus on those individuals who are at high risk of hospital or institutional admission, and who are amenable to preventive care, these 'impactability' models can enhance the cost-effectiveness of any necessary interventions.

Case-finding has been specifically used to support long-term conditions management. By predicting the populations most at risk of emergency admissions, those people within a community who would most benefit from targeted interventions can be identified – typically through at-home case management by a multi-disciplinary group of care professionals. The ability to use data and information to stratify populations according to need has been used in many care settings as a core strategy to reduce unnecessary hospitalisations and promote health and wellbeing in the community for people with complex chronic illnesses (see Box 13.2).

Box 13.2 Three European examples of case-finding technologies to support integrated care

Virtual wards in England: Many National Health Service (NHS) organisations in England use computer models (called "predictive models") to help them identify individuals who are at high risk of future hospital admissions. In certain parts of the NHS, such people are being offered extra support through a system of "virtual wards". The aim of these wards is to prevent unplanned admissions by providing multi-disciplinary case management in the community. The virtual wards work just like a hospital ward, using the same staffing, systems and daily routines, except that the people being cared for stay in their own homes. An evaluation of the costs and benefits of this approach in three communities – in the city districts of Croydon and Wandsworth, and in the county of Devon – was undertaken (Lewis et al., 2011). Early evidence suggested that the effective use of patient data can support better integration and co-ordination of care across organisational boundaries and provide a more personalised service to patients (Goodwin et al., 2010).

Integrated home care in Finland: In the South Karelia District in Finland, integrated home care has been advanced through the use of web cameras, broadband and video phones that enable different health and social care professionals to share data and provide rapid responses to patients in need of care. In the pilot phases of the initiative, 185 patients participated together with a general practitioner, two full-time nurses, several part-time home-care workers, as well as several IT engineers and data analysts. Results showed patients felt an increase in their sense of security, a reduced sense of isolation, used medication less and remote consultations were about 50 per cent more economical than usual care (Tepponen and Hammar, 2011).

eHealth units in Greece: In Athens, an eHealth unit at Sotiria's Hospital has been created to store and analyse data collected by the patient and home care nurses in a common shared electronic file available to the multi-disciplinary team and to the patients. This has enabled more effective multi-disciplinary decision-making at the point of care with the patient (Mastroyiannakis, 2010).

eHealth and long-term conditions management in the home

The evidence base for telehealth and telecare, particularly the remote management of people with long-term chronic illness, is under-developed; this lack of evidence has contributed to slow uptake of the technology across Europe (Clark and Goodwin, 2010). However, many good case examples exist that demonstrate the benefits of supporting people with long-term conditions through technology. Box 13.3 provides one such example from the Veterans Health Administration (VHA) in the US and its Care Coordination/Home Telehealth (CCHT) programme. The CCHT approach has achieved better outcomes for individuals and reduced system costs.

Outlook

In spite of the apparent simplicity of the meaning of integrated care, achieving it is an intrinsically complex process involving changes in core organisational, managerial, professional and system level aspects. This makes it difficult to identify best practices and limits opportunities for transferability of successful experiences.

ICT have been gradually introduced as supportive tools in integrated care because of the potential of these technologies to describe structured processes, support the co-ordination of activities and facilitate communication among different actors. However, their adoption has been slow. Only solutions in the areas of home automation (domestic robotics or domotics) or telecare can be termed mainstream.

Box 13.3 Case study: the VHA's Care Coordination/Home Telehealth programme

The Veterans Health Administration (VHA) implements a medical assistance programme for American veterans through outpatient clinics, hospitals, medical centres and long-term health and social care facilities. The aim of this programme is to provide non-institutional care services for the rising number of elderly veterans with chronic care needs; to improve coordination of their care and to avoid unnecessary admission to long-term institutional care. CCHT is now a routine service that uses home telehealth and disease management technologies in care management, designed to support veteran patients (aged over 65 years); 95 per cent of users are male.

The main conditions managed are diabetes mellitus, hypertension, congestive heart failure and chronic obstructive pulmonary disease (COPD). A smaller number of veterans are currently being treated for depression. Care co-ordinators, who are usually nurses or social workers, receive specific training and manage between 90 and 150 patients. Eligible patients are offered the choice whether to receive CCHT-based care. When a patient is enrolled, the care co-ordinator selects the appropriate home health technology, gives the required training to the patient and caregiver and reviews telehealth monitoring data, providing active care or case management on a continuous basis.

The most commonly used technology is a messaging/monitoring device (in 85 per cent of cases), followed by videotelemonitors (11 per cent) and videophones (4 per cent). Messaging devices present disease management protocols that contain text-based questions for patients to answer, helping the care co-ordinators assess patients' health status and disease self-management capabilities. Biometric devices record and monitor vital signs data. Videophones and videotelemonitors support audio–video consultations at the home.

Promoting patient self-management is a fundamental component of the CCHT model and the messaging devices are key to this. Care co-ordinators intervene as necessary in accordance with specific alerts (for example, if there is a change in a patient's symptoms, they help the patient self-manage by phone or through institute care/case management).

Impact of the programme

In serving more than 30,000 patients, CCHT is probably the largest and most integrated example of home telehealth in the US and, indeed, internationally. Analysis of data obtained from a cohort of 17,025 CCHT patients in 2008 showed a reduction in bed days of care and in hospital admissions, a high satisfaction rate and a substantial cost savings.

Home telehealth has been adopted across the VHA as a cost-effective way of managing chronic care patients in both urban and rural settings.

Sources: (Darkins et al., 2008; Kubitschke et al., 2010).

By and large, it seems that both integrated care and eHealth are in need of a larger number of solid cases that demonstrate their value within a given co-ordinated care process and in a variety of contexts. This should be accompanied by a review of the regulatory framework for their adoption and supported by comprehensive programmes promoting change and innovation.

The European Commission is actively promoting such change and innovation through its European Innovation Partnership on Active and Health Ageing, in particular by means of the partnership's B3 Action Group on Integrated Care. The group constitutes an inclusive European-wide forum for the exchange of practices around the practicalities of adoption, replication and scale-up of integrated care. It has set two ambitious goals (European Commission, 2013): (1) making available programmes for chronic conditions/case management in at least 50 regions by 2015, available to at least 10 per cent of the target population (patients affected by chronic diseases in the regions involved); (2) scaling-up and replicating integrated care programmes, supported by innovative tools and services, in at least 20 regions in 15 Member States based on validated, evidence-based cases (2015–2020).

Another important sign of maturity in the field of integrated care is the growth of professional networks, dedicated journals and conferences. In this respect, the International Foundation for Integrated Care (IFIC) is expanding. It is a "not for profit network that crosses organisational and professional boundaries to bring people together to advance the science, knowledge and adoption of integrated care policy and practice" (IFIC, 2013).

Taken as a whole, the time seems to be ripe for the extension of integrated care programmes and accompanying ICT.

References

Ali, M.K., Shah, S. and Tandon, N. (2011), "Review of electronic decision-support tools for diabetes care: a viable option for low- and middle-income countries?", *Journal of Diabetes Science and Technology* 5(3): 553–570.

Anchala, R., Pinto, M.P., Shroufi, A., Chowdhury, R., Sanderson, J., Johnson, L., Blanco, P., Prabhakaran, D. and Franco, O.H. (2012), "The role of Decision Support System (DSS) in prevention of cardiovascular disease: a systematic review and meta-analysis", *PLoS.One* 7(10): e47064.

Anderson, G. and Horvath, J. (2004), "The growing burden of chronic disease in America", *Public Health Reports* 119 (3): 263–270.

Berwick, D.M., Nolan, T.W. and Whittington, J. (2008), "The triple aim: care, health, and cost", *Health Affairs (Millwood.)* 27 (3): 759–769.

Billings, J., Dixon, J., Mijanovich, T. and Wennberg, D. (2006), "Case finding for patients at risk of readmission to hospital: development of algorithm to identify high risk patients", *British Medical Journal* 333 (7563): 327.

Billings, J., Carretero, S., Kagialaris, G., Mastroyiannakis, T. and Meriläinen-Porras, S. (2013), "The role of information technology in long term care for older people", in Leichsenring, K, Billings, J. and Nies, H. (eds) *Long-Term Care in Europe. Improving Policy and Practice*. Palgrave Macmillan: Basingstoke.

Bodenheimer, T. (2008), "Coordinating care – a perilous journey through the health care system". *North England Journal of Medicine* 358 (10): 1064–1071.

Carretero, S., Stewart, J., Centeno, C., Barbabella, F., Schmidt, A., Lamontagne-Godwin, F. and Lamura, G. (2012), *Can Technology-Based Services support Long-term Care Challenges in Home Care?* Joint Research Centre, JRC77709.

Clark, M. and Goodwin, N. (2010), *Sustaining Innovation in Telehealth and Telecare*. The King's Fund, London.

Coleman, K., Austin, B.T., Brach, C. and Wagner, E.H. (2009), "Evidence on the Chronic Care Model in the new millennium", *Health Affairs (Millwood.)* 28 (1): 75–85.

COM, (2007), Commission of the European Communities, *A Lead Market Initiative for Europe*. Brussels, COM(2007) 860 final.

COM, (2010), Commission of the European Communities, *A Digital Agenda for Europe*. Brussels, COM(2010) 245 final/2.

Darkins, A., Ryan, P., Kobb, R., Foster, L., Edmonson, E., Wakefield, B. and Lancaster, A.E. (2008), "Care Coordination/Home Telehealth: the systematic implementation of health informatics, home telehealth, and disease management to support the care of veteran patients with chronic conditions", *Telemedicine Journal and EHealth* 14 (10): 1118–1126.

Divall, P., Camosso-Stefinovic, J. and Baker, R. (2013), "The use of personal digital assistants in clinical decision making by health care professionals: a systematic review", *Health Informatics Journal* 19 (1): 16–28.

Edgren, L. and Barnard, K. (2012), "Complex adaptive systems for management of integrated care", *Leadership in Health Services* 25 (1): 39–51.

European Commission (2013). European Innovation Partnership on Active and Healthy Ageing. https://webgate.ec.europa.eu/eipaha. 2013. 27 August 2013. (Electronic Citation)

Georghiou, T., Steventon, A., Billings, J., Blunt, I., Lewis, G. and Bardsley, M. (2011), *Predictive Risk and Health Care: An Overview*, London: Nuffield Trust.

Goodwin, N. (2013), "Understanding integrated care: a complex process, a fundamental principle", *International Journal of Integrated Care* 13: e011.

Goodwin, N., Curry, N., Naylor, C., Ross, S. and Duldig, W. (2010), *Managing People with Long-Term Conditions*, London: The Kings' Fund.

Goud, R., van Engen-Verheul, M., de Keizer, N.F., Bal, R., Hasman, A., Hellemans, I.M. and Peek, N. (2010), "The effect of computerized decision support on barriers to guideline implementation: a qualitative study in outpatient cardiac rehabilitation", *International Journal Medical Informatics* 79 (6): 430–437.

Graafmans, J. and Brouwers, T. (1989), "Gerontechnology, the modelling of normal aging" in *Human Factors and Ergonomics Society Annual Meeting*. Human Factors and Ergonomics Society, pp. 187–190.

Gunter, T.D. and Terry, N.P. (2005), "The emergence of national electronic health record architectures in the United States and Australia: models, costs, and questions", *Journal of Medical Internet Research* 7 (1): e3.

Ham, C. (2010), "The ten characteristics of the high-performing chronic care system", *Health Economics, Policy and Law* 5 (1): 71–90.

Hofmarcher, M., Oxley, H. and Rusticelli, E. (2007), *Improved Health System performance through better care coordination*, OECD. Directorate for employment, labour and social affairs. Health Committee, 30.

IFIC (2013), International Foundation for Integrated Care. http://www.integratedcare-foundation.org/. 2013. International Foundation for Integrated Care. 27-8-2013. (Electronic Citation).

Kubitschke, L., Cullen, K., Müller, S., Delaney, S., Garies, K., Dolphin, C., Frenzel-Erkert, U., Wynne, R., Lull, F. and Rauhala, M. (2010), ICT & Ageing – European Study on Users, Markets and Technologies. Final Report. Available at http://www.ict-ageing.eu/ict-ageing-website/wp-content/uploads/2010/D18_final_report.pdf.

Lewis, G.H. (2010), "'Impactibility models': identifying the subgroup of high-risk patients most amenable to hospital-avoidance programs", *Milbank Quarterly* 88 (2): 240–255.

Lewis, G., Bardsley, M., Vaithianathan, R., Steventon, A., Georghiou, T., Billings, J. and Dixon, J. (2011), "Do 'virtual wards' reduce rates of unplanned hospital admissions, and at what cost? A research protocol using propensity matched controls", *International Journal of Integrated Care* 11: e079.

Mastroyiannakis, T. (2010), eHealth Unit Sotiria Hospital. Case report. Interlinks Project. (Grant 223037) http://interlinks.euro.centre.org/model/example/EHealthUnitOfSotiriaHospital. (Electronic Citation)

McDonald, K.M., Sundaram, V., Bravata, D.M., Lewis, R., Lin, N., Kraft, S., McKinnon, M., Paguntalan, H. and Owens, D. K. (2007), *Care Coordination (Volume 7 of Closing the Quality Gap: A Critical Analysis of Quality Improvement Strategies)*, Agency for Healthcare Research and Quality, Rockville, MD, Technical Review 9.

Mitchell, N., Randell, R., Foster, R., Dowding, D., Lattimer, V., Thompson, C., Cullum, N. and Summers, R. (2009), "A national survey of computerized decision support systems available to nurses in England", *Journal of Nursing Management* 17 (7): 772–780.

Montenegro, H., Levcovitz, E., Holder, R., Ruales, J. and Suárez, J. (2011), *Integrated Health Service Delivery Networks: Concepts, Policy Options and a Road Map for Implementation in the Americas*. Washington, D.C.: Pan American Health Organization (PAHO), p. 4.

Nancarrow, S.A., Booth, A., Ariss, S., Smith, T., Enderby, P. and Roots, A. (2013), "Ten principles of good interdisciplinary team work", *Human Resources for Health* 11 (1): 19.

Nolte, E. and McKee, M. (2008), "Integration and chronic care: A review", in Nolte, E. and McKee, M. (eds) *Caring for People with Chronic Conditions. A Health System Perspective.* Maidenhead: Open University Press, pp. 64–91.

Ouwens, M., Wollersheim, H., Hermens, R., Hulscher, M. and Grol, R. (2005), "Integrated care programmes for chronically ill patients: a review of systematic reviews", *International Journal for Quality in Health Care* 17 (2): 141–146.

Pruitt, S., Annandale, S., Epping-Jordan, J., Fernández, J., Khan, M., Kisa, A., Kaplow, J., Nuño, R., Reddy, S. and Wagner, E. (2002), *Innovative Care for Chronic Conditions: Building Blocks for Actions: Global Report*. Geneva, Switzerland: Noncommunicable Diseases and Mental Health, World Health Organization, c2002.

Stans, S.E., Stevens, J.A. and Beurskens, A.J. (2013), "Interprofessional practice in primary care: development of a tailored process model", *Journal of Multidisciplinary Healthcare* 6: 139–147.

Tepponen, M. and Hammar, T. (2011), ICT solutions and new health technology facilitating integration in home care. http://interlinks.euro.centre.org/model/example/ICTSolutionsAndNewHealthTechnologyFacilitatingIntegrationInHome%20care. Interlinks project (Grant 223037). (Electronic Citation)

Valentijn, P.P., Schepman, S.M., Opheij, W. and Bruijnzeels, M.A. (2013), "Understanding integrated care: a comprehensive conceptual framework based on the integrative functions of primary care", *International Journal of Integrated Care* 13: e010.

Vazquez, M.L., Vargas, I., Unger, J.P., Mogollon, A., Silva, M.R. and Paepe, P. (2009), "Integrated health care networks in Latin America: toward a conceptual framework for analysis", *Rev.Panam.Salud Publica* 26 (4): 360–367.

Wagner, E.H., Davis, C., Schaefer, J., Von, K.M. and Austin, B. (1999), "A survey of leading chronic disease management programs: are they consistent with the literature?" *Managed Care Quarterly* 7(3): 56–66.

Wagner, E.H., Austin, B.T., Davis, C., Hindmarsh, M., Schaefer, J. and Bonomi, A. (2001), "Improving chronic illness care: translating evidence into action", *Health Affairs (Millwood)* 20 (6): 64–78.

Zwarenstein, M., Goldman, J. and Reeves, S. (2009), "Interprofessional collaboration: effects of practice-based interventions on professional practice and healthcare outcomes", *Cochrane Database of Systemic Reviews* 3: CD000072.

14
The eHealth Contribution to Person-Centred Care

Dipak Kalra, Jörg Artmann, Veli Stroetmann and Niels Boye

Introduction

Patients and healthy individuals can play an active role in their own health management. They also increasingly want to do so. Indeed, there are growing societal pressures to recognise the central role of members of the public as informed and autonomous partners in making various decisions about their personal healthcare: these include the safety, efficacy and acceptability of treatment choices; and service priority setting. Individuals can acquire considerable expertise in managing their own illnesses and preventing ill health if they are given the appropriate resources. People's participation in healthcare includes a spectrum of activities that covers clinician-directed monitoring (self-testing), patient tailoring of treatment (self-management) and fully autonomous prevention and information and communication technology (ICT) assisted-care (otherwise known as the co-production of health).

This chapter illustrates facets of citizen participation in healthcare and the role of ICT tools in facilitating this participation. It begins with an introduction to the management of chronic diseases and shows how the role of the patient in this context is changing from being a passive recipient of care to a shaper of his/her own care and health outcomes. Then the role of ICT tools in this process is discussed. Next, future-oriented scenarios for patient-centred care are presented. Finally, the chapter closes with reflections on how eHealth solutions can be scaled up. Although this chapter concentrates on the European context, many of its insights have far-reaching implications for global health, as the experience of multiple chronic conditions also grows worldwide.

Chronic disease management and eHealth

The burden of chronic diseases on the healthcare systems of the industrialised nations is well known. Non-communicable diseases – mainly cancer, cardiovascular diseases, diabetes and chronic respiratory diseases – are responsible for about two-thirds of deaths worldwide. The impact of conditions such as chronic heart failure on Western economies – due to prolonged absence from work and disability – can be measured in billions of Euros (Bloom et al., 2011). The current design of most Western healthcare systems is focused on the reactive treatment of acute diseases. It is often ill equipped to address the complex factors leading to the initial onset and slow development of chronic diseases.

In this context, chronic disease management seeks to provide a more holistic response to the needs of patients who experience a chronic condition. This approach is exemplified in different ways across Europe: either a general practitioner plays a gatekeeping role or joint doctors' offices enable patients to see different specialists in a single visit (these are sometimes referred to as polyclinics). The second of these two approaches is particularly important for conditions such as diabetes, which affects a patient's different organs and where "small" incidents, such as a foot infection, can have serious consequences for more widespread or urgent health-related developments.

Due to the slow, gradual development of chronic conditions, it is useful to visualise progress in four separate transitions: from being healthy; to borderline health; to acute disease and eventually to chronic illness (Meglic and Brodnik, 2010). The particularly great challenge for patients who have developed risk factors – and hence for their healthcare systems – is their potential for a transition into an irreversible cycle of chronic illness.

Once the patient has entered the cycle of chronic illness, the condition cannot be reversed. Disease management is therefore at the heart of chronic disease care. It has been suggested by Levich that patient self-management should be at the core of all chronic disease management (Levich, 2007). By encouraging patients to act as leaders of their own health surrounded by a team of supportive healthcare professionals, bodily functioning, health outcomes and quality of life can all be maintained or improved. For such an approach to remain inclusive of all patient profiles, different levels of patient engagement need to be supported. Ultimately, the proportion or share of healthcare provider responsibility to patient responsibility is currently being debated.

To achieve appropriate levels of engagement and empowerment, an effective health management programme with educational and supportive interventions should be established. The Chronic Care Model developed by Edward Wagner and his colleagues at the MacColl Institute in Seattle in the United States of America (US) suggests that productive interactions between informed, activated patients and a well prepared, proactive practice team will produce improved outcomes (ICIC, 1998). However, to create these optimal conditions, certain elements need to be in place in the health system and wider community. ICT-based solutions are a key element in this model. Clinical information systems allow healthcare professionals to search patient history, track patient progress and document health outcomes and goals.

Goldstein, DePue and Kazura suggest that clinical information systems, such as pre-visit health-risk appraisal instruments, questionnaires or interactive computer-based systems can be used more widely to improve outcomes (Goldstein et al., 2009). Such ICT-based solutions provide a swift means of aiding patient education and counselling interventions. Additionally, the use of patient assessments prompts clinicians and patients to address issues of self-management during consultations. Assessments and action plans also support patients because they serve as reminders towards the achievement of health goals (Goldstein et al., 2009). The availability of these tools electronically, such as via a patient accessible electronic health record or portal (particularly one that can deploy reminders), increases their chance of success. Thus, the action plan or assessment is more effective.

Effective self-management programmes can be aligned with the required input elements of the Chronic Care Model: self-management support; delivery system design; decision support and clinical information systems. Three of the recommended components cited below pertain directly to ICT-based solutions (Lorig et al., 2000):

- Remote management capabilities (telephone, email, home monitoring);
- Case management with remote communication based in the team office;
- An electronic medical record to ensure continuity and integration of care.

These three tools provide a means for communication with the disease management team, both between patients and healthcare professionals, and among health professionals. The communication possibilities presented by such ICT-based solutions as an integrated (shared) electronic health record (EHR) are essential for team-delivered care. The need for a team-based approach has been made apparent by Graf and colleagues (Graf et al., 2012) who point out that no single physician can manage all the activities involved. Instead, a multidisciplinary team operating according to redesigned workflows is required. It is argued that it is only once these elements are in place that ICT-based solutions can be used as support tools (Graf et al., 2012).

Chronic disease management is further complicated by the existence of multiple morbidity (or multi-morbidity) – that is, when a patient is experiencing several chronic conditions at the same time – as it expands considerably the issues associated with a single chronic disease: "Patients with multi-morbidity are more likely to die prematurely, be admitted to hospital, and have longer hospital stays than those with single conditions. They have poorer quality of life, loss of physical functioning, are more likely to experience depression, and to be receiving multiple drugs with consequent difficulties with adherence"

(Smith et al., 2012). Unfortunately, multi-morbidity "is the norm rather than the exception in primary care patients and will become more prevalent as populations age" (Mercer et al., 2009). Currently, 49 per cent of European women and 39 per cent of European men aged over 50 experience more than two chronic diseases (HEIDI Wiki https://webgate.ec.europa.eu/sanco/heidi/index.php/Heidi/Population_group-specific_health/Elderly#Data_sources). The prevalence of patients with co-existing chronic diseases means that the effectiveness of solutions focused on single diseases is limited. Rather, integrated care models, which combine services from across the health and social care sector to build a personalised solution, are required. Managing the combination of these services so that they fit into a personal patient pathway – that is, a co-ordinated sequence of care interventions by different healthcare professionals – requires dedicated healthcare teams with redesigned workflows and ICT support.

ICT solutions such as EHRs can be used to provide timely and accurate information; allow supportive and educational interventions for patients' self-management of their health; monitor patients' progress; assess patients' needs; and provide a point of contact to other health team members. It is perhaps this last point that is most important. In order for patients to become active and effective members of their own disease management team, access to the reassurance and encouragement of healthcare staff, particularly in the early stages of a disease, is as essential as any other element. Once patients have gained confidence and experience in managing their health, they will rely on this less. This idea is elaborated by Hibbard and colleagues (Hibbard et al., 2004) who point out that activation is developmental in nature: first, patients must believe in the importance of their role; then they must obtain the confidence and knowledge to take action; next they must take action and finally they must maintain the lifestyle changes of these actions – even under stress. Recent studies confirm the link between patient activation and improved health outcomes (Greene and Hibbard, 2012).

European policy-makers increasingly recognise the significance of chronic disease management and the important role ICT can play in supporting it. For example, in Ireland a policy on the prevention and management of chronic disease has been launched. This policy describes the best practice which aligns with many of the aspects identified in the earlier section, including: "The use of information systems and registers to plan and evaluate care for individuals with chronic disease" (Department of Health, 2008). Disease management programmes, which focus on specific diseases, use co-ordinated care elements across the delivery system. Examples that include the use of ICT as a support tool have been developed across Europe, including in Denmark, France, Germany, the Netherlands, Sweden and the United Kingdom (UK) (Nolte et al., 2009). Across Europe, a number of small-scale pilot studies on integrated care have also taken place using evidence-based medicine, supported by electronic protocols and clinical pathways.

Integrated care as person-centred care

The term *integrated care* has different meanings according to the context in which it is used. This section presents examples of attempts to structure this concept and delimit it from other concepts, such as co-ordinated care or linked care. This section briefly summarises the role of ICT applications in the delivery of integrated care. The role of integrated care pathways as formal representations of care processes is also described.

There are different perspectives on integrated care and the processes that are required to achieve it. It is important to consider both the policy motivation to implement integrated care against the background of chronically ill patients, as well as the conceptual elements of integrated care.

A policy brief on integrated care and telehealth published by the World Health Organization (Stroetmann et al., 2010) puts the problem as follows: "Demographic change, rising incidence of chronic disease and unmet needs for more personalised care are trends that demand a new, integrated approach to health and social care. Professionals must work across sectors as a team with common goals and resources to deliver a coordinated response to each citizen's care requirements. Advanced information and communications technology gives a major new opportunity to realise care integration, superseding today's chain of disjointed responses to discrete threats to health." According to Nolte and McKee: "chronic illness requires complex models of care, involving collaboration among professions and institutions that have traditionally been separate" (Nolte and McKee, 2008).

Integrated care can be visualised on a continuum of efforts to link and co-ordinate care. At the highest level, integrated care involves multi-disciplinary teams, common records and the pooling of funds.

This level of integration is an ideal response to patients with high (or complex) needs. In contrast, the lowest level of integration would only seek to ensure that doctors in the primary care sector are informed through the receipt of discharge letters about patients that are leaving a hospital. Such co-ordination between two different care settings is only a basic prerequisite and does not yet include any form of agreement on a care plan. The maximum level of integration would provide a "one stop shop" response to the health needs of the patient: care would be delivered in one or many settings through a single entry point by an agreed set of health and social care professionals co-ordinating their work (Leutz, 1999).

Lloyd and Wait provide another typology of integrated care models that partly echoes the concepts already presented above (Lloyd and Wait, 2011). They distinguish between the following five dimensions of integrated care:

- Shared information among professionals from different sectors
  This model uses greater sharing of patient information among health and social care professionals to facilitate the treatment of patients in a co-ordinated fashion, minimise data storage costs and reduce problems that result from separate information systems;
- Standardised communication protocols and formats
  Defined protocols and formats are used to improve communication between health and social care professionals, and facilitate a more seamless and integrated care process;
- Single assessment processes incorporating multi-disciplinary assessment
  This involves a single, multi-disciplinary assessment of users' needs for health and social care. Single assessment processes reduce the number of assessments that a patient undergoes, and provide a central point of information from which to co-ordinate care;
- Defined pathways of care
  This model uses clearly defined multi-disciplinary pathways of care, incorporating both health and social care;
- Single access points to care
  This model seeks to limit the number of "access points" at which users receive care (ideally to a single access point), so as to reduce the number of professionals and organisations that patients have to deal with. Such a single point of access model may in the future be supported by software solutions that point a user to the relevant contacts in each care-seeking situation.

It is worth noting that the five elements build on each other to culminate in defined pathways of care. Nevertheless, these elements must rely on prior infrastructure, shared goals and a joint needs assessment.

The role of eHealth in facilitating integrated care and self-care

Integrated care clearly has a co-ordination and communication need that can realistically only be met by modern ICT tools. This section presents the rationale for, and the potential of, the use of eHealth services to achieve integrated care. Ultimately, the use of these ICT tools needs to be embedded in a revised healthcare delivery process, sustained by the joint commitment of all relevant stakeholders.

The seamless sharing of information across the continuum of care is one of ten key principles for successful health systems integration (Suter et al., 2009). Care communication and the sequencing of events are also requirements that call for ICT support (Rijken et al., 2008). Indeed, as the World Health Organization brief on telehealth and integrated care (Stroetmann et al., 2010) states: "ICT applications, or eHealth, can enable patient data to be safely shared, clinical pathways and service delivery processes to be coordinated, knowledge to be generated from structured data, and results to be merged into an evolving standard of care provided jointly by...health and social care services."

Central to this new approach of offering services that respond to needs in a person-centred manner are supportive infrastructural arrangements (like shared EHRs), which enable healthcare information management.

A further step is the use of Personal Health Systems (PHS) (Stroetmann et al., 2011a). The concept of PHS is understood as a system of personal technical devices that collects and communicates healthcare data of the patient, such as blood sugar levels, blood pressure, body weight or similar and respective solutions and services provided to the customer (patient, citizen). On the basis of such systems, it is possible to offer interventions such as telemonitoring, telephone services or tele-consultation. This adds substantial benefits to the existing ICT services by supporting relationships and enhancing the dialogue between different health and/or social care providers (Stroetmann et al., 2011b).

With the help of messaging systems that exchange structured data among computer systems, notifications about a patient's hospital admission and discharge can be transmitted to local authorities, primary care doctors and relevant home care providers, leading to better co-ordination of health and care services.

Ultimately, a comprehensive eHealth strategy can capitalise on the full potential of telehealth, in order to cope better with growing demands of an ageing society challenging healthcare systems (Stroetmann et al., 2010).

ICT support for care integration and co-ordination

Despite initial developments towards better integration of healthcare and social care practices, today's healthcare and social care systems are still far from being integrated as a result of their systemic silo structures. Different professional cultures (for example, both academic and non-academic training takes place) and funding schemes have contributed to these silos.

The potential of ICT-enabled forms of support, such as telecare and telehealth, could be exploited in a more effective way if these silos were more systematically embedded within a "whole systems" approach to health and social care. This whole systems approach implies the bringing together of different services, organisations and parts of care provision, notably the health and social care services that have traditionally been separated.

What are the technical requirements to achieve a whole systems approach to care delivery? The components can be grouped according to two major types of activities:

- Data sharing and co-ordination;
- Real-time communication.

The data-sharing and co-ordination ICT building blocks deal with all aspects related to health and clinical data exchange among the care providers and the structured delivery of services along a patient pathway. These therefore include, as components, an integrated care record or another form of shared EHR. A workflow engine (Huser et al., 2010) and joint scheduling are examples of co-ordination tools among carers and, finally, a number of monitoring services exist that can collect health and lifestyle data from the patient.

Alongside this data sharing and co-ordination aspect, real-time communication building blocks are also necessary to set up an integrated care delivery service. The communication components have an inter-agency dimension, which, on the one hand, allows different care providers to communicate and to hold joint case conferences. On the other hand, they have a joint-response dimension, when they allow local care providers to raise ad hoc requests that require a joint response.

The current maturity of each of these components differs, which makes it all the more important for local or regional initiatives to carefully define what the desired changes in the care delivery process are and how best to achieve them.

From integrated care to co-production of health

The preceding section focused on the use of ICT tools to care for patients in a more structured and informed way. However, ICT can also serve as an information and communication provider to engage chronically ill and healthy citizens in the co-production of their own health environment. This section presents an illustrative (fictitious) scenario of person-centred care. The scenario shows the potential value that an ICT-enabled re-design of healthcare services around a patient can provide both to the patient and to the providers.

Although fictitious, this scenario is inspired from many real integrated care initiatives across Europe. In these case studies, the personalisation of healthcare delivery was usually a response to the management of people's specific chronic conditions with a view to enable patients to become co-producers of their own health. The key eHealth enablers that would be needed in order to deliver the scenario are then discussed in up to six possible dimensions (where they are relevant to the specific scenario). Just five enablers are discussed in relation to this scenario about integrated care for Elsa, an elderly patient (Box 14.1).

Box 14.1 A scenario for person-centred care: integrated care for an elderly patient

Elsa is 79 years old, she is Danish, and has a light cognitive impairment, type II diabetes, congestive heart failure and insomnia. Her complicated medical treatment is supervised by a district nurse with inputs from two outpatient clinics and her general practitioner via the Danish shared medical record (Fælles Medicin Kort – FMK). However, Elsa does not often adhere to the pre-packed medication that she is prescribed, due to her cognitive impairment and because she often feels uncomfortable when taking all the drugs.

One night Elsa slips on the way to the toilet on a carpet in her flat and breaks her left hip. She is taken to hospital, operated on and introduced to rehabilitation to ensure that she becomes mobile again. Elsa continues to take most of her medications for her chronic diseases while in the surgical department, and she is discharged on more than ten different drugs. The surgical treatment was excellent and the mobilisation effective.

The district nurse receives a discharge "warning" about Elsa's departure from hospital three days before. She visits Elsa at the hospital and receives permission to check her apartment and contact her daughter to obtain yet more information. She runs her present medication though a poly-pharmacy check through an application developed by the Danish Institute for Rational Pharmacotherapy, inputting information about Elsa's fall, hip fracture, kidney function, age, gender, diabetes II and mild congestive heart disease for parameterisation of the model. The model suggests a dexascan for osteoporosis and change of pain, insomnia and diuretic treatments. The suggestions proposed by the model are communicated to Elsa's general practitioner. The nurse also visits Elsa's apartment and goes through it for obstacles – both for Elsa, and the intelligent iWalker (rollator) with which Elsa has been equipped. She arranges to have the apartment cleaned up and books a technician to install sensors in the kitchen and at the door, and screens in the sleeping and sitting rooms.

When Elsa returns home, her daughter, the nurse and a physiotherapist with the iWalker and a small bicycle-like treadmill are all physically present in the apartment. The doctor joins in via tele-presence. A retired nurse is also there. She will assist Elsa as a "buddy" during Elsa's immediate period back at home. In the first week, this means that the nurse will spend up to three hours a day, to go through the routines and configure the system and the sensor network for Elsa's needs. One of her tasks is to co-ordinate with providers and social contacts in what is called Elsa's personal "ecosystem", her social network of family, friends and neighbours. The district nurse will come once a day for the first week and so will the therapist. The general practitioner co-ordinates the medical treatments, including the new treatments for osteoporosis. Elsa's training is soon supervised semi-automatically by the physiotherapist via video technology and by occasional visits. The "buddy" and Elsa go through a range of applications from the Danish eHealth library and configure them for Elsa's social and medical conditions. Elsa learns to control blood glucose herself and uses an application for her own empowerment on decisions with regard to her diabetes. An automatic pill dispenser is added to the technology in Elsa's home. The doctor monitors the treatment via tele-presence and biochemical tests and occasionally adjusts the dosage accordingly.

All of the actions and plans of the members of this virtual care team, and data feeds from the various monitoring devices, are integrated into Elsa's shared medical record. Care planning tools are configured to alert specific members of the team if there are assessments or interventions that are due for their attention, and provide a kind of instant messaging to enable point-to-point communication inside the team. A supportive environment for daily activities intended for light cognitive impairment is configured using the wireless sensor network in the apartment. The computer technology is also used to support Elsa's social activities and enables her to use public transportation and banking, and to easily get in contact with her general practitioner and social services.

Key enablers of person-centred care

In terms of the scenario about the integrated care recommended for this elderly patient, five key enablers are immediately evident. They are healthcare business and service models; healthcare ICT marketplace and procurement models; ICT standards and effectiveness; workforce skills and societal engagement combined with empowerment and value. The implications of how each enabler works are described here in detail.

Healthcare business and service models

The Elsa scenario describes a sophisticated package of care that involves multiple professionals who collaborate in part through human means and in part through the use of monitoring devices, assistive technologies and online collaboration tools. This package of care has substantial capital costs (for example, the procurement of the electronic care planning tools and mobile devices carried by all of the health professionals, and the physical objects installed in Elsa's apartment). It also has substantial revenue costs as a number of different healthcare actors will need to dedicate time each week to help keep Elsa in her own home. In addition to the health-related services, a number of social care services (such as home help and meals provision) may also need to be factored in to an overall costing model for Elsa's care in the community.

Today, few healthcare or integrated care systems would allow the nursing home budget that has been saved to be used to offset the costs of this package of community care services. A complication with this model that may arise in some European countries is that individuals may be expected to contribute financially (for example, by selling their existing home) to the costs of residential care but not to the costs of the provision of care in the community.

In the Elsa scenario, the outcome of the person-centred care is higher quality of life, recruitment of alternative co-producers of health and wellbeing, and a shift of the point of activity and data integration very close to Elsa, who is the ultimate client.

This transition requires a novel service model and some investments in needed structures. The return on investment is more difficult to assess and may require alternative thinking in terms of business or service models, as nursing home facilities and personnel are not resources that can be easily redeployed. Furthermore, the scenario requires a consensus in society about the acceptable price tag on gaining "two more healthy years", which is the current European Commission expectation for the effects of the active and healthy ageing initiative as part of the European Innovation Partnership (European Commission, 2013).

Health ICT marketplace and procurement models

The safe monitoring of Elsa's home requires several sensors to be placed inside rooms and connected to domestic appliances. Thus, they will function in a co-ordinated fashion in order to trigger appropriate signals if Elsa becomes immobile or has a fall, but they will avoid false alarms and other noise. Ideally, it should be possible to procure a single coherent bundle of products and associated information services and have them installed, and to ensure integrated training for healthcare staff about the smart home as a whole rather than on a per device basis. An integrated maintenance contract would also be helpful.

In most situations, an integrated ecosystem like the Elsa scenario tends to occur only in research projects and pilots. In such cases, the technology package is usually predetermined by the consortium partners. This scenario, both for Elsa and for many other patients like her, would be best served by having an adaptable profile of interoperable products and services that could be bundled together under a single financial, contractual and accountability framework.

ICT standards and effectiveness

The many different products installed in Elsa's home all need to be able to interoperate with her EHR and with the care planning system that is tracking her situation and generating alerts. This requires a combination of information representation standards (information models and messages) and semantic standards so that the trigger conditions across the different devices can be co-interpreted by the care planning and monitoring applications. The required localisation effort, although theoretically possible, currently does not scale up and would not permit ad hoc combinations of products to work together as needed.

Workforce skills

Several of the members of this virtual team will need to be trained in how to configure many different home devices and how to interpret the various signals that they generate. This will include knowing when to appropriately react to a possible adverse situation, and when to recognise false alarms and spurious readings from individual devices.

Societal engagement, empowerment, value

This scenario assumes that it is more desirable for Elsa, her family and the community in general for her to remain at home than in a nursing home or equivalent. The devices and the support of the nurse buddy will enable Elsa to have greater autonomy, and allow her to continue living independently, possibly for a few more years.

Engaging patients as co-producers of health

As shown in the Elsa scenario, ICT tools can be a force for sophisticated care integration. Yet it is possible to look wider than just a limited view of the individual patient. Patients can be engaged as co-producers of their own health.

The paradigm that is called the co-production of health is about using ICT as a tool for collaboration and communication on health issues among an extended group of stakeholders. These stakeholders are those relevant to the health and the care of a specific person or patient and who help to create a supportive environment for the patient's self-care and healthy behaviour. This co-production environment has the potential to shift the focus from thinking about a person as one living with a chronic condition to one leading a rich, independent life. This reduces individuals' dependency on professional services and releases organisational capacity to be spent on those people who are more dependent on professional services.

A citizen avatar, which is a computer-generated visual representation of an individual, can be used to visualise health information. In a future co-production environment, this data would be extracted from a clearly delimited range of citizen-led activities, and would be supplemented by a smaller range of healthcare professional-dominated activities. This continuum is represented in Figure 14.1.

Through data that are semantically enriched – in other words, that are accompanied by meta-information to convey its meaning for computers – it is possible to represent the existing knowledge about a person's health and augment it through new incoming data. Personalised care, which is based on the parameterisation of knowledge, and guidance in the context of each single individual, relies on this semantically enriched data.

The promise of a co-production of health environment is that – through the use of ICT – medical evidence can be used throughout the digital health continuum. At the co-production end of the continuum (from lifestyle activities to rehabilitation and training), there is a possibility – using the same equipment, software and virtual health team – to stimulate a flexible and personal response to all the related health challenges. Thus, co-production is not just relevant to the part of the continuum that is professionally dominated in a hospital or telemedicine setting.

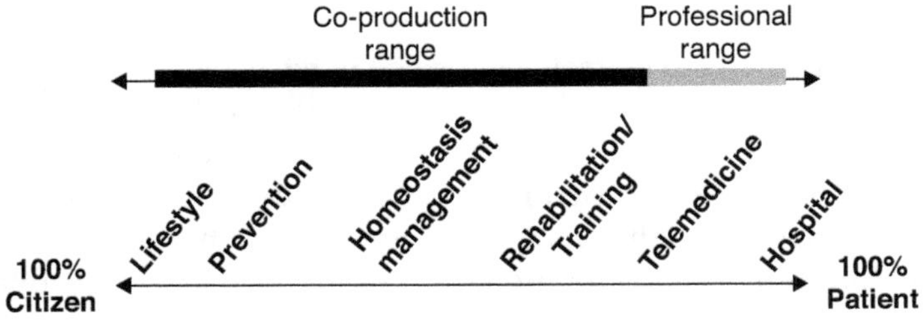

Figure 14.1 The digital health continuum
Source: © Niels Boye 2013.

This digital health continuum concept may prompt a rethinking of chronic disease management, a term that is often used to describe shared care models that co-ordinate the provision of professional healthcare from different sources.

Future patient-centred healthcare systems need to harness the potential of IT solutions much more in the co-production range of a digital health continuum. Starting to facilitate such a focus will free up resources for the type of care that truly requires professional attention in highly specialised hospitals.

Future challenges implicit in scaling up ICT solutions to enable person-centred care

Person-centred care models will usually require quite radical health and social care service redesign. Care pathways will need rethinking to properly support multiple chronic conditions and to be genuinely person-centred (in other words, capable of being tailored to personal preferences as well as to personalised parameters). Few preventative measures and lifestyle behavioural interventions are presently provided or funded by health systems. Hence, new reimbursement models will be needed to encourage health services to invest in the delivery of preventive and monitoring interventions, and to commit to educating patients to become empowered in self-care.

The Elsa scenario relied on several innovative uses of health ICT solutions. Although these are to be envisaged in the future, they exist today only in relatively few circumstances. Even where the components of such solutions do in fact exist today, they often do not interoperate well, and have to be procured and brought together in a piecemeal fashion to provide the many functionalities of a smart home.

Novel models of procurement and a more responsive marketplace may be required in order to scale up multi-component ICT solutions. For example, industry partnerships (such as virtual consortia or just-in-time consortia) may be required to design and deliver relevant, holistic, end-to-end eHealth services. The quality labelling of ICT solutions, in terms of their adoption of standards, information governance and security measures, as well as their functional capabilities, will also be vital to enable informed purchasing decisions. This is an important impetus to develop new kinds of criteria for the quality and safety of self-care devices and applications. There are many standards, produced by different bodies, which are often relatively isolated in their scope and specificity. As a consequence, they may fit together poorly, and they may require ad hoc profiling and localisation in order to achieve end-to-end connectivity. Examples of poor fit include semantic standards (such as terminology systems), structural standards (such as information models) and messaging standards. It is therefore important that in the future, standards bodies put substantial effort into identifying and aligning relevant interfacing standards so that their adoption can be holistic and solution-oriented rather than artefact-specific.

There is now a recognised need to enhance the ICT and health informatics skills of the healthcare workforce both above *and* beyond the training in the information systems that they are using on a daily basis.

Patient-centred care also requires educating healthcare professionals in how best to identify individuals who will be capable of self-management; how best to deliver appropriate education and ongoing support; how to manage escalation of any concerns and how to work with a community of patients who wish to share information transparently. Health professionals and other staff will need to understand how professional accountability and medico-legal liability evolve in the context of patient empowerment and patient choice.

Patients and healthy citizens will also need education in terms of health, diseases and treatments and in some aspects of health informatics. The latter will include how to appraise Internet resources and scientific publications, how to navigate and understand individual electronic health records and how to use health ICT solutions.

Less tangible, but probably just as important, are the attitudinal and behavioural changes needed in the culture of healthcare delivery that will enable eHealth solutions to thrive. Examples of such cultural and attitude changes include:

- Codes of professional practice in supporting self-caring patients;
- The acceptance and governance of citizen-contributed health information;
- Promoting the value of data "not collected here";
- Professional risk management of shared clinical decision-making;
- Healthcare organisational risk and accountability for shared-care services.

Last but certainly not the least, action is needed by governments, health system payers and providers, industry and patient associations to accelerate the adoption of innovative eHealth solutions. In particular, governmental level intervention is probably needed to modify the accountability of healthcare systems so as to allow for shared responsibility with patients and citizens. Action is needed at a European level to ensure that the forthcoming Data Protection Regulation (anticipated in 2014, but with no set date as yet) will enable rather than disable the sharing of personal health information in support of better quality eHealth services.

Disclaimer

The European Commission co-funded projects on whose work this chapter is based are eHealth Innovation Thematic Network [Grant Number 270986];

SmartCare Pilot Type A [Grant Number 270986]; ProeHealth [Grant Number 30-CE-0387926/00-81]; SmartPersonalHealth [Grant Number 248419] as well as the Renewing Health project [Grant Number 250487].

The information and views set out in this publication are those of the author(s) and do not necessarily reflect the official opinion of the European Union. Neither the European Union institutions and bodies nor any person acting on their behalf may be held responsible for the use made of the information contained in this chapter.

References

Bloom, D.E., Cafiero, E.T., Jané-Llopis, E., Abrahams-Gessel, S., Bloom, L.R., Fathima, S., Feigl, A.B., Gaziano, T., Mowafi, M., Pandya, A., Prettner, K., Rosenberg, L., Seligman, B., Stein, A.Z. and Weinstein, C. (2011), *The Global Economic Burden of Non-Communicable Diseases,* ed. Geneva: World Economic Forum.

Department of Health (2008), Tackling Chronic Disease – A Policy Framework for the Management of Chronic Diseases http://www.dohc.ie/publications/tackling_chronic_diease.html. [Accessed 26 September 2013].

European Commission (2013), About the European Innovation Partnership on Active and Healthy Ageing http://ec.europa.eu/research/innovation-union/index_en.cfm?section=active-healthy-ageing&pg=about.[Accessed 15 October 2013].

Goldstein, M.G., Depue, J. and Kazura, A.N. (2009), "Models of provider–patient interaction and shared decision making", in Shumaker, S.A., Ockene, J.K., Riekert, K.A. (eds) *The Handbook of Health Behavior Change,* 3rd edition. New York: Springer.

Graf, T.R., Bloom, F.J., Jr., Tomcavage, J. and Davis, D.E. (2012), "Value-based reengineering: twenty-first century chronic care models", *Primary Care* 39 (2): 221–240.

Greene, J. and Hibbard, J.H. (2012), "Why does patient activation matter? An examination of the relationships between patient activation and health-related outcomes", *Journal of General Internal Medicine* 27 (5): 520–526.

Hibbard, J.H., Stockard, J., Mahoney, E.R. and Tusler, M. (2004), "Development of the Patient Activation Measure (PAM): conceptualizing and measuring activation in patients and consumers", *Health Services Research* 39 (4 Pt 1): 1005–1026.

Huser, V., Peissig, P.L., Christensen, C.A. and Starren, J.B. (2010), "PS1-21: Evaluation of commercial workflow engine for modeling clinical processes in quality improvement and decision support", *Clinical Medicine and Research* 8 (1): 46–46.

Improving Chronic Illness Care (ICIC) (1998), The Chronic Care Model, http://www.improvingchroniccare.org/index.php?p=The_Chronic_Care_Model&s=2. [Accessed 26 September 2013].

Leutz, W.N. (1999), "Five laws for integrating medical and social services: lessons from the United States and the United Kingdom", *Milbank Quarterly* 77 (1): 77–110, iv–v.

Levich, R.B. (2007), "Self management in chronic illness", in Nuovo, J. (ed.) *Chronic Disease Management..* New York: Springer Science.

Lloyd, J. and Wait, S. (2011), *Integrated Care: A Guide for Policy-Makers,* ed. London: Alliance for Health and the Future.

Lorig K., Holman L.K., Sobel H., Laurent D., González V. and M., Minor (2000), *Living a Healthy Life with Chronic Conditions: Self Management of Heart Disease, Arthritis, Diabetes, Asthma, Bronchitis, Emphysema, and Others,* ed. Palo Alto: Boll Publishing.

Meglic, M. and Brodnik, A. (2010), "Electronic environments for integrated care management case of depression treatment" (ed.) *Ubiquitous Health and Medical Informatics: The Ubiquity 2.0 Trend and Beyond* IGI Global.

Mercer, S.W., Smith, S.M., Wyke, S., O'Dowd, T. and Watt, G.C. (2009), "Multimorbidity in primary care: developing the research agenda", *Family Practice* 26 (2): 79–80.

Nolte, E., Knai, C. and McKee, M. (2009), *Managing Chronic Conditions: Experience in Eight Countries,* ed. Copenhagen: WHO European Observatory on Health Systems and Policies.

Nolte, E. and McKee, M., eds (2008), *Caring for People with Chronic Conditions. A Health System Perspective.* Berkshire: Open University Press.

Rijken, M., Jones, M., Heijmans, M. and Dixon, A. (2008), "Supporting Self-Management", in Nolte, E. and McKee, M. (eds) *Caring for People with Chronic Conditions. A Health System Perspective.* Berkshire: Open University Press.

Smith, S.M., Soubhi, H., Fortin, M., Hudon, C. and O'Dowd, T. (2012), "Managing patients with multimorbidity: systematic review of interventions in primary care and community settings", *British Medical Journal* 345: e5205.

Stroetmann, K.A., Kubitschke, L., Robinson, S., Stroetmann, V., Cullen, K. and McDaid, D. (2010), *How Can Telehealth Help in the Provision of Integrated Care?* ed. Copenhagen: World Health Organisation.

Stroetmann, V., Thiel, R., Stroetmann, K.A., Wilson, P., Romao, M. and Strubin, M. (2011a), "Understanding the role of device level interoperability in promoting health – Lessons Learned from the SmartPersonalHealth Project", *Yearbook of Medical Informatics* 6 (1): 87–91.

Stroetmann, V., Thiel, R., Wilson, P., Romao, M., Parisot, C., Zoric, M., Strübin, M. and Stroetmann, K. (2011b), *Enabling Smart Integrated Care: Recommendations for Fostering Greater Interoperability of Personal Health Systems,* ed. Luxembourg: Office for Official Publications of the European Communities.

Suter, E., Oelke, N.D., Adair, C.E. and Armitage, G.D. (2009), "Ten key principles for successful health systems integration", *Healthcare Quarterly* 13 Spec No: 16–23.

15
HIT: The Leadership Role of Hospitals

Antoine Geissbühler, Josep M. Piqué and Magdalene Rosenmöller

Introduction

Hospitals have a crucial role to play in realising the full potential of eHealth, with a high level of leadership and governance called for inside the hospital and beyond. Together with an academic, two health sector executives, leading figures in the field of eHealth from two of the most innovation-driving and first-rate hospitals in Europe, have joined forces in this chapter. They reflect on the importance of information technology (IT) in hospitals and the implementation of highly integrated IT systems in their respective institutions, the Hospital Clínic, Barcelona, and Hôpitaux Universitaires, Geneva.

Healthcare challenges call for IT solutions

Healthcare systems around the world are faced with enormous challenges, on both the demand and supply sides that are transforming the way care is delivered. Many tertiary care hospitals have taken the lead in this transformation as drivers for innovation. Among the most discussed challenges is the global ageing population leading to a rising number of multiple, chronic conditions that are increasing demand for cure and care services. The growing availability of costly new drugs, medical technologies and devices puts an additional burden on already strained healthcare budgets. Healthcare institutions struggle with the seemingly impossible task of facilitating access to high quality of care at the right time and place together with limited financial resources, while being aware that more expensive care does not always mean better care (OECD, 2009).

The fragmented environment in which most healthcare institutions operate does not assist in this endeavour. This ongoing perspective of silos does not promote the necessary co-ordination of care that chronic patients need. Furthermore, it constitutes a significant barrier to the active role that patients can play as co-creators of health, and hampers the opportunities of institutions to re-shape the service offering accordingly. Old-fashioned payment systems, such as fee-for-service reimbursement schemes, perpetuate this state of affairs and often lead to unnecessary, additional or more expensive services.

Yet chronic conditions require well-organised, multi-disciplinary care processes, in which providers from diverse levels of care combine forces in a territorial care concept, and where they are accountable for their actions in terms of health outcomes. Co-ordination across primary and specialised care settings is achieved through teamwork, with each member contributing to the overall aims through a unique set of expertise and skills, and performing delegated, well-defined roles.

Co-ordination of care is enabled by the intelligent use of health information technology (HIT). HIT can provide a practical means of achieving good communication and support through decision-making tools, or it can anticipate potential harmful events for patients. It paves the way for a shift from the traditional form of reactive medicine to a more preventive and predictive approach, whereby the onset of diseases can be averted and exacerbations of chronic illnesses avoided, all of which contribute positively to more efficient health systems.

In a process-oriented care approach, HIT allows for a better understanding of professionals' actions and encounters with patients. Information technologies make it possible to bring together transversal data over a patient's life, providing information on quality, health output and real cost of diseases. This facilitates precise calculations on cost-benefit or cost-opportunity, and all the information necessary to take better decisions regarding the introduction of new technologies, drugs or procedures.

This central role of information technology in healthcare is providing connectivity between different healthcare actors, making co-operation and co-ordination around a given patient the emergent new paradigm.

Electronic health records: Connecting patient information as a basis for care co-ordination

The integration of health information systems is essential in supporting shared care in hospitals, enabling care provision to mobile individuals and making regional health care systems more efficient.

The electronic health record (EHR), a set of documents containing clinical and administrative information regarding a particular patient, is a key tool in underpinning communication and decision-making in daily care practice. In an integrated care paradigm, these features are increasingly demanded by healthcare professionals, who need seamless accessibility to information regardless of its location and format; in other words it should no longer be a challenge if the patient record information is distributed across multiple sites, held in a variety of electronic formats or represented as a mixture of narrative, structured, coded and multimedia entries.

Simple as it may sound, combining data from heterogeneous sources is in fact a complex and time-consuming task. Ensuring the proper interoperability of clinical information systems implies addressing aspects of functionality, presentation, terminology, data representation and semantics. Only well-designed systems are robust and reliable enough to foster communication and data use for healthcare delivery, research and management. This quest for interoperability is high on the European policy agenda. Indeed, the European Directive 2011/24/EU on patients' rights in cross-border healthcare (European Commission, 2011) is intended to provide a solution to the current lack of standards, allowing quicker and easier access to confidential information by the relevant professionals, while mitigating the risk of health data – from different sources, and collected throughout a lifetime – being accidentally exposed or easily distributed to unauthorised parties (Kierkegaard, 2011).

Despite its intrinsic importance in contributing to communication and co-ordination among health actors, it must be acknowledged that the rate of adoption of EHRs has been, and continues to be, lower than initially anticipated. Poor user-friendliness and a perception of the record as a tool for administration and billing, rather than as being useful for clinical work, have been two issues that have militated against the record's wider acceptance among health professionals. There is a need to raise awareness about the potential of HIT in supporting a model of care that is more responsive to patients' needs, based on the co-ordination of care, workflow efficiency, teamwork, clinical decision support and population health management. All of these are areas that offer great potential, when associated with improved HIT use, as has been experienced in a series of initiatives, such as Linkcare and Nexes, implemented in the Hospital Clínic Barcelona (see Box 15.1).

Box 15.1 The Linkcare and Nexes initiatives at the Barcelona Hospital Clínic

Linkcare (the Integrated Health Care Shared Knowledge Community for Health Care Professionals) was founded in 2010 by the Hospital Clínic Barcelona, and is supported by its Research Foundation. The Hospital Clínic Barcelona is a university tertiary hospital, belonging to the Catalan Network of Public Hospitals (XHUP). It is active in care provision research, teaching and innovation. Linkcare was established with the aim of channelling health and chronic care knowledge and products developed in the hospital to the market, particularly where they contribute to increased quality of life and cost containment. Linkcare is in the privileged position of being able to capitalise on market opportunities and accelerate the delivery of connected health and care solutions. The company has developed a portfolio of products and services that contribute to state-of-the-art innovative healthcare delivery solutions and embrace the evolution of medicine and technology.

Nexes (Supporting Healthier and Independent Living for Chronic Patients and [the] Elderly) operates among different European partners, with its main objective being to identify strategies for the extensive deployment and adoption of integrated care services for chronic patients. Supported by HIT, it is based on the assumption that HIT provides value for patients, generates efficiencies and sustainability at a systems level and contributes to fostering the ability of European healthcare systems to face the growing challenges of chronic conditions. It concentrates on properly standardised patient-centred interventions, covering a wide spectrum of care co-ordination. It has a strong focus on prevention, disease modulation and the bridging of healthcare with social support so as to overcome fragmentation between healthcare and community services. Insights gained here contributed to the Initiative for Chronic Care Conditions endorsed by the World Health Organization (WHO).

Source: www.linkcare.es

HIT in population-based care: An outlook for the future of health

Primary care practices play an increasingly important role in population health, by encouraging prevention and healthy lifestyles. They are also an important element in chronic care management, supporting patients in taking care of their needs and carrying out their own care, while maintaining their autonomy by staying at home and avoiding unnecessary hospital stays. The move from reactive and acute symptom care to proactive planned care for both healthy and chronically ill populations is important and would not be possible without HIT, which enables effective population-based care and the reporting of quality metrics. EHRs will in the future help identify which patients in a population may need particular services. Registries are another critical tool for population health management: they are an area where HIT applications could be better developed and integrated with EHRs (Gliklich and Dreyer, 2010).

Advances in human genomics are of crucial importance not only for supporting individual care, but also for prediction and prevention in population health, even though more time is needed for its real potential to be realised. High-quality long-term clinical information repositories are already being built to cross-match structured data with the genomic profile and to allow for prediction of outcomes associated with a specific treatment or procedure, in order to avoid ineffective treatments and undesirable adverse effects and the consequent costs.

An additional and high-value aspect of structured electronic health information is its use for research purposes. High volume and excellent quality information is of crucial importance for the pharmaceutical industry, with a view to surveillance and post-commercial follow-up of medications with different individual responses in various settings. It enables the identification of specific response factors to a medication or procedure, according to the genomic profile of the patients concerned. It also fosters the accurate measurement of health outcomes as a tool for reviewing the effectiveness of clinical pathways in view of improving the quality of services.

The conditions for realising real benefits from the use of structured data are (i) the high quality of recorded data, including regular audit of data entry; (ii) continuous maintaining and updating of the data; (iii) controlled, coded access to all professionals who are able to add or extract information; (iv) the commitment by patients to be active participants in maintaining and updating their own data; (v) the commitment by professionals to use the data in the framework of multi-disciplinary teams, while care is based on defined pathways, clinical evidence and workflows which are regularly reviewed in light of new evidence. Although some institutions are starting to implement systems that allow for the exploitation of electronic structured data, the impact and all possible use of this data will be realised only slowly.

Better incentives for better use of HIT

Still, HIT faces enormous challenges. Today's financial incentives seldom reward patient-centred care; instead, fee-for-service reimbursement encourages EHRs to be used for the documentation of billable events rather than for tasks that are important to the quality of care, such as proper co-ordination among different health-care stakeholders, and timely and effective care transitions. Instead, payment innovations, such as bundled payments, fees for performance, and mandates for aggregating care in organisations, may encourage providers to share accountability for health and other outcomes. Proper payment systems could encourage clinicians to demand HIT capabilities that would better support their tasks in improving patients' health, making those activities important for the success of healthcare organisations.

There is huge potential for improvement and innovation in the HIT field, with large investments needed in order to generate the benefits needed for improving population health and achieving real improvements for health systems. To better understand how to accomplish this, it is important to look into how HIT is implemented in the hospital setting.

Implementing IT in hospitals – governance and leadership

For more than a century, hospitals have been at the centre of the production of health care. Unsurprisingly, this is where the first healthcare information systems were developed and where they produced successful results, improving efficiency of care and reducing mortality, morbidity and cost in these institutions (Amarasingham et al., 2009). Meanwhile, electronic patient records have been introduced in the field of ambulatory medicine, notably in countries with socialised primary care (Bates, 2005) or in integrated delivery networks, such as Kaiser Permanente (Garrido et al., 2005).

These two domains, as well as many other related services – such as home care and social care, and supporting services such as laboratory and imaging – are expected to connect with each other, in order to secure the multiple transitions and interactions needed in care delivery processes (Cook et al., 2000; Moore et al., 2003; Coleman and Berenson, 2004). Transitions are becoming increasingly frequent and risky in an environment where the complexity and fragmentation of care processes is intensifying as a result of a number of challenges such as financial constraints, demographic changes and the escalation of medical technologies (Tooke, 2011).

Patients and their network of informal caregivers are expecting – and are likewise expected – to play a more active role in the co-ordination of health care. This process of patient empowerment can be facilitated significantly by modern healthcare IT tools, which are assisting the evolution from professional-centric systems to "informed-patient care", and, eventually, to "patient-informed care" (Geissbühler, 2012). Hospitals play an important role in enabling implementation and overcoming challenges in the institution itself and in the wider area, managing uptake and connection; hospital strategy and IT governance are therefore crucial.

Different aspects of HIT governance

Most eHealth systems have a scope that spans institutional borders. This cross-institutional spanning implies that governance cannot function as it does inside a single organisation. Instead, it must seek to bring together and organise stakeholders who might not necessarily feel comfortable working together, as they may have differing perspectives on a particular project's goals and on the means to achieve them. Indeed, different stakeholders such as patients, providers, regulators and payers do have conflicting interests, most notably when it comes to sharing financial resources and sensitive information, and to financing.

The financing of eHealth systems can be problematic in terms of both capital investment and operational system costs. Less fragmented public health systems and integrated delivery networks have an easier task, but investment decisions are usually difficult as financial benefits are not evident and those paying for the system are not always the ones reaping the financial rewards. This dilemma might be magnified as systemic and organisational change continues in the health/eHealth fields.

Initial investments in terms of eHealth infrastructure, software development and deployment are significant and sometimes risky. In most successful cases, these are made by regional or national governments, sometimes in the form of a public–private partnership. In order to sustain operational costs, sound economic models should be developed. Current economic modelling is somewhat unconvincing, and only a few examples exist of well-documented returns on investment, whether in financial terms or in the sense of quality or safety of care (Black et al., 2011). This counterbalancing of today's apparent lack of evidence seems to be particularly relevant within the framework of modern socioeconomic constraints.

In terms of privacy protection, governance needs to manage two areas of potential, inevitable tension: between, on the one hand, the transparency that can be provided by such systems, and which could enable better care co-ordination, better decision-making for health systems management, and even more efficient research and industrial development; and, on the other hand, the desire for personal data protection of both citizens and care professionals. Empirical observations suggest that the point of equilibrium for such a tension depends significantly on societal factors and, in particular, on the level of trust that citizens place in their government (Geissbühler, 2013). Policymakers in particular anticipate that it is feasible to build an argument which either reduces or eliminates the dilemmas involved (Andoulsi and Wilson, 2012).

It is therefore important that a clear political mandate be formulated when initiating an eHealth project, with key societal determinants taken into account. For example, the Geneva Health Information Exchange (HIE) was initiated several years after a scandal erupted regarding secret files on Swiss and foreign citizens that were kept illegally by the Swiss Federal Department of Justice and Police (Ganser, 2005). In the Geneva area, there was therefore a high degree of sensitivity about privacy protection and some level of mistrust towards the government. In order to facilitate the adoption of the project, Geneva's regional authorities explicitly requested that the HIE would have to stay under the control of each participating citizen, would not enable centralisation of health information and that participation would be optional both for citizens and for care providers (in other words, it would imply a double opt-in).

Box 15.2 The Geneva Health Information Exchange Project: e-toile

The e-toile project aims at connecting all Geneva health system stakeholders via a community healthcare information network. This health network combines public and private healthcare services, improved continuity and co-ordination of care. One goal is to empower patients to assume an increased understanding of their conditions as well as a more active role and participation in their care, while the common infrastructure provides an added value to consumers.

The system is based on the following four key concepts:

- all participating professionals provide (voluntarily) information for continuity of care;
- a patient smart card gives access to the information;
- access is based on the notion of the therapeutic relationship, with the joint presence of both the patient and health professional;
- healthcare information remains at its source, the point of care; it can be consolidated virtually but not centralised.

Four initial services built on the e-toile platform include:

- a distributed, shared electronic patient record;
- secure communication between health-care professionals;
- e-prescription (including a shared treatment plan which brings together prescription (medical), dispensation (pharmacist) and administration (home nurse) information, and facilitates medication reconciliation during care transitions);
- collaborative, multi-professional dashboards for chronic disease management for conditions such as diabetes and heart failure.

Source – www.swisspost.ch/ehealth (Geissbühler, 2013)

Another important foundation for eHealth projects is the creation of a consensus-building platform. Given the various tensions that must be managed in order to foster trust and acceptance of eHealth systems, rules and policies cannot be imposed unilaterally but must be negotiated by representatives of different actors. Establishing representativeness is in itself a challenge: for example, should citizens be represented by consumer organisations or by patient organisations? Healthy consumers would most likely value privacy more than transparency, whereas patients, and in particular patients with chronic conditions – having generally been exposed to the insufficiencies of care co-ordination – are likely to have a more nuanced and tolerant position regarding privacy. The age and computer literacy of stakeholder representatives could also have a strong influence on their values with regard to data privacy and protection, as members of the social-web generation have a more relaxed attitude with regard to disclosing personal data than earlier generations.

In general, a consensus-building platform is hosted outside of the participating organisations, either in the form of an association, foundation or a separate business entity. The main output of this platform is a set of important principles that underpin the eHealth system. Examples of such key principles include: (i) the mode of participation (mandatory participation, opt-in, opt-out) for providers and patients; (ii) the access control model (such as identification, authentication and consent); (iii) definition of roles, rules for access, exceptions for emergency situations; and, (iv) the certification of the participating organisation and surveillance mechanisms. Often, the platform monitors the progress of projects and verifies that the implementation remains consistent with the founding principles.

Trust as a basis for good HIT

Trust is an important element in the implementation of eHealth. The validation of key principles and the formalisation of rules and policies are important steps in building trust and fostering acceptance. There are several examples of large projects that have been delayed or stalled due to a lack of attention to these processes (Ströher and Honekamp, 2011).

In many European countries, the formalisation of this trust is achieved through the creation and approval of new laws, which, in general, have been based on existing data protection laws, but have also clarified how key principles of privacy, data security, oversight and sanctions apply in the specific domain of eHealth. Even though there is still limited public attention paid to these issues, the process usually generates significant debates among stakeholders. Advances have been made at European level (Dumortier and Verhenneman, 2012; Wilson and Kolitsi, 2012). One mechanism, used for transnational projects where legal frameworks differ from country to country, is the establishment of a contract between stakeholders, usually in the form of a "circle of trust". On the basis of accepted policies and procedures, such a circle defines the rights and duties of each participant, in particular with relation to security and privacy. These have been successfully used in large regional and European-wide eHealth networks such as epSOS (Albertini and Orsi, 2010) and ALIAS (Direzione Generale Sanità, 2012).

Implications for the IT leadership of healthcare institutions

Implementation of IT and eHealth is somewhat disruptive for healthcare (Topol, 2013), where hospitals have often assumed a leadership role for the surrounding ecosystem, as a result of their leaders' understanding of the wider range of disciplinary needs, for example, clinical, economic, organisational and social, and the requirement to overcome certain traditional barriers and constraints. Healthcare IT, including clinical information, is now professionalised; electronic medical records are increasingly considered to be a commodity, even though their deployment and meaningful use might remain challenging.

Assuming its leadership and governance role, hospital management needs to place emphasis on the clinical and economic impact of healthcare IT. Here all health professionals need to play a stronger role in leading IT strategy in clinical, managerial and economic terms, steering tools towards the production of measurable benefits, sometimes to the detriment of in-depth informatics analysis and design. Within an institution, these tasks are frequently spread among several teams and committees, and professional "mediators" (for example Chief Medical Information Officers), well-versed in health informatics, help to connect the worlds of care production, informatics and management on a wider scale.

The "walls" of hospitals are starting to dissolve, due to a shift towards shorter inpatient stays, ambulatory treatments, the monitoring of patients at home rather than in clinical settings, and, last but not least, the development of patients and their informal care-givers into people who are more proactive and demanding participants in the health care team.

The traditional barriers that used to stratify the various flows of healthcare information between organisations are rapidly disappearing. This transition challenges not only the architecture of information systems – or more appropriately the "urban planning" or enterprise architecture of organisations) – but also the consistency of the semantics of the information exchanged. Traditional models centred on transitions of care, generally implemented through rigid, unsophisticated interfaces, or through institution-centric portals, are rapidly losing their relevance. The ability of highly integrated systems to provide enough agility and scalability, while maintaining consistency and integrity of information, is challenged by the rapid growth of a new ecosystem of web and mobile applications, characterised by extreme individualisation, decentralisation, diversity and more open-access to data or "data liberation" (eHealth Taskforce, 2012).

In addition to dealing with technological and informatics constraints, organisations must also learn to cope with rules and policies that are defined in other contexts, whether they are political, regulatory or commercial, and to integrate them into their own environments. The challenges of aligning local policies and procedures with those of a wider network are typically encountered when dealing with the consistent identification of stakeholders across organisations or with the compatibility of roles and access rules in multiple settings. An *a priori* agreement on standards would be ideal, but this is rarely achieved due to the relative immaturity of appropriate norms in these domains. Nevertheless, large transnational projects, such as epSOS (Albertini and Orsi, 2010) and pragmatic standardisation mechanisms such as Integrating the Healthcare Enterprise (IHE) (www.ihe.net), are paving the way for this necessary harmonisation at political, legal, organisational and technical levels.

Conclusions

HIT plays a central role in healthcare by providing connectivity between different healthcare actors, and allowing the co-operation and co-ordination around a given patient needed in the emerging new paradigm of increasingly integrated care settings. Hospitals and healthcare providers play an important role in the realisation of the full benefits of IT in healthcare, not only within their own institutions but also in the wider care context. To achieve the full potential of IT, sound IT governance is paramount.

References

Albertini, E. and Orsi, G. (2010), Smart Open Services for European Patients. Open eHealth initiative for a European large scale pilot of patient summary and electronic prescription. Milan, Lombardy, EPSOS European Patients Smart Open Services.

Amarasingham, R., Plantinga, L., et al. (2009), "Clinical Information Technologies and Inpatient Outcomes: a Multiple Hospital Study", *Archives of Internal Medicine* 169 (2): 108–114.

Andoulsi, I. and Wilson, P. (2012), "Understanding Liability in eHealth: Towards Greater Clarity at European Union Level", in George, C., Whitehouse, D. and Duquenoy, P. (eds) *eHealth: Legal, Ethical and Governance Challenges* Heidelberg: Springer-Verlag.

Bates, D.W. (2005), "Physicians and ambulatory electronic health records", *Health Affairs* 24 (5): 1180–1189.

Black, A., Car, J., et al. (2011), "The impact of eHealth on the quality and safety of health care: a systematic overview", *PLoS Med* 8 (1): e1000387. doi: 1000310.1001371/journal.pmed.1000387.

Coleman, E. and Berenson, R. (2004), "Lost in transition: challenges and opportunities for improving the quality of transitional care", *Annals of Internal Medicine* 140: 533–536.

Cook, R., Render, M., et al. (2000), "Gaps in the continuity of care and progress on patient safety", *British Medical Journal* 320: 791–794.

Direzione Generale Sanità (2012), ALIAS Alpine Hospitals Networking for Improved Access to Telemedicine Service. ALIAS Project Final Booklet. Real telemedicine services through a Virtual Hospitals Network. Milan, Italy, Region of Lombardy.

Dumortier, J. and Verhenneman, G. (2012), "Legal regulation of electronic health records: a comparative analysis of Europe and the US", in George, C., Whitehouse, D. and Duquenoy, P. (eds) *eHealth: Legal, Ethical and Governance Challenges*. Heidelberg: Springer-Verlag.

eHealth Taskforce (2012), eHealth Task Force Report Redesigning Health in Europe for 2020. Brussels, European Commission.

European Commission (2011), Directive 2011/24/EU of the European Parliament and of the Council of 9 March 2011 on the application of patients' rights in cross-border healthcare. Official Journal of the European Union. Brussels, European Commission.

Ganser, D. (2005), "The British Secret Service in neutral Switzerland", *Intelligence and National Security* 20 (4): 553–580.

Garrido, T., Jamieson, L., et al. (2005), "Effect of electronic health records in ambulatory care: retrospective, serial, cross sectional study", *British Medical Journal* 330 (581).

Geissbühler, A. (2012), "eHealth: easing transitions in health care", *Swiss Medical Weekly* 142: 13599.

Geissbühler, A. (2013), "Lessons learned implementing a regional health information exchange in Geneva as a pilot for the Swiss national eHealth strategy", *International Journal of Medical Informatics* doi:pii: S1386-5056(1312)00201-00208. 00210.01016/j.ijmedinf.02012.00211.00002. [Epub ahead of print].

Gliklich, R.E. and Dreyer, N.A. (2010), *Registries for Evaluating Patient Outcomes: A User's Guide*, 2nd edition. Rockville: US Agency for Healthcare Research and Quality.
Kierkegaard, P. (2011), "Electronic health record: wiring Europe's healthcare", *Computer Law & Security Review* 27 (5): 503–515.
Moore, C., Wisnievsky, J., et al. (2003), "Medical errors related to discontinuity of care from an inpatient to an outpatient setting", *Journal of General Internal Medicine* 18: 646–651.
OECD (2009), *Health at a Glance 2009: OECD Indicators*. Paris, OECD.
Ströher, A. and Honekamp, W. (2011), "ELGA – the electronic health record in the light of data protection and data security", *Wien Med Wochenschr* 161(13–14): 341–346.
Tooke, J. (2011), *The Future of Healthcare in Europe*. London: University College London.
Topol, E.J. (2013), *The Creative Destruction of Medicine: How the Digital Revolution Will Create Better Health Care*. New York, Perseus Books.
Wilson, P. and Kolitsi, Z. (2012), "Support of eHealth Applications by Legal Systems in Europe", *European Journal for Biomedical Informatics* 8 (2).

16
Recent US Experience with Health ICT

Don Eugene Detmer

Introduction

Over the past 25 years in the United States of America (US), Electronic Health Records (EHRs) and EHR systems have moved from an interest and priority of a few enthusiasts to becoming a central pillar in national health policy. The aim is now for a learning healthcare system that engages all relevant stakeholders. This chapter reviews the high points of how this substantial shift in policy, technology and practice has come to pass. The perspective is that of an informed player who has been engaged in these processes as well as been a witness to these activities and developing benchmarks. The health domains covered include care, research and education. Both the prospects and challenges going forward are discussed, including the importance of harmonising efforts across the globe. In sum, the prospects remain favourable despite the complexity involved and some daunting policy challenges.

Fifty years of US health information technology development

In the US EHRs development took place mostly in academic hospital settings, in contrast to European developments in the 1960s to 1980s where the more extensive concentration was on general practice environments plus a few academic centres (Detmer, 2000). US awareness focused initially on business operations, laboratory results reporting, decision-making and picture archiving. As data storage and processing capabilities improved, attention turned to medical care applications to improve decision support, physician order entry and clinical notes (Berner et al., 2005).

By 1989, sufficient progress had occurred for the Institute of Medicine to support a study looking at the potential for computers to improve medical care and clinical records. This resulted in a 1991 report (Dick and Steen, 1991). A supplementary version of the report was published in 1997, *The Computer-Based*

Patient Record: An Essential Technology for Health Care (Dick et al., 1997). The initial report attracted substantial attention, particularly within the hospital system of the US Veterans Administration, as well as in those nations with national systems of care. The 1997 edition helped to underscore in particular the progress that had been made in Europe. The report reviewed users and uses of EHRs, technology and the way forward. It identified a set of functions that such records should meet. Importantly, the committee sought to concentrate not on the technology but rather on shifting the focus from the source of clinical notes, written or produced for example, by the physician, nurse or pharmacist, to an integrated approach based on supporting management of the patient problems (hence the report's name, which is related to the computer-based patient record). The report therefore made an early contribution to shifting later Institute of Medicine reports towards patient-centred care while ensuring that EHRs were seen as crucial to substantial quality improvements in the future (Dick et al., 1997; Institute of Medicine, 2001).

During this era, larger hospitals in the US, in concert with their in-house academic informaticians, made great progress with their research and development activities through the support of grants from the National Library of Medicine of the National Institutes of Health. These efforts, which began with the funding of four centres in 1972, included formal training programmes encompassing biomedical informatics. They led to the deployment of more functional electronic record systems in addition to other benefits. Competition for these grants remains high today. Over the years, recipients acting as centres for excellence have formed the core of this research and development process (National Library of Medicine, 2013). By 1997, the desirability of EHRs and even data exchanges (first known as regional health information organisations) were accepted both by the establishment and early adopters as the wave of the future. Despite this interest, widespread adoption and improvement of electronic health record (EHR) functions, such as physician order entry, were slow to be diffused into practice settings because financing – and especially the challenge of managing implementation – were emerging as issues (Lorenzi and Riley, 2004). Nevertheless, substantial growth in the number of EHR vendor products occurred during this 20-year period. The lack of clear policies governing use and transmission of personal health data was, however, seen as a major limiting factor to widespread adoption. By the mid-1990s, the Administrative Simplification provisions of the US Health Improvement Portability and Accountability Act (HIPAA) mandated the Secretary of the Department of Health and Human Services to develop regulations for the privacy and security of EHRs (National Research Council, 1997). This approach differed from how these policies developed in Europe (Dumortier and Verhenneman, 2013).

Despite the benefits of these efforts, which have improved the regulation of privacy and security in general, there have been five persistent significant limitations of HIPAA and the dominant Washington world perspective. They have been: 1) proscription from a national system of uniform personal health identifiers, which impacts negatively on privacy, security, quality, safety and efficiency by reducing the quality of data and increasing the costs to authenticate identity; 2) a continued patchwork of conflicting privacy laws at the level of the individual states relating to health data, as these laws are not overridden by federal law; 3) a peculiar unintended consequence that allows access to identifiable patient data for quality care improvement but prevents the equivalent access for quality research; 4) a striking lack of a serious commitment to amend policy that assures uniform simplified access to personal health data for legitimate biomedical and public health research and 5) a lack of protection of data across other potential users and uses of person-specific data, until partially addressed in 2009 through the Health Information Technology for Economic and Clinical Health (HITECH) legislation (Detmer, 2010a). The HITECH provisions of the American Recovery and Reinvestment Act of 2009 were included both to pump billions of dollars into a flagging national economy and to tip the use of EHRs and EHR systems towards system-wide adoption. Thus, hospitals and physicians' offices receive major financial rewards for two purposes: linking their systems to the Center for Medicare and Medicaid Services for automated reimbursement; and creating a shift from paying simply for when services are delivered or procedures performed to payment based on meeting quality criteria and standards of professional practice (so-called, value-driven payment systems) (Simborg et al., 2013).

Between 1996 and 2000, the National Committee on Vital and Health Statistics also began laying out a conceptual plan for a national health information infrastructure using a model that envisioned computer-based medical, public health and personal health records that would have sufficient levels of common language so that they would be interoperable (Detmer, 1997). Standards were making progress both in technical sophistication and adoption at the federal level, as evidenced by the Standard Nomenclature of Medicine (SNOMED) and Logical Observation Identifiers Names and Codes (LOINC).

Both communication and co-operation between Europe and America regarding standards and other issues relating to eHealth were growing. Whereas SNOMED was developed by the American College of Pathologists, Read codes were added to it to assure a much more robust representation of primary care terminology. The US government then underwrote a national licence so that SNOMED could be used by all US care institutions without charge. The National Library of Medicine also funded a research team for creating LOINC. LOINC has proven to be a robust database that has emerged as a universal standard for identifying medical laboratory observations.

This collaboration continues (National Committee on Vital and Health Statistics, 1998). A final roadmap for activity that builds on a 2012-dated major agreement between the European Union and the US to support future collaboration on health ICT was launched in Spring 2013 (Commonwealth Fund, 2004; Europe's Information Society, 2013; Health Info Technology, 2013). The challenge of competing national standards such as the Clinical Procedure Terminology of the American Medical Association and International Classification of Disease/SNOMED – Clinical Terms is just one excellent example of how much work remains to be done. There is also the ongoing challenge of implementing International Classification of Diseases (such as ICD-9 and ICD-10) in the US. The American Medical Informatics Association's web publication *The Standards Standard* offers readers a way to see what is underway in this field (AMIA, 2013).

Meaningful use of electronic health records, and more

Despite rhetorical exhortation for EHRs by three presidents – most notably George W. Bush who in 2004 called for an EHR by 2014 for every American – few federal financial incentives existed in the past to support physicians and hospitals to make the transition to becoming "paper-free" institutions. In 2004, an Office of the National Coordinator for Health Information Technology was created, but it had little budget or authority to create change since financial incentives were simply not aligned. Despite a Presidential Commission on System Interoperability, connectivity and data exchange, standards have remained a nagging problem even with the recent progress and genuine interest in making such standards international (Commission on System Interoperability, 2005). The HITECH provisions of the American Recovery and Reinvestment Act of 2009 created payment incentives for those settings that demonstrated the capabilities for "meaningful use" of EHRs (as stipulated by the government) rather than simply owning the requisite computer infrastructure (Simborg et al., 2013). Meaningful use was defined as a set of functionalities that included automated billing for payment and quality reporting as well as decision support and patient engagement through electronic means to be implemented in stages (Office for Health Info Technology, 2013). Initial financial incentive payments are intended to change to deductions from expected payments as the programme matures in the latter part of this decade.

Inter-provider communications across secure networks have made progress since a group of federal and non-federal entities began exchanging information in 2009 over the Nationwide Health Information Network (NwHIN), which is now called the eHealth Exchange; Healtheway, Inc. is its governance group.

HITECH includes facilitation through both CONNECT open-source software and DIRECT PROJECT that offers standards (The Nationwide HIM, 2013). Data exchange among hospitals, physicians, patients and other care entities is a highly desired functionality for EHR systems in the US, and there are clear lessons to be learned from other nations (Payne et al., 2011). Meanwhile, much earlier, in 2001 Canada committed substantial national resources to support an Infoway initiative to enhance data exchange and EHRs. As the Canadian health system is based on care organised by the country's individual provinces, progress has generally been most notable in the wealthier parts of the nation, particularly in Alberta. Both in Canada and the US, commitment to the capability of secure record transfers is still evident as a national priority. However, progress has not been equal in all US states or Canadian provinces. Regional characteristics produce multiple reasons for the lag of some geographic areas behind others. The US Center for Disease Control and Prevention has a public health information network that is tied to the meaningful use programme, and also links together multiple activities across communities and other health resources (Canada Health Infoway, 2013).

The US$ 12.5 billion that was dispersed under the HITECH programme to hospitals and physicians by early 2013 has dramatically increased the pace of adoption of EHRs. Implementation and use now include three-quarters of office-based physicians and over two-thirds of group practices (Hsaio and Hing, 2012; US PHIN, 2012). Furthermore, the passage into law of the Accountability and Affordability Act of 2010, known more colloquially as ObamaCare, has served to cement the will of the federal government that health information technology is essential for America's evolving healthcare system. Despite criticisms that the meaningful use requirements are either too detailed and/or demanding, and that charges for reimbursement are potentially inflated through electronic "up-coding", as well as other concerns, commitment to the vision of widespread use of EHRs remains (Simborg et al., 2013).

The American EHR Partners surveys of EHR use and satisfaction with vendor products offer ongoing updates of both product functionalities and experiences (Goedert, 2012). As implementation has moved from a small group of early adopters to a more widespread late adoption group, satisfaction with EHRs has decreased somewhat. Importantly, these surveys (American EHR Partners, 2013) show that, without a commitment to at least three hours of training prior to early use, satisfaction levels drop substantially. With training, use is generally accepted and eventually appreciated. User interface issues remain significant, however. Part of this challenge relates to the requirements that payment agencies place on clinicians with respect to patient encounter notes or clinical progress reports. Often the documentation required to ensure payment has only a marginal relationship with the clinical data requirements needed by physicians to guarantee good clinical care (Simborg et al., 2013). The American Medical Informatics Association is calling for a major effort to anticipate and manage these, and other, unintended consequences emerging from implementation of the health information technology and HITECH provisions. It seeks to separate the data requirements necessary for payment and system performance from those required by the healthcare team to offer high-quality, safe care (McGowan et al., 2012).

To this end, the American College of Surgeons has embarked on a strategy that envisions ongoing collaborations with EHR vendors to automate as much as possible direct data capture of the information in EHRs. This would be used for direct transfer to a variety of registries relating to cancer, trauma, quality management, payment data, data transfer essential for care co-ordination and data essential for continued professional certification and licensure. The professional associations of cardiologists, cardiovascular surgeons and vascular surgeons are awakening to the potential of EHRs to offer major benefits to their memberships through eHealth opportunities. The goal is a data ecosystem that streamlines the movement of data essential to a learning healthcare system that can evolve over time towards a more robust co-ordinated data infrastructure. To compare outcomes accurately among hospitals and surgeons will require a harmonisation of terminology and agreement on standards in computable language. Automated data capture will be a big step forward (Cusack et al., 2013). Examples of the fields in which such data could be captured and where national quality standards currently exist include surgical site infections and surgery in elderly patients (American College of Surgeons, 2013). Progress with e-Measures will take time, but experience and insight into how this can be accomplished is being gained (Terhilda et al., 2013).

The HITECH meaningful use provisions include criteria relating to communications between patients and their caregivers, particularly in Phase 2 of the implementation of the law. At that stage, at least 50 per cent of patients should be connected with their clinicians in terms of EHR-based personal data either through secure patient web portals or other arrangements. Various factors have led to a rise in the use of personal health records. They include the maturation of the Internet, a more knowledgeable ("savvy") information technology (IT)-using patient population, a rising incidence in chronic illnesses associated with an aging population and younger physicians who are more accustomed to using social media.

Two models of the use of EHRs predominate (Detmer et al., 2008). In the free-standing model, patients enter the data into a web-based product that holds the information; patients and others – such as family members – may also add information to it. In the second model, the record is under the provider's control: via a portal, patients have access to either their complete record or parts of it. Varying degrees of interactivity are possible. The portal approach is gaining in numbers. Over time, it is most likely to become the dominant method of engaging patients (HIMSS EHR Usability Task Force, 2009).

Latest developments in US health information technology

Two other eHealth developments have gained a foothold in terms of broader public interest. The first relates to the sharing of detailed personal health data to foster advanced research into better treatment of specific diseases. PatientsLikeMe is one such company that enables the sharing of data (PatientsLikeMe, 2013). The second area of growing consumer health development is genetic testing as an early manifestation of personalised medicine. 23andme is representative of the kind of company involved in this field (23andme, 2013). At the national level, the Blue Button Plus initiative from the Office of the National Coordinator for Health Information Technology builds on the Blue Button initiative of the Veterans Administration. This initiative will allow patients to obtain a copy of their EHR at the press of a "blue" button on the computer screen (Blue Button Plus, 2013). This mechanism is likely to have a dramatic impact on increasing connectivity and content. All these developments result in creating larger and larger accumulations of person-specific health information. The second involves the collection and management of large datasets and the potential that they have for better health and healthcare fits the current penchant for calling all such datasets, "big data". Although there is no clear definition of just what comprises "big data", the sense is that the analysis of large datasets will be useful for a variety of purposes. It is most likely to become essential for "personalised medicine" in which treatment options will be attuned to an individual's genetic profile and adjusted to the person's relevant life experiences. At least two major uses of big data are translational bioinformatics and data analytics for healthcare system improvements in quality, efficiency and safety. Examples are emerging where large datasets have offered very important insights into major problems such as cancer and heart disease, for example, research relating to rosiglitazone (Avandia) and myocardial infarction risk (Hornbrook et al., 2005; Brownstein et al., 2009). Efforts to find ways to scale patient EHR data across research institutions have been given a big boost through the aegis of the Clinical Translational Science Awards of the National Institutes of Health (NIH, 2013). Important efforts at "scaling", such as Informatics for Integrating Bioinformatics & the Bedside (I2B2), enable single queries to be asked of datasets that are distributed over a number of collaborating hospitals. However, there are still many knotty issues that remain regarding the compatibility of detailed data models and semantics (I2B2, 2013).

Arguably, no discipline in the health professions has had as dramatic, rapid and widespread a growth as biomedical and health informatics. The demand for workforce personnel in this field ranges from such disciplines as computer science, health information management, translational bioinformatics, research informatics, clinical informatics, to public health informatics (Detmer, 2013).

The HITECH legislation via the Office for National Coordinator community college workforce programme sought to train 10,000 individuals per year capable of supporting implementation and use of EHRs: the postings for health IT jobs regularly exceeds 10,000 for this domain alone. In addition, the developments in human genomics, proteomics and epigenetics have reformulated two sets of scientific subsections into popular and growing informatics disciplines: translational bioinformatics and research informatics. These disciplines owe their major recent boost in interest to the Clinical and Translational Science Awards and the Human Genome Project. The Clinical and Translational Science Awards seek to increase collaborative research across laboratories, clinics, hospitals and communities so that worthwhile discoveries are both fostered and implemented much more quickly. Becoming a part of routine translational bioinformatics, clinical and public health practices create demand for skilled informaticians across the entire spectrum of informatics disciplines. Indeed, there is growing workforce demand worldwide (Detmer, 2010b). Equally impressive has been the development of clinical informatics as a formally recognised area of specialisation in medicine, osteopathy, nursing and other clinical health disciplines. Nursing informatics was the earliest to engage in the clinical domain related to IT use. Nursing and other health professions are now seeking to assure an advanced inter-professional clinical informatics training and certification programme in order to keep pace with advancing knowledge and skills. The aim is to make it an inter-professional advanced clinical informatics training and certification programme and include all members of the healthcare team so that they share a largely common set of informatics knowledge, skills and attitudes. Through the leadership of the American Medical Informatics Association and the American Board of Preventive Medicine, working together with other collaborating boards, nearly 500 informally trained clinical informaticians become formally certified in the subspecialty of Clinical Informatics in January 2014 in Clinical Informatics (Detmer et al., 2009; Detmer, 2010). An intriguing and commendable effort, that engages most of the health professional associations, is underway to guarantee a common set of knowledge and skills. It includes informatics for all health professional students during their formative educational experiences. This idea had its origin at the Institute of Medicine Educational Summit in 2003, when a set of core competencies was identified as essential to bridging the chasm in quality of care in the US healthcare system. The competencies include providing patient-centred care, working in interdisciplinary teams, employing evidence-based practice, applying quality improvements and utilising informatics (which is the term used in the report itself) (Greiner and Knebel, 2003).

Three other areas relating to health information technology are now receiving greater attention in the US. They relate to the safety of EHRs and Health Information Exchanges (HIEs), the continued growth and development of clinical decision support systems and the growing negative impact that privacy regulations are having on research productivity and costs. In 2011, the Institute of Medicine released a report examining how health information technology (EHRs and Health Information Exchange systems) was performing with respect to patient and system safety (Patient Safety and HIT, 2012). The report's conclusions were that current performance is not meeting expectations. Yet, federal regulatory agencies have a major task ahead of them to address these needs without making the situation either freeze or deteriorate. The report has resulted in focused attention to the challenge by the Office for National Coordinator and the Food and Drug Administration (Office of the National Coordinator for IT, 2013).

Despite its challenges, adaptive clinical decision support is an extremely important area of informatics. The American Medical Informatics Association produced a White Paper in 2007 for the Office for National Coordinator and the Agency for Health Research and Quality that has been used by the government to frame activities in the area (Osheroff et al., 2007). A summary of current challenges and barriers shows that progress has been made along the lines of the roadmap described in the 2007 report (Lyman et al., 2010; The Center for Patient Safety Research and Practice, 2013). A growing number of reports and groups are drawing attention to the negative impact that privacy regulations are having on the capacity to perform biomedical, clinical and public health research (Nass et al., 2009; PCAST Report to President Obama, 2010; Smith et al., 2012). At the time of writing, there is little evidence that this trend will be reversed anytime soon. It remains an issue internationally (Lowrance, 2012).

The influential 2001 Institute of Medicine report, *Crossing the Quality Chasm: A New Health System for the 21st Century*, generated real momentum for information technology and informatics as a critical feature for the future of healthcare (Committee on Quality of Health Care in America, 2001). A decade later, the underpinning premises of that report were enhanced through the development of a learning healthcare system, one supported by a digital infrastructure (Olsen et al., 2007; Grossman et al., 2011). Although it is known that ICT can be transformational, getting to that point is a challenge (The Blue Ridge Academic Health Group, 2008). Most recently, in 2012, the capacity of American healthcare to consume resources with less than enviable outcomes has generated an Institute for Medicine report, entitled *Best Care at Lower Cost*. Its first major recommendation focuses squarely on securing a proper digital infrastructure (Smith et al., 2012).

The overriding aim of policy today in the US is to achieve an economically sustainable and continuously learning healthcare system. It would be supported by a data and communication infrastructure that creates "natural paths" and encourages patients to live healthier lives and manage their chronic illnesses more conscientiously. At the same time, it would help clinicians to create cost-effective ways to support individual patients as well as groups of patients and communities who share similar conditions. In parallel, it could support improvements with respect to the social determinants of health. Using health information technology to secure greater value from healthcare investments is the agenda for those committed to health, healthcare and informatics. The result is anticipated to be essential processes for best outcomes at the lowest cost through at least four means: improved communications; satisfaction; engagement and research breakthroughs.

References

23andme.com (2013), See https://www.23andme.com/. [Accessed 28 March 2013].

American College of Surgeons (2013), NSQIP Hospital Compare. See http://www.facs.org/hospitalcompare/. [Accessed 28 March 2013].

American EHR Partners (2013), See http://www.americanehr.com/Home.aspx. [Accessed 28 March 2013].

AMIA (2013), American Medical Informatics Association: *The Standards Standard.* See http://www.amia.org/news-publications/standards-standard. [Accessed 28 March 2013].

Berner, E.S., Detmer, D.E. and Simborg, D. (2005), "Will the wave finally break? A brief view of the adoption of electronic medical records in the United States", *Journal of the American Medical Informatics Association* 12 (1): 3–7.

Blue Button Plus (2013), See http://www.healthit.gov/patients-families/faqs/what-blue-button-america. [Accessed 28 March 2013].

Brownstein, J.S., Murphy, S.N., Goldfine, A.B., Grant, R.W., Sordo, M., Gainer, V., Colecchi, J.A., Dubey, A., Nathan, D.M., Glaser, J.P. and Kohane, I.S. (2009), "Rapid identification of myocardial infarction risk associated with diabetes medications using electronic medical records", *Diabetes Care.* 2010 Mar; 33 (3): 526–531. doi: 10.2337/dc09-1506. Epub Dec 15.

Canada Health Infoway (2013), See https://www.infoway-inforoute.ca/index.php. [Accessed 28 March 2013].

Commission on System Interoperability (2005), Ending the Document Game. *US National Library of Medicine.* See http://endingthedocumentgame.gov/. [Accessed 28 March 2013].

Committee on Quality of Health Care in America (2001), IOM report, Crossing the Quality Chasm: A new health system for the 21st century. *National Academies Press,* Washington, DC. [Accessed 28 March 2013].

Commonwealth Fund (2004), See http://hpm.org/en/Surveys/CMWF_New_York__USA/04/Strategy_for_Electronic_Health_Records.html. [Accessed 28 March 2013].

Cusack, C.M., Hripcsak, G., Bloomrosen, M., Rosenbloom, S.T., Weaver, C.A., Wright, A., Vawdery, D.K., Walker, J. and Mamykina, L. (2013), "The future state of data capture and documentation: a report form AMIA's 2011 Policy Meeting", *Journal of the American Medical Informatics Association* 20 (1): 134–140.

Detmer, D.E. (1997), "The future of IAIMS in a managed care environment: a call for private action and public investment", *Journal of the American Medical Informatics Association* 4(2): S65–S72.

Detmer, D.E. (2000), "Information technology for quality healthcare: a summary of United Kingdom and United States experiences", *Quality in Health Care* 9 (3): 181–189.

Detmer, D.E., Bloomrosen, M., Raymond, B. and Tang, P. (2008), "Integrated personal health records: transformative tools for consumer-centric care", *BMC Medical Informatics and Decision Making* 8:45–72.

Detmer D.E. (2009a), Information technology for quality healthcare: a summary of United Kingdom and United States experiences. *Qual Health Care* 9(3): 181–189.

Detmer, D.E., Lumpkin, J.R. and Williamson, J.J. (2009b), "Editorial: defining the medical subspecialty of clinical informatics", *Journal of the American Medical Informatics Association* 16: 167–168.

Detmer, D.E. (2010a), "Activating a full architectural model: improving health through robust population health records", *Journal of the American Medical Informatics Association* 17: 367–369.

Detmer, D.E. (2010b), Capacity Building in e-Health and Health Informatics: A Review of the Global Vision and Informatics Educational Initiatives of the American Medical Informatics Association. *Yearbook of Medical Informatics.* International Medical Informatics Association. pp.101–105. IMIA & Schattauer.

Detmer, D.E., Munger, B.S. and Lehmann, C.U. (2010), "Medical informatics board certification: history, current status, and predict impact on the medical informatics workforce", *Applied Clinical Informatics* 1: 11–18.

Detmer, D.E. (2013), "Information Technology and Informatics", in C. Guest, W. Ricciardi, I. Kawachi and I. Lang (eds) *Oxford Handbook of Public Health Practice*, 3rd Ed. Oxford: Oxford University Press, Chapter 2.2, pp. 84–89.

Dick, R. and Steen, E.B. (eds) (1991), *Institute of Medicine. The Computer-Based Patient Record.* Washington DC: National Academy Press.

Dick, R., Steen, E.B. and Detmer, D.E. (eds) (1997), *Institute of Medicine. The Computer-based Patient Record.* Washington DC: National Academy Press.

Dumortier, J. and Verhenneman, G. (2013), "Legal regulation of electronic health records: a comparative analysis of Europe and of the US", in George, C., Whitehouse, D. and Duquenoy, P. (eds) *eHealth: Legal, Ethical and Governance Challenges*, Heidelberg: Springer-Verlag, pp. 25–56. See http://link.springer.com/chapter/10.1007/978-3-642-22474-4_2. [Accessed 28 March 2013].

Europe's Information Society (2013), Thematic Portal. EU–US cooperation in eHealth – main elements of a joint roadmap for activities under the MoU identified. See http://ec.europa.eu/information_society/newsroom/cf/itemdetail.cfm?item_id=8146 and http://www.healthit.gov/policy-researchers-implementers/eu-and-us-step-cooperation-ehealth-and-health-it. [Accessed 28 March 2013].

Goedert, J. (2012), Research Tracks Physician IT Adoption in 2012, Health Data Management, 28 Sept. http://www.healthdatamanagement.com/news/ehr-electronic-health-records-practice-management-physicians-45043–1.html. [Accessed 28 March 2013].

Greiner, A.C. and Knebel, E. (eds) (2003), *Health Professions Education: A Bridge to Quality.* Washington, DC: IOM, National Academies Press.

Grossman, C., Powers, B. and McGinnis, J.M. (eds) (2011), *Digital Infrastructure for the Learning Healthcare System.* Washington, DC: National Academies Press. [Accessed 28 March 2013].

Health Info Technology (2013), Office of the National Coordinator for Health Information Technology. Draft Executive Summary. February. See

http://www.healthit.gov/policy-researchers-implementers/eu-and-us-step-cooperation-ehealth-and-health-it. [Accessed 28 March 2013].

HIMSS EHR Usability Task Force (2009), Defining and testing EMR usability: principles and proposed methods of EMR usability evaluation and rating. Healthcare Information and Management Systems Society (HIMSS), Chicago.

Hornbrook, M.C., Hart, G., Ellis, J.L., Bachman, D.J., Ansell, G. and Greene, S.M. (2005), "Building a virtual cancer research organization", *Journal of the National Cancer Institute Monographs* 35: 12–25.

Hsiao, C.J. and Hing, E. (2012), Use and characteristics of electronic health record systems among office-based physician practices: United States, 2001–2012. *NCHS data brief*, no 111. Hyattsville, MD: National Center for Health Statistics. http://www.cdc.gov/nchs/data/databriefs/db111.htm. [Accessed 28 March 2013].

I2B2 (2013), Informatics for Integrating Biology and the Bedside. See https://www.i2b2.org/. [Accessed 28 March 2013].

Institute of Medicine (2001), *Crossing the Quality Chasm: A New Health System for the 21st Century*. Washington DC: National Academy Press.

Lorenzi, N.M. and Riley, R.T. (2004), *Managing Technological Change: Organizational Aspects of Health Informatics*. 2nd ed., New York: Springer.

Lowrance, W.W. (2012), *Privacy, Confidentiality, and Health Research*. Cambridge University Press.

Lyman, J.A., Cohn, W.F., Bloomrosen, M. and Detmer, D.E. (2010), "Clinical decision support: progress and opportunities", *Journal of the American Medical Informatics Association* 17: 487–492.

McGowan, J.J., Cusack, C.M. and Bloomrosen, M. (2012), "The future of health IT innovation and informatics: a report from AMIA's 2010 policy meeting", *Journal of the American Medical Informatics Association* 19 (3): 460–467.

Nass, S.J., Levit, L.A. and Gostin, L.O. (eds) (2009), *Institute of Medicine Report, Beyond the Health Privacy Rule: Enhancing Privacy, Improving Health through Research*. Washington, DC: National Academies Press.

National Committee on Vital and Health Statistics (1998), Assuring a Health Dimension for the National Information Infrastructure. A Concept Paper by the National Committee on Vital and Health Statistics, presented to the U.S. Department of Health and Human Services Data Council, October 14, Washington, D.C. http://www.ncvhs.hhs.gov/hii-nii.htm. [Accessed 28 March 2013].

NIH (2013), National Institutes of Health, National Center for Advancing Translational Sciences. See http://www.ncats.nih.gov/research/cts/ctsa/ctsa.html. [Accessed 28 March 2013].

National Library of Medicine (2013), University-based Biomedical Informatics Research Training Programs. See https://www.nlm.nih.gov/ep/GrantTrainInstitute.html. [Accessed 28 March 2013].

National Research Council (1997), *For the Record: Protecting Electronic Health Information*. Washington, DC: The National Academies Press.

Office for Health Info Technology (2013), Office of the National Coordinator for Health Information Technology. Meaningful Use. See http://www.healthit.gov/policy-researchers-implementers/meaningful-use. [Accessed 28 March 2013].

Office of the National Coordinator for IT (2013), *HIT and Patient Safety*. See http://www.healthit.gov/policy-researchers-implementers/health-it-and-patient-safety. [Accessed 28 March 2013].

Olsen, L., Aisner, D. and McGinnis, J.M. (eds) (2007), *Roundtable on Evidence-based Medicine, The Learning Healthcare System*. Washington, DC: National Academies Press. [Accessed 28 March 2013].

Osheroff, J.A., Teich, J.M., Middleton, B., Steen, E.B., Wright, A. and Detmer, D.E. (2007), "A roadmap for national action on clinical decision support", *Journal of the American Medical Informatics Association* 14: 141–145.

Patient Safety and HIT (2012), *Committee on Patient Safety and Health Information Technology; Institute of Medicine. Health IT and patient safety: building safer systems for better care*. Washington D.C.: National Academies Press, See http://www.nap.edu/catalog.php? record_id=13269. [Accessed 28 March 2013].

PatientsLikeMe (2013), See http://www.patientslikeme.com/. [Accessed 28 March 2013].

Payne, T.H., Detmer, D.E., Wyatt, J.C. and Buchan, I.E. (2011), "National-scale clinical information exchange in the United Kingdom: lessons for the United States", *Journal of the American Medical Informatics Association* 18(1): 91–98.

PCAST Report to President Obama (December 2010), Realizing the Full Potential of Health Information Technology to Improve Healthcare for Americans: The Path Forward. See http://www.whitehouse.gov/sites/default/files/microsites/ostp/pcast-health-it-report.pdf. [Accessed 28 March 2013].

Simborg, D.W., Detmer, D.E. and Berner, E.S. (2013), "The wave has finally broken: now what?" *Journal of the American Medical Informatics Association* March 28 (online) see http://jamia.bmj.com/content/early/2013/03/27/amiajnl-2012-001508.abstract. [Accessed 28 March 2013].

Smith, M., Saunders, R., Stuckhardt, L. and McGinnis, M. (eds) (2012), *Institute of Medicine report, Best care at lower cost: the path to continuously learning health care in America*. Washington, D.C.: National Academies Press. [Accessed 28 March 2013].

Terhilda, G., Kumar, S., Lekas, J., Lindberg, M., Kadiyala, Whippy A., Crawford, B. and Weissberg J. (2013), "e-Measures: insight into the challenges and opportunities of automating publicly reported quality measures", *Journal of the American Medical Informatics Association* (http://dx.doi.org/10.1136/amiajnl-2013-001789).

The Blue Ridge Academic Health Group (2008), Advancing Value in Health Care: The Emerging Transformation Role of Informatics. Report 12. See http://whsc.emory.edu/blueridge/publications/reports,html. Emory University, Atlanta. [Accessed 28 March 2013].

The Center for Patient Safety Research and Practice (2013), See http://www.patientsafetyresearch.org/. [Accessed 28 March 2013].

The Nationwide HIM (2013), Health Information Network. Direct Project and CONNECT Software, DHHS, ONC, http://healthit.hhs.gov/portal/server.pt?open=512&mode=2&objID=3340. [Accessed 28 March 2013].

US PHIN (2012), Public Health Information Network. See http://www.cdc.gov/phin/. [Accessed 28 March 2013].

17
Reshaping Health in a World of Mobile Phones

Patricia Mechael, Ada Kwan, Avrille Hanzel and Chelsea Hedquist

Introduction

This chapter focuses on the role that mobile technologies play in health, particularly with regard to how the ubiquity of mobile telephony is reshaping health and creating new possibilities for a healthier future. Although mHealth and eHealth are readily grouped together and are closely linked, mHealth offers a unique opportunity to strengthen eHealth (Vital Wave Consulting, 2009) through its communications and mobility capabilities and broader reach into the general population. In order to provide a holistic understanding of the current and future states of mHealth, this chapter begins with a brief description of the importance of communication through history and how mobile technologies offer an instant form of communication to the modern-day world. The current state of mHealth is then illustrated through a number of examples of ways in which mHealth can be used as a tool for improving healthcare and health systems, as well as a description of primary actors within the increasingly interconnected ecosystem of mHealth. Based on the current state of mHealth, recommendations are then provided for the field on how various areas should move forward to most effectively achieve mHealth's full potential. All experience, knowledge and lessons learned are provided from the perspective of the mHealth Alliance (referred to as the Alliance), which is hosted by the United Nations Foundation (www.mhealthalliance.org).

Communicating over large distances: Then and now

In West Africa, drums were once the only way to communicate across large distances. Over the course of history, humans have devised creative ways to communicate over great distances, often shaping sound and light into transmittable signals or using animals and birds to carry messages. The creation of different tools to communicate over great distances highlights the important role that human communication has played in the history and survival of mankind.

There has been a progressive development of wireless telecommunication and messaging. This ranges from the invention of the telegraph and use of signalling patterns developed in the 1840s, to the fixed-line telephone in the 1870s, to the invention of e-mail in the 1970s (and its increased uptake among the general public in the 1980s), to the invention of the mobile phone in 1973 (and its mass uptake in the 2000s).

From the late 20th century, instant synchronous and asynchronous communication began to explode in popularity and has continued to do so ever since. At the end of 2011, there were more than 6 billion mobile phone subscriptions for a worldwide population of over 7 billion (International Telecommunication Union, 2012). This growing number has created an extensive web of contacts supported by expanding mobile networks. Mobile network infrastructure is also extending into parts of the world where there has been no previous mode of communication, and the concept of being unreachable is quickly disappearing.

Remarkably, this is the case for both rich and poor. In low- and middle-income countries, home to over 75 per cent of the world's mobile phone subscriptions (International Telecommunication Union, 2012), mobiles are more readily available than potable water and electricity. Connectivity is a newly pervasive concept, enabling people who make less than a dollar a day and people who have never before seen a doctor to have access to people and information any time, anywhere.

The growing availability of mobile phones has started to have a positive impact on the health sector. Individuals in low- and middle-income countries often face challenges such as poor knowledge of basic disease prevention and health promotion as well as inadequate access to health services, while the health systems themselves suffer from insufficient capacity and critical shortages of trained health personnel and supplies. The expansion of mobile network coverage offers opportunities to improve access to and delivery of health information and services for the general population, to increase knowledge and training of health professionals and to provide real-time monitoring data to health systems administrators and policy-makers. Innovation and technology offer limitless opportunities for advancements in this rapidly growing field.

Current state of mHealth

mHealth is defined by the World Health Organization's (WHO) Global Observatory for eHealth (GOe) as "medical and public health practice supported by mobile devices, such as mobile phones, patient monitoring devices, personal digital assistants and other wireless devices" (WHO, 2011). mHealth is no longer in its infancy and has generated significant interest from stakeholders, including national Ministries of Health, bi-lateral and multi-lateral agencies, non-profit organisations, mobile network operators, pharmaceutical companies and donors (WHO, 2010).

If leveraged appropriately and strategically through effective partnerships, mobile technologies hold great potential to improve access to health services, to enhance the quality of service delivery and to empower individuals to improve their own health, accelerating improvements in health outcomes throughout the world. These outcomes range from supporting the achievement of the United Nations' Millennium Development Goals (MDGs), to improving non-communicable disease management and the health burden of an ageing global population. In a 2010 WHO GOe report, the status of mHealth was assessed across 114 countries. This report categorised efforts where mobile technologies were used in a wide variety of health settings, including call centres, emergency and disaster management, mobile telemedicine, appointment reminders, community mobilisation and health promotion, mobile patient records, information access, patient monitoring, health surveys and data collection and decision support systems. Across the WHO's member states, 83 per cent reported offering an mHealth service, and many of the countries had between four and six mHealth programmes. The mHealth services that were the most popular were health call centres (59 per cent), emergency toll-free telephone services (55 per cent), the management of emergencies and disasters (54 per cent) and mobile telemedicine (49 per cent) (WHO, 2010). A recent assessment of the field identified more than 400 mHealth projects aimed at Millennium Development Goal (MDG) 4 (to reduce child mortality), MDG 5 (to reduce maternal mortality) and MDG 6 (to combat HIV/AIDS, malaria and other communicable diseases) (WHO, 2010). These global partnerships and collaborations, especially those using mobile phones and other information communication technologies (ICTs), collectively have the potential to save millions of lives throughout the world.

Many strategies are currently being employed to leverage mobile technologies to tackle a wide range of health challenges; the most common strategies in low- and middle-income countries aim to make strides in maternal, newborn and child health, as well as in HIV/AIDS. mHealth offers many unprecedented options, from encouraging healthy behaviours to replacing traditional pen-and-paper reporting methods. Some strategies include motivating risk-reducing behaviour change among at-risk populations, increasing awareness of a stigmatised health matter among the general population, offering distance learning options for healthcare professionals, equipping frontline health workers with point-of-care protocols that can save lives during home visits and both real-time disease surveillance and mobile-phone-based data collection options. Limitations that had previously faced communities in remote areas or communities without sufficient health training are beginning to be addressed and overcome through the rapid increases in advancements in the field of mHealth.

To illustrate some of the possible uses of mobile technologies in improving health and wellness, six types of uses are described below and related project case studies are show-cased. The topics together provide a brief snapshot of the current state of mHealth projects, specifically in Africa and Asia (see Box 17.1 where the topics are covered in the same sequence of topics).

1. *Social accountability and behaviour change* – Although health awareness and related campaigns have played an important role in the history of public health, the rise in mobile phones represents an opportunity to increase the reach and availability of information related to health education and awareness. Mobile technology offers a vehicle to carry information and improve social accountability and knowledge levels, as well as the quality and availability of health services that can encourage and empower individuals to make informed decisions about healthy lifestyle choices and prompt the health system to improve provision of those services.

2. *Diagnostic and treatment support* – Mobile technologies for diagnostic and treatment support have two main user groups. First, mobile technologies are used by health workers to access protocols, transmit test results and implement point-of-care support tools (for example, drug information and guidelines). The second user group includes patients who use mobile technologies, typically through SMS reminders, to prompt them to take their medications or attend appointments.

3. *Disease and epidemic outbreak tracking* – Surveillance systems often rely on pen-and-paper methods for reporting. These reports can take weeks or months to arrive at their eventual destination. In emergency situations, such as during a disease outbreak, a proper response to address a health issue or to contain a disease from spreading cannot be orchestrated adequately when notification is delayed. Thus, surveillance tools that offer real-time information can strengthen a surveillance response. Because location data are commonly built into mobile phones, information can be mapped geographically and easily visualised.

4. *Supply chain management and anti-counterfeit drug services* – The ability of mobile phones for immediate exchange of information has been leveraged in supply chain management of medicine and commodities. When supply is running low or when there is a shortage of a stock item ("stock-outs"), health facilities can contact their distributors to replenish missing stock. Mobile technologies are also being used in detecting and reporting on counterfeit drugs.

5. *Remote data collection* – Health facilities are often required to systematically report to district or national levels of government, often using pen-and-paper methods that pose challenges, including delivery delays by weeks or months after the time period captured by the report, possible loss of or damage to the report or the long distances involved preventing the physical delivery of the

report. Mobile technologies can make data entry easier and convert data into an electronic format, reducing time and costs.

6. *Health care worker communication and training* – Health worker shortages and lack of motivation among health professionals handicap the delivery of effective health interventions throughout the world. For example, a report by Save the Children has shown that 38 per cent of newborn deaths could be prevented by providing training and support for midwives, offering a set of interventions that has been proven effective (Save the Children, 2011). This training can translate into saving around 1.3 million babies each year. For this reason, mobile technologies are being considered as a means to transmit knowledge, information and protocols that can support health extension workers when they make visits to households that have difficulty accessing facility-based health services.

Box 17.1 Case studies

U Report in Uganda – behaviour change

Developed by the United Nations International Children's Emergency Fund (UNICEF), this text-based application targets the general population, enabling individuals to educate one another on topics such as female genital mutilation, disease outbreaks and safe water issues. It also allows each user to report on and discuss issues important to him or her, which health administrators and practitioners can then analyse. Mobile Alliance for Maternal Action (*MAMA*) in Bangladesh, South Africa and India and the Mobile Technologies for Community Health (*MoTECH*) in Ghana are additional examples of behaviour change related to maternal and child health.

Project Mwana in Zambia – diagnostic support

Timely care is crucial for reducing mother-to-child transmission of HIV and Mwana uses mobile networks to transmit infants' HIV test results in a usually slow turnaround context, made possible through collaboration across the Ministry of Health, UNICEF, Boston University affiliate the Zambia Centre for Applied Health Research and Development and the Clinton Health Access Initiative (UNICEF Innovation, 2013). Available in 62 facilities at the end of 2012, it aims to scale up to 200 facilities across the country. The project's two objectives – to strengthen early infant diagnosis and improve the rate of postnatal follow-up – are aligned with the country's health strategies. The project uses text messaging to immediately transmit test results to facilities, as well as a mobile phone application to remind mothers of appointments and other clinic visits. Other examples include the decision support work of *D-Tree International* and *mCheck*, which empower health workers with tools to improve diagnostic and treatment for a range of maternal and child health conditions.

mTrac in Uganda – outbreak tracking

Rapid diagnostics for malaria using paper-based reporting proved insufficient in addressing positive cases in a timely and accurate fashion (Asiimwe et al., 2011).

The availability of a widespread mobile phone network was the base for an mHealth monitoring system called *mTrac*. The Uganda Ministry of Health designed the system with support from UNICEF and Foundation for Innovative New Diagnostics (FIND) Diagnostics. It tracks disease outbreaks, health system delivery and supply distribution through text messaging, using citizen feedback, an anonymous hotline and public dialogue sessions to populate the database. One hundred and forty clinics across two districts with low set-up and operating costs substantially improved speed and accuracy of reporting (Asiimwe et al., 2011). Other examples include the strategic application of *Magpi* (formerly *EpiSurveyor*) as well as a range of hotlines and platforms used in countries such as Mexico and China to monitor and track outbreaks of diseases such as H1N1 or Avian Flu.

Sproxil in Nigeria – fighting counterfeit drugs

Sproxil was first implemented in Nigeria, and is now due to be extended to India and Kenya. It offers a method to verify the legitimacy of a medicine upon purchase in countries where counterfeit drugs lead to an alarming number of deaths or harmful effects. After purchasing medicine, a person can send a text message with a unique code to *Sproxil's* server, which checks the source of the medicine and then returns a response of its authenticity to the sender. The system has begun to improve trust in the health system among those who are particularly vulnerable to insecure drug supply chains. Other examples of supply chain management systems include John Snow International's *cStock* and *SMS for Life*.

Open Data Kit (ODK) in Kenya – remote data collection

The open-source mobile data collection toolkit, *Open Data Kit* (ODK), is used in Kenya to support a home-based HIV counselling and testing programme, jointly run by the United States Agency for International Development (USAID) and the Academic Model for the Prevention and Treatment of HIV (AMPATH) (Hartung et al., 2010). ODK allows a choice of tools and customisation to fit a user's need: AMPATH uses ODK for data collection such as tracking the immunisation status of children, or identifying pregnant women without antenatal care. Data collected are easily transferred via mobile phone to their medical records system, avoiding paper-based transfer (Hartung et al., 2010). Other examples include *FormHUB*, created by the Earth Institute at Columbia University, a free mobile tool to administer surveys and collect data, and *Magpi*, developed by *DataDyne*, collecting data through mobile phones and transmitting them to a cloud-based platform (Schuster and Perez Brito, 2011).

Mobile Academy in Bihar, India – health education

This mobile-phone-based service implemented in Bihar, India, by the Bill and Melinda Gates Foundation allows community health workers to play short messages with health tips to the women they visit: 200,000 community health workers attending a total of 27 million women of childbearing age (BBC Media Action, 2013). The programme includes the "Mobile Academy" – a mobile-phone-based training option for health workers, to improve their communication skills and to refresh their knowledge of life-saving behaviours, with interactive voice response technology enabling interaction. Another example is *CommCare* by Dimagi, combining case management with educational multi-media content for counselling households.

The increasingly interconnected mHealth ecosystem

The world is benefitting from an increasingly interconnected ecosystem made possible by increased networks for communication, particularly mobile networks. The field of mHealth exists in a subset of this larger ecosystem, referred to as the mHealth ecosystem, which is an evolving web of individuals and organisations who are using mobile technologies in a variety of ways to strengthen health systems and improve health and wellness throughout the world. This rapidly evolving field demands strong leadership and collaboration across many different stakeholders in order to leverage existing resources effectively and avoid duplication of efforts. Although inherently necessary, co-ordination and standardisation pose the biggest challenges to the seamless integration of mHealth into health systems. Capacity building among health and industry decision-makers, managers and practitioners is vital to overcoming this challenge and strengthening the enabling environment for mHealth. As demand for mHealth services rapidly increases, significant work is required to assess the educational and skills development needs of both government and non-government organisations.

Despite a global surge in programmes and initiatives, mHealth has not yet reached its full potential. Apart from capacity, there are several persistent gaps in the enabling environment that need to be addressed before mHealth can reach both global and national scale, namely in the areas of increased, better research and evidence, sustainable financing mechanisms, technology integration and global and national policy-making.

mHealth evidence

In the past decade, the field of mHealth has experienced some growing pains as a result of the high expectations that inevitably accompany initial enthusiasm. The field of mHealth will continue to encourage best practices informed by useful evidence generated from rigorous evaluations, and the growing trend of establishing a knowledge base for mHealth will continue. This knowledge base includes not only evidence from thorough studies that can help understand the ways in which mHealth can contribute in meaningful ways, but also the sharing of lessons learned that can reduce improper implementation.

As described in the Bellagio eHealth Evaluation Declaration of 2011, inappropriate implementation can "divert valuable resources and even cause harm". Indeed, the WHO has created the mHealth Technical Expert Review Group (mTERG) to guide governments and other mHealth implementers on evidence-based strategies (Labrique et al., 2012). Two literature reviews (Free et al., 2013a,b) reported that although many studies exist, they are of poor quality with few having low risks of bias and even fewer demonstrating clinically significant benefits. An identified challenge is that the field of science moves at a slower pace than the quickly advancing field of mHealth. In the near future as evaluation becomes more ingrained into mHealth projects, it is predicted that metrics and thresholds will be developed and agreed upon, which can support efforts in building the evidence base for informed decision-making and investments.

Sustainable financing models

There no easy answer to the question "Who pays?" and funding and sustainable business models in mHealth are currently lacking. However, an expected shift in donor funding linked to pilots towards sustaining efforts past the pilot stage may help support the financial sustainability of mHealth projects. Additionally, in some contexts, exploration into governmental support and business models, and the adoption of these, can help keep mHealth projects financially viable.

Effective business models will certainly vary according to context. Some governments may offer certain services for free in some circumstances, and in other contexts, individuals may be accustomed to purchasing health services out of pocket. Generally speaking, prevention services, which are often earmarked from public healthcare budgets and supported by taxes, will not generate as much revenue as laboratory or treatment services. mHealth projects may be better off financially as a result of obtaining governmental support or similar mechanisms for funding.

Sending text messages and making voice calls generate recurrent costs. Therefore, many implementing agencies are concerned about financial viability. Across the field, mHealth projects are often funded through donors, but a growing number are creating business models with revenue generation. For the larger scale programmes, partnerships are being created with mobile network operators, which sometimes subsidise costs per message or call for large package bundles. In public health, scale is often necessary to optimise both health impacts and cost efficiencies. Although empirical evidence supporting this is lacking in the field of mHealth, it can be seen over and over again in health and other sectors that increasing the number of clients served corresponds to decreasing costs per client.

A 2013 report by the mHealth Alliance and Vital Wave Consulting explored sustainable financing models for mHealth, with a focus on the relationships of implementers, funders and economic buyers, and the value propositions for each of these parties in regard to mHealth (mHealth Alliance and Vital Wave Consulting, 2013). Long-term financing sustainability for mHealth is not just about finding the right models, but also establishing a process of balancing the value chain on an ongoing basis through effective monitoring and evaluation. Although projects at the pilot phase will likely rely on seed funding, implementers and funders will need to make sure plans and structures are in place so that evidence-based value can be demonstrated to future buyers in order to ensure financial sustainability. Additionally, it is recommended that ongoing communicative relationships are developed with players throughout the value chain, mainly with governments, mobile network operators and other economic buyers. This close communication will help maintain a clear understanding between parties about risks and barriers in the value chain from the start, and will assist in anticipating any changes in interests as projects grow towards scale. Developing a value chain that motivates economic buyers to remain engaged in the long term requires incentives, as well as proactive and continued monitoring and rebalancing of the value chain.

Technology standards and interoperability

Standards and interoperability are becoming popular topics of discussion as interest grows around eHealth and mHealth.

Interoperability relates to not only the architecture of the systems, but also standards that govern health data concepts, patient identification, data processing protocols and mechanisms for secure sharing of patient data that preserve confidentiality. In contrast to eHealth, mHealth has lower and fewer legacy barriers to overcome in order to establish interoperable architectures. However, for mHealth to be nested within eHealth (more specifically, in health information systems, such as health records or health management information systems), implementers must be alert to the risk of rendering meaningful systems static because of a lack of technical standards and interoperability.

In mHealth, technology-related and other standards must be developed and also effectively implemented. Currently, standards are often non-existent or not strongly encouraged in low- and middle-income countries. This poor adoption of standards causes similar systems to be deployed competitively. This has resulted in duplicated or overlapping systems that function in silos. There are greater implications for interoperability and the larger eHealth systems over time, particularly if the intent is to scale up.

Aside from encouraging wider access to and use of standards for mHealth in low- and middle-income countries, the next steps in moving towards strong standards will involve improving at least six domains of activity. They involve enhancing the evidence base of how specific packages of standards can work towards achieving health systems goals, building the capacity and increasing standards access, ensuring that standards are adopted in low- and middle-income countries, engaging and mediating use of standards in low- and middle-income countries, encouraging co-ordination across the mHealth ecosystem and strengthening governance in mHealth and the larger field of eHealth (Payne, 2013). To facilitate this movement, donors and governments can encourage best practices in various ways. This can be done through funding that is tied to the use of interoperability standards, policy and supporting efforts to develop in-house capacity in collaboration with local governments and academic institutions. Additionally, a means of facilitating dialogue among the widely varied stakeholders who are involved in the process of designing, evolving and regulating standards is to hold multi-stakeholder meetings on these topics (Payne, 2013).

mHealth strategies and policies

As the impact and effects of mHealth are increasingly supported by evidence, a strong argument emerges for Ministries of Health around the world to support mHealth-specific strategies and policies at a national level. To date, there have been several governments that have supported the integration of mHealth into their national health programmes, including those of Ethiopia, Kenya, Nigeria, Rwanda, Tanzania and Uganda, among others. The box below shows examples of how the governments of Ethiopia and Nigeria are looking towards mHealth as a tool for improving their health services.

As health systems become more mobile and services are expanded to incorporate personal health information, privacy and security policies will become increasingly important. The mHealth Alliance has worked with Thomson Reuters Foundation's TrustLaw Connect Initiative, Baker & McKenzie, Merck and law firms from seven countries, to conduct a landscape analysis of mHealth privacy and security issues on the national and country levels (mHealth Alliance, 2012). Results of the study show that few countries have explicit policies on either mHealth specifically or personal health information in general. Key recommendations include the development of Model Laws at the global level that can be adopted for use by low- and middle-income countries as well as integrating privacy checks and encryption technology for data transmission into software and hardware.

Box 17.2 mHealth policies

Ethiopia

Driven by the desire to improve maternal and child mortality and access to life-saving interventions, Ethiopia decided in 2011 to extend services on community and family levels (The Bellagio eHealth Evaluation Declaration, 2011). Health extension workers were integrated into the health system and their information and communication were to be met with mHealth. With the support of the Bill and Melinda Gates Foundation, needs were mapped (family planning, lack of skilled birth attendants, poor referral systems, poor supply management), and an mHealth framework developed (Vital Wave Consulting, 2011). Although most health extension workers had their own mobile phone, coverage was low, with only 8 per cent of the population having a subscription, mostly concentrated in urban areas. Thus, local level mHealth solutions (text messaging for training) needed to go alongside macro-level improvements (data collection). Phasing in the strategy over a five-year timespan, the effectiveness of mHealth was first demonstrated with one group of health workers, then extended to build a larger, more robust system.

Nigeria

At the end of 2012, the Nigerian Federal Ministry of Health launched the Saving One Million Lives (*SOML*) initiative to address preventable causes such as maternal child mortality. Prioritising strategic integration of ICTs and partnering with the mHealth Alliance, Intel, GSMA and other organisations, a situational analysis of ICTs, mHealth and eHealth and the enabling environment was undertaken to develop a proper strategy of integrating ICTs into the *SOML* initiative. While an mHealth plan was being developed, early opportunities for scale were identified to translate into immediate results, such as scaling up mobile and web-based facility reporting, district health information software system (DHIS2), integrating the use of mobile money into a conditional cash transfer programme (with financial incentives for using health services) and integrating mobile phones into the tracking systems for improving supply chain management for priority commodities related to the SOML initiative.

Integration with other mobile services

As more and more individuals in low- and middle-income countries engage with the business, health, agriculture and financial sectors through mobile phones, the integration of mHealth with other mobile services is increasingly considered, thus expanding options for mHealth. The most obvious option is to develop an add-on with mobile money options, such as *mPesa*, a mobile banking service that expanded from Kenya into Afghanistan, India, South Africa and Tanzania, and is used for payment of health workers, management of health insurance, and/or the processing of conditional cash transfers to improve the uptake of healthy behaviours. Smart integration with other mobile services can encourage individuals to adopt money-saving behaviours, especially in cash economies where getting sick and paying out of pocket can cause a fall into poverty. Changamka Ltd in Kenya, for example, has led the field with a mobile option for insurance – a medical smart card that allows low-income Kenyans to prepare for any income shocks that result from unexpected health expenses. Cards can be purchased in local shops and loaded through *mPesa*, without any registration. Additional options under consideration include direct engagement through common platforms and access to services across sectors.

Future visions for mHealth

Mobile technologies have transitioned from the questions of "if" to "what" and now "how". Health systems and the individuals that they serve are becoming increasingly empowered through mobile phones and other mobile devices. Taking into consideration the trends in the field and the Alliance's ongoing efforts, the following are predictions and a call to action to inform the future state of mHealth.

The ways in which mobile phones are used in terms of health capitalise on a variety of features that range from voice calls and text messages to mobile applications that are supported by data transmissions and the mobile web leveraging general packet radio service (GPRS), 3G and 4G network infrastructure, global positioning systems (GPS), Bluetooth and the ability to link up to more complex backend systems (Mechael et al., 2010; Istepanian et al., 2011). Additionally, the technologies behind sensors and other location-aware features are being developed rapidly, resulting in a push towards the Internet of Things. This is leading to more robust and media-rich applications development as well as the integration of multiple platforms and remote sensing that will drive greater support for individuals to manage their own health as well as health workers to have more point-of-care diagnostic and treatment guidance. The integration of mobile applications is resulting in a more service delivery-oriented health system with data capture for real-time monitoring and decision-making. This and performance-based financing for health are two innovations that are revolutionising how health information and services are being designed and accessed.

The continuing development of cheaper, more rugged and simple smartphones will accelerate. The coming decade may witness many more developments with tablets, mobile learning (Chib et al., 2010; Holzinger et al., 2005; SunStar Manila, 2012), mobile money (Jack and Suri, 2011; Mondato, 2013), wireless monitoring (Bielli et al., 2004), context-aware platforms (Broens et al., 2007), applications and games on both non-smartphones and smartphones and radio and television transmission to mobile handsets (International Telecommunication Union, 2010). Technological advances will move quickly to enable faster wireless broadband through both new and existing technologies with 4G, and when 5G is introduced. Additionally, linkages to more sophisticated back-end systems will be more common. The field of mHealth is having a significant impact on the broader eHealth field, and is in many ways making eHealth a more viable strategy for low- and middle-income countries in the form of distributed systems that are able to support individuals and health workers alike, as well as with facilities, district health offices and national health programmes. The implications that these options have for improving coverage, efficiencies in health, and responsiveness of the health system are profound at the global level.

At the beginning of 2012, the mHealth Alliance revised its strategy and business plan to support the field more effectively in realising the full potential of mobile technology in improving health outcomes and wellbeing for low- and middle-income countries. Five focus areas based on identified gaps in scale and sustainability were identified, namely: improvement of the evidence base for mHealth, integration of standards and interoperability in health information systems, identification and promotion of sustainable financing models, research and sharing of effective policies that support mHealth and community capacity building to design and deploy user-centred mHealth programmes (mHealth Alliance, 2012). These five programme areas are the fundamental building blocks of the enabling environment needed for mHealth to fully mainstream into health systems, and significant collaborations and efforts are underway to advance each of them.

The predictions for mHealth correspond to the global efforts driving their acceleration, a few programmes, platforms and approaches that are achieving national scale and coverage of target populations as well as movements towards the enabling environment needed for such technologies to thrive.

Conclusion

Although people throughout the world no longer have to rely on methods such as drums or carrier pigeons to communicate, individual communities continue to struggle with getting effective health interventions to the people who need them the most. mHealth is having a profound impact on global health efforts, including the Millennium Development Goals. Ministries of Health, donors and the private sector are increasingly recognising the growing power of mobile technology to positively improve access to health information and services, improve quality of care, create efficiencies and empower individuals and health workers towards achieving better health.

Actors in the mHealth ecosystem, including the general population, health professionals and the health sector, implementers and entrepreneurs in mHealth, governments, various non-profit and civic society organisations, donors, researchers and telecommunication operators, are moving towards coming together to form effective partnerships and collaborations for collective action to advance the field. Through these partnerships, we will see more and better research linking mHealth to eHealth. It will involve improved health outcomes, greater systems integration and adoption and promotion of standards, increases in sustainable funding and business models driving mHealth investments, greater capacity to design and implement mHealth systems and policies that align technology for health targets and protect the privacy and security of personal health information.

Countries that have already integrated mHealth into policy and national strategies may soon be joined by other countries beginning to engage in similar activities. Although significant challenges remain, emerging trends in global health indicate that mHealth is mainstreaming and scaling rapidly, and the enabling environment is beginning to catch up with the technology.

References

Asiimwe, C., Gelvin, D., Lee, E., Amor, Y.B., Quinto, E. and Katureebe, C. (2011), "Use of an innovative, affordable, and open-source short message service-based tool to monitor malaria in remote areas of Uganda", *The American Journal of Tropical Medicine and Hygiene* 85 (1): 26–33.

Bellagio eHealth Evaluation Declaration (2011), Consensus Statement of the Global eHealth Evaluation Meeting.

BBC Media Action (2013), Empowering community health workers in Bihar: Mobile Academy and Mobile Kunji, http://www.bbc.co.uk/mediaaction/where_we_work/asia/india/india_sdp_empowering_chw_ma_mk.html. [Accessed 1 November 2013].

Bielli, E., Carminati, F., La Capra, S., Lina, M., Brunelli, C. and Tamburini, M. A. (2004), "Wireless health outcomes monitoring system (WHOMS): development and field testing with cancer patients using mobile phones", *BMC Medical Informatics and Decision Making* 4 (7).

Broens, T., Van Halteren, A., Van Sinderen, M. and Wac, K. (2007), "Towards an application framework for context-aware m-health applications", *International Journal of Internet Protocol Technology,* 2 (2): 109–116.

Chib, A.I., Lwin, M.O., Lee, Z., Ng, V.W. and Wong, P.H.P. (2010), "Learning AIDS in Singapore: examining the effectiveness of HIV/AIDS efficacy messages for adolescents using ICTs", *Knowledge Management & E-Learning: An International Journal* 2 (2): 169–187.

Free, C., Phillips, G., Galli, L., Watson, L., Felix, L. and Edwards, E. et al. (2013a), "The effectiveness of mobile-health technology-based health behaviour change or disease management interventions for health care consumers: a systematic review", *PLoS Med* 10 (1): e1001362.

Free, C., Phillips, G., Galli, L., Watson, L., Felix, L. and Edwards, E. et al. (2013b), "The effectiveness of mobile-health technologies to improve health care service delivery processes: A systematic review and meta-analysis", *PLoS Med* 10 (1): e1001363.

Hartung C., Anokwa Y., Brunette W., Lerer A., Tseng C. and Borriello G. (2010), Open Data Kit: Tools to Build Information Services for Developing Regions. Paper presented at the International Conference on Information and Communication Technologies and Development (ICTD 2010), London, December 2010. See: http://opendatakit.org/wp-content/uploads/2010/10/ODK-Paper-ICTD-2010.pdf. [Accessed 1 November 2013].

Holzinger, A., Nischelwitzer, A. and Meisenberger, M. (eds) (2005), Mobile phones as a challenge for m-Learning: Examples for mobile interactive learning objects (MILOs), 3rd International Conference on Pervasive Computing and Communications Workshops (PerCom 2005 Workshops).

International Telecommunication Union (2012), *Measuring the Information Society.* Geneva: International Telecommunication Union.

International Telecommunication Union (2010), World Telecommunication/ICT Development Report. Geneva: International Telecommunication Union.

Istepanian, R., Philip, N., Wang, X.H. and Laxminarayan, S. (2011), "Non-telephone healthcare: the role of 4G and emerging mobile systems for future m-Health systems", *Community Medical Care Compunetics* 2: 9–16.

Jack, W. and Suri, T. (2011), *Mobile Money: The Economics of M-Pesa.* Cambridge, MA: National Bureau of Economic Research.

Labrique, A., Vasudevan, L., Chang, L.W. and Mehl, G. (2012), "Hope for mHealth: More 'y' or 'o' on the horizon"? *International Journal of Medical Informatics* S1386–5056(12): 00240-00247.

Mechael, P., Batavia, H., Kaonga, N., Searle, S., Kwan, A. and Goldberger, A. (2010), *Barriers and gaps affecting mHealth in low and middle income countries: Policy white paper: The Earth Institute.* Columbia University and the mHealth Alliance.

mHealth Alliance (2012), Annual Report. See: http://www.mhealthalliance.org/media-a-resources/annual-report. [Accessed 1 November 2013].

mHealth Alliance and Vital Wave Consulting (2013), Sustainable Financing for Mobile Health (mHealth): Options and opportunities for mHealth financing models in low and middle-income countries. Washington, D.C., mHealth Alliance; Palo Alto, CA: Vital Wave Consulting. See: http://www.mhealthalliance.org/images/content/sustainable_financing_for_mhealth_report.pdf. [Accessed 1 November 2013].

Mondato, L.L.C. (2013), Can mobile money enhance access to healthcare? http://mondato.com/en/articles/can-mobile-money-enhance-access-to-healthcare. [Accessed 1 November 2013].

Payne, J.D. (2013), *The State of Standards and Interoperability for mHealth among Low- and Middle-Income Countries*. Washington, DC: mHealth Alliance.

Save the Children (2011), *Missing Midwives*. London, UK: Save the Children UK.

Schuster, C. and Perez Brito, C. (2011), Cutting Costs, Boosting Quality and Collecting Data Real-Time – Lessons from a Cell Phone-Based Beneficiary Survey to Strengthen Guatemala's Conditional Cash Transfer Program. World Bank. (166)

SunStar Manila (2012, March 15), Text2Teach connects students to a more interactive learningenvironment.Seehttp://www.sunstar.com.ph/manila/local-news/2012/03/15/text2teach-connects-students-more-interactive-learning-environment-2113. [Accessed 1 November 2013].

UNICEF Innovation, Project Mwana (2013), http://www.unicefinnovation.org/projects/project-mwana. [Accessed 1 November 2013].

Vital Wave Consulting (2009), *mHealth for Development: The opportunity of mobile technology for healthcare in the developing world*, Washington D.C. and Berkshire UK: United Nations Foundation-Vodafone Foundation Partnership.

Vital Wave Consulting (2011), *mHealth in Ethiopia: Strategies for a New Framework*. Palo Alto, CA: Vital Wave Consulting.

Wang, C.S. (2010), "Mobile and wireless technologies applying on sphygmonameter and pulsimeter for patients with pacemaker implementation and other cardiovascular complications", *Jorunal of Biomedical Science and Engineering* 3: 47–51.

World Health Organization (2010), *The World Health Report: Health Systems Financing: The Path to Universal Coverage*. Geneva, Switzerland: World Health Organization Press.

World Health Organization (2011), mHealth: New Horizons for Health through Mobile Technologies, Geneva, Switzerland: World Health Organization Press.

18
eHealth in Drug Discovery and Disease Research

Mats Sundgren

Introduction

Information technology is transforming the way healthcare is developed, delivered and documented, making available detailed information such as phenotypes and genetic data and holding the promise of making a great contribution to medical research. A part of this fast changing landscape is eHealth. eHealth is becoming increasingly important for the pharmaceutical industry, offering remarkable enhancement opportunities for the clinical research sector. Electronic health records (EHRs), interconnected through healthcare networks, have the potential to interact richly with research platforms while complying with all applicable legal, regulatory and ethical standards and policies. This chapter explores the great potential of eHealth to the field of drug discovery and development.

Current challenges of the life sciences industry

We stand on the brink of a golden age of medical insights. The amount of available information is expanding exponentially. Information technology (IT) is radically transforming the way healthcare is developed, delivered and documented. At present, the practice of health care generates, exchanges and stores huge amounts of patient-specific information. In addition to the traditional clinical narrative, databases in modern health centres automatically capture structured data relating to all aspects of care, including diagnosis, medication, laboratory test results and radiological imaging data (DiMasi et al., 2003). The concept of eHealth, which is defined here as the intersection of medical informatics, public health and business (as a result of which health services are delivered or enhanced through the use of the Internet, applications and related technologies such as electronic health records) is also becoming increasingly important for the life science industry. It offers remarkable enhancement opportunities for biomedical research. Strategic imperatives of the life science industry are already interfacing with various eHealth opportunities: these include drug discovery, systems biology, disease understanding, translational science, personalised medicine and the acceleration of clinical research development programmes (Hermosilla et al., 2013).

Brief overview of current challenges

Current unmet medical needs, an ageing society and extended life expectancy are contributing to unprecedented organisational and economic pressures on healthcare systems and on the life science industry. The development of new medicines is critical to delivering improvements in healthcare and to meeting the new demands that are arising. Yet innovation in the pharmaceutical industry is characterised by high fixed costs incurred over a period of years before any returns from the fruits of the research and development (R&D) effort are realised. The incentives for firms to engage in the discovery and development of new therapies, therefore, depend critically on containment of expected R&D costs, as well as on the returns that can be expected from successful innovation (DiMasi et al., 2002).

The discovery and development of new medicines which are effective and safe for routine use in patients have become increasingly complex, labour intensive and challenging. Drug discovery and development is a multivariate process aiming at designing stable, potent compounds with high therapeutic efficacy and low toxicity. One challenge is the innovation output. The number of new molecular entities approved by the United States of America (US) Food and Drug Administration were less than one per company annually for nine of the largest pharmaceutical companies during the period 2005–2010. With a continuous increase in R&D spending during the same period, the annual amount had reached US$ 60 billion by the end of 2010 (Bunnage, 2011). Published studies have used time-periods that range up to 12–15 years with a cost per drug to market of around US$ 1.8 billion (Paul et al., 2010).

Another challenge is the attrition rate of research projects. In each step of the drug discovery process, many potential drugs are excluded. The cost of development increases rapidly on each step of the ladder towards approval: thorough evaluation of drug hits and leads is important for identifying failing compounds at an early stage. There is currently a 95 per cent attrition rate in the clinical phases (Paul et al., 2010). If this could be decreased by only a few percentage points, and undesired compounds excluded at a slightly earlier stage, significant efforts and resources could be saved. Moreover, clinical research programmes have increased by both complexity and size – the average cost of clinical trials has increased threefold between the years 2000 and 2012 (CMR International, 2012). The result of all these issues is that the industry is facing a difficult situation. Patents on many high revenue products are expiring, and the marketplace has become much more competitive with significant restrictions on reimbursements and more demanding regulatory demands.

The life science information landscape

Today's computer science concepts, tools and theorems are moving into the very fabric of science. Scientific computing platforms and infrastructures make possible new kinds of experiments that were impossible only 20 years ago. A key example is the use of eHealth solutions which allow pervasive monitoring using miniature devices, chips and wireless networks to monitor patients (for example, glucose and lipids). These can provide measurement of animals or humans in real time (Microsoft Research, 2006).

The use of such technologies, as well as other advances in eHealth, is driving an explosion in the generation of high-quality scientific and health information. This information, supported by an almost infinite storage in clouds of processors, allows far greater availability and shareability of data. However, these opportunities demand new skills that can support, or at best combine, traditional scientific disciplines with computer science and multivariate modelling and informatics (in other words, information science, information technology, algorithms and social science) to manage the deluge of data. This, in turn, drives a new emphasis in the life science industry on connecting systems and making data interoperable across different platforms. It has led some external voices, like *The Economist* (2009), to claim that "Interoperability is king." This suggests that a key to success in eHealth in the life science industry hinges on how internal information can be connected with the external world, including healthcare and patients, to share and make use of different information types or systems. The trend is clear: succeeding in these areas requires a new level of information sharing and exploitation capability that connects internal and external health information in a much more dynamic and seamless way than before.

Moreover, the accelerated interest in the development of eHealth services holds the promise of becoming an important interface for delivering key information to medical research and drug discovery. The implications for the life science industry and healthcare are huge. Therefore, it is important to ensure that appropriate computer science skills are integrated into life science research. In addition, adequate scientific computing platforms, which can manage the deluge of data that are produced, should be available at all stages of new drug development. A good example of such a platform is one which would enable the interconnection of health information repositories, such as electronic health records, from many different hospitals to support medical research through patient recruitment and drug safety monitoring. Such interconnection, however, demands not only suitable technological platforms that conform to interoperability standards, but also a new set of multi-disciplinary skills (for example, technical, organisational, informatics and legal) that provide viable interoperability of data among organisations in an ethical and safe way.

The life science worldview of information

The pharmaceutical industry not only produces drugs but it also supplies "informed materials" (in other words, the rich and complex informational material environment preceding a drug product even before it is launched). This clearly demonstrates that the rules of engagement in new drug development will become heavily dependent on information management.

Today, the pharmaceutical industry world of information can be divided into three domains. First is the "internal information domain", which generates and refines scientific information to shape future products. Second is the "external regulated information domain", which connects (with controlled access) to scientific databases and health information (for example, clinical trials). And, third is the "external open information domain", which is a fast moving external open domain, accessible through the Internet that is becoming a vital source of strategic value regarding safety and science information (such as scientific discussion forums, patient communities and blogs) (Sundgren, 2011).

From a new drug development perspective, a competitive edge can be gained by connecting all three of these information domains. Thus, the combination and use of health information technology (HIT) and eHealth services generated in the external environment will become central to new drug development business models (see Figure 18.1). It is in this context that the life science industry is facing a key transitional period of adapting to new governing logics of science-based innovation in which the sense-making of new technology and health data production will play a pivotal role (Styhre and Sundgren, 2011).

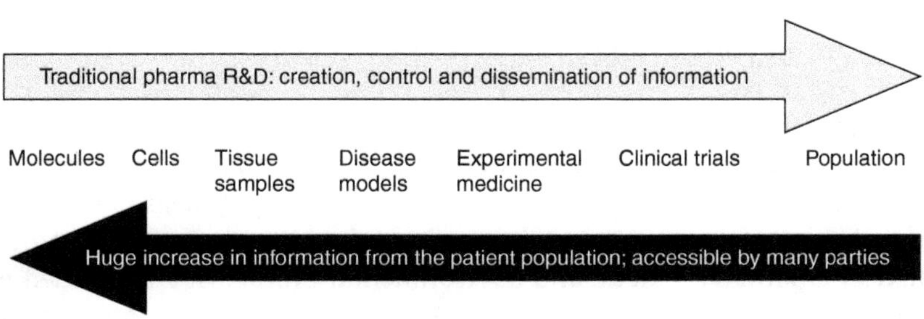

Figure 18.1 Different impact of eHealth and external health data on the drug development process
Source: Author's figure.

What eHealth offers life sciences

The advent of eHealth services[1] that involve trustworthy access and the re-use of large amounts of health data will have a significant impact on the pharmaceutical industry. Key challenges such as attrition rates (in other words, translational research) can be significantly improved by enhancing the predictability and validity of bridging pre-clinical animal models with rich, real world patient data. For late stage development eHealth services hold the promise of considerably improving design, specificity and execution in clinical trial programmes by targeting the appropriate patients. Another example of how eHealth services will become important in order to interact in a more profound way in the drug development process is in the area of personalised medicine and, ultimately, personalised healthcare (Lehner et al., 2012).

One key area of eHealth to improve science-based innovation

The approach of evidence-based medicine has revolutionised medicine during the past 50 years. However, results from large population-based studies are not always applicable to a specific individual. Physicians generally take into account specific characteristics – such as age, gender, height, weight, diet and environment – when evaluating an individual patient. Recent developments in a number of molecular profiling technologies, including proteomic profiling analysis and genomic/genetic testing, allow the development of personalised medicine and predictive medicine, which is the combination of comprehensive molecular testing with proactive, personalised preventive medicine. It is hoped that personalised medicine will enable healthcare providers to focus their attention on factors specific to an individual patient so as to provide individualised care.

In order to enhance science-based innovation capabilities, many pharmaceutical companies, if not all, have placed Personalised Health Care, translational science, personalised medicine and HIT at the top of their strategic research agendas. These disciplines are interconnected with each other and will play an important role in new drug development during the coming years.

Personalised Health Care can be broadly defined as the use of new therapies to better manage a patient's disease or predisposition towards a disease. It aims to achieve optimal medical outcomes by helping physicians and patients choose the disease management approaches most likely to work best in the context of a patient's genetic and environmental profile. In a simplified way, related disciplines such as Personalised Medicine and Translational Research can be seen as enablers of personalised healthcare, which will contribute to improved health outcomes as new genetic and genomic markers of health and wellness and disease risk are identified. Such approaches may include genetic screening programmes that more precisely diagnose diseases and their subtypes. Alternatively, they may help physicians select the type and dose of medication best suited to a certain group of patients, either to improve efficacy or minimise toxicity. Progress in personalised healthcare thus depends on personalised medicine, which can link defined biology from mechanism to disease. A commonly used phrase is translating bench science to bedside clinical practice or dissemination to population-based community interventions. This dramatic change has come about in recent years as a result of the genomics and bioinformatics revolution. Patients provide the biological specimens from which "disease signatures" can be identified. These are then used to develop diagnostics and drugs targeted at disease subgroups.

Thus, the new information landscape not only enables personalised healthcare but also allows different approaches in life science to combine scientific and health data to create breakthrough models to better understand diseases. It facilitates a new approach to life sciences research that is significantly removed from the blockbuster paradigm that aims for "one size fits all" products. It provides a gateway to mitigate the attrition challenge. The importance of personalised healthcare, and the connecting scientific disciplines, points to the growing need for an increased understanding of the driving forces that will change the limited assumptions and current logic of the pharmaceutical and biotechnology industries. The healthcare providers, governments and the boundary-spanning nature of future activities and challenges will also necessitate innovations in management models, systems and approaches (Hermosilla et al., 2013).

Two illustrations of how eHealth can play an important role in drug development

Two fictional scenarios, targeted at supporting new drug development, aim to illustrate how future eHealth services could support personalised medicine and subsequent clinical development. They provide examples of why eHealth services are a core component of the future of life science, personalised medicine and, ultimately, personalised healthcare. Even though these scenarios are fictional, hopefully these and similar eHealth services can become a reality in a couple of years' time. The technology already exists to make them a reality, but the organisational environment is still evolving. The point of these simple illustrations is to exemplify a valid need for these services in life science and to highlight the gaps and challenges in making such scenarios a reality.

Box 18.1 Scenario one: eHealth services to enhance disease models and biomarkers

Let us assume that the goal for a pharmaceutical company is to develop a set of diagnostic tools and biomarkers[2] for a diabetes project that has emerged from discovery research. The development of the diagnostic tools has been primarily driven by the pharmaceutical company, and a majority of data has been derived internally, but the diagnostic tool itself has been developed by an external subcontractor. The project then proceeds with patient recruitment in order to test the validity of the tool as an aid to a more patient-specific response to diabetes. In a traditional approach, suitable diabetes patients would be recruited through primary care or specialist care providers who would be asked to identify suitable candidates through their patient lists.

In an eHealth-enabled personalised medicine approach, collaboration would begin far earlier in the process. The R&D of the diagnostic tool would start as collaboration in the healthcare environment. As a joint venture, it would allow very close connection with patients in the early stages of research. During the entire R&D phase, the diagnostic tool would be supported by sophisticated re-use and data mining of health information from EHRs and other record systems. The clinical phase would proceed directly from the collaboration, based on a finely tuned selection of patients, which has been made possible by re-using information from the EHRs. The clinical studies would be carried out in a real-life setting that involves devices and sensors (such as implanted glucose monitors) to monitor key indicators in real time. Some patients would also carry out their own tests and the resulting information would also become available in real time. Outcome research-related aspects would be supported through mobile devices.

The clinical programme can be seen as a real-time interaction patient evaluation that will allow much more information to be captured than is usually the case in clinical trials. During the final phase of personalised medicine (that is, the diagnostic and drug phase), the established platform of collaborating with healthcare institutions and regulatory bodies would offer new ways to categorise work and efforts. It would enable the next step in bringing medicine into the personalised healthcare perspective (Sundgren, 2011).

Box 18.2 Scenario two: improving clinical study design by eHealth services

A pharmaceutical company is preparing for a phase III randomised comparative[3] clinical trial as part of the approval process for a new medicine. Today, phase III studies are often conducted at more than one medical centre or clinic and involve a large patient group. They can usually involve around 3,000 patients, but can include more than 15,000 depending on the disease or medical condition studied. These complex studies are costly and lengthy; just the patient recruitment phase can last for 12 months or more.

An important step prior to starting such a trial is the development of the study protocol. The study protocol outlines the study hypothesis, and is coupled with a wide range of assumptions/variables that need to be answered. The protocol includes inclusion and exclusion criteria of patients, description of intervention (what, how), concomitant therapy, examination procedures (baseline, follow-up, outcome assessment), biomarkers and the statistical methodology for the targeted number of patients. The study protocol is the result of careful consideration and iteration on the part of experts and assessment of previous knowledge and studies. The next step is to start the recruitment of eligible patients for the study. This lengthy process is done by knowledgeable physicians in the project who use their established external networks (for example, through local marketing companies and academic institutions) to connect with medical investigators at hospitals, and/or the help is obtained from contract research organisations that make use of either advertising tailored to local audiences or relationships with particular investigators at hospitals or clinics. After 18 months, the recruitment process is completed, and the study progresses.

So how would the above scenario be different if the protocol feasibility and recruitment approach were done by the assistance of eHealth services? First of all, during the first step of the study design and protocol development, the project team would use a specialised eHealth service for study optimisation by re-using EHR data. A federated trusted third-party service provider would allow trustworthy real-time access to 500 hospital sites in Europe, North America and Asia. The study team would send queries through an Internet interface application and obtain instant responses of de-identified health data about the numbers of patients across multiple sites, whose EHR information suggests that they would meet draft eligibility inclusion criteria for a study and not match any of its exclusion criteria. After some degree of iteration, the project team would refine these criteria in the draft protocol in order to assure that the protocol provides feasible and sufficient recruitment into the study. Next, for patient identification and recruitment, the team would use another EHR re-use service. This would enable a network of hospitals to precisely identify the patients in its EHR repository who match an issued protocol, for finer-grained examination of these patients' EHR against the protocol.

The end result of this scenario is an EHR-based screening list for review by a group of study physicians/nurses; it does not involve automatic inclusion in the study. Within two months the project team has not only refined a valid study protocol supported by extensive real-world data, but also has access to a confirmed list of hospitals, physicians and staff ready to take the next step in enrolling the patients for the study.

The challenges of using eHealth in the life sciences

An important aspect for a discussion on eHealth services is scalability. Scalable solutions involve not only the importance of making use of large amounts of high-quality health data (such as EHRs), but also the cost factor. Moreover, the success factor involved in developing scalable and sustainable eHealth services is the need to create a win–win–win situation (often referred to as a "triple win") for all stakeholders involved (for example, political players, regulatory bodies, the life science industry and patients). This single, most important, success factor implies a number of aspects that must overcome current major barriers and challenges (Geissbühler et al., 2013).

The re-use of EHRs in eHealth services is a representative challenge. It provides a departure point to discuss other major challenges for scalable eHealth services such as the two scenarios selected on disease models and biomarkers, and clinical study design.

The notion is that aggregated and anonymised EHR data (at local, regional and national levels) has the potential to bring great benefits to public health, clinical research and evidence-based knowledge. But why have these benefits not emerged as reality?

There are at least four major levels of challenges that need to be addressed. These include the policies, technologies, collaboration models and new business models involved (Sundgren, 2011).

Policy level – A number of challenges exist at the policy level: for example, privacy and public health, and harmonisation of legislation and accreditation in the face of disparities. As eHealth services build on the sharing of various types of health data, they raise a number of privacy concerns. Yet sharing data is essential for public health, longitudinal patient care and life science research. Therefore, it is of key importance that the policy-makers concerned grapple with the competing interests of personal privacy and population health in order to develop a policy landscape in which sharing EHRs and health data re-use can be undertaken in a trusted way, backed up by suitable safeguards. In Europe, the challenge is to encourage the harmonisation of the European Union (EU) Member States' interpretations of healthcare data privacy legislation, in order to define good practice that can facilitate trustworthy re-use of EHRs for medical and life science research (Sundgren, Wilson and deZegher, 2009). Moreover, there is a need to establish accreditation mechanisms for the stakeholders involved in eHealth services (such as data holders, service developers and service receivers) to ensure that the shared data is in compliance with the ethical, regulatory and data protection policies and requirements that can be adaptable on regional and national levels.

Technical level – At this level, evident challenges include: standardisation; transparency and openness; interoperability; understanding in face of a diversity of languages spoken/written; and the quality of data. Without agreement on general IT concepts, technical standards of EHR data (as well of life science concepts and models), platforms/interfaces, the connection to individual and isolated and disparate EHR systems will delay scalable solutions. Transparent and open source software tools that support interoperability and integration among EHRs, and among EHR entries basic research data, are needed (Curtis et al., 2012). Technical interoperability of eHealth machines and data will also help address the cost containment demands of healthcare in order to allow the various re-use opportunities mentioned earlier. This would require electronic machines to exchange and manipulate patient data. All those involved in health services must then understand and act on this information, even when operating using different languages. Another challenge from a life science perspective is to promote standards that will promote the quality of data.[4]

Collaboration level – Increased and enhanced collaboration is important for various reasons. Scalable eHealth services that can provide benefits to life science and at the same time can provide a range of tangible and far-reaching benefits for the patient, health care and the public health sector, will have the best opportunities to succeed (Goldman, 2012). This calls for new kinds of collaboration mechanisms among stakeholders (for example, the patient, the public health sector and the life sciences and IT industries). In order for this collaboration to take place, incentives are needed to ensure that actors and data can connect and that data can be used. This requires many important improvements, such as common terminologies for data (for example, EHR data and clinical research elements), an ability to interface different technical platforms and the use of agreed information models and open standards. Today it is difficult to connect pharmaceutical companies (that are conducting numerous clinical trials in very different domains) to the large number of hospitals that have heterogeneous legacy EHRs and many different clinical data warehouses. Semantic interoperability platforms must provide a formal and unambiguous representation of clinical data across domains in order to match query specifications to routinely collected clinical data. Achieving broad-based, scalable and computable semantic interoperability across multiple domains requires the integration of multiple standards that, therefore, must be mutually consistent, coherent and cross-compatible. Unfortunately, standards in this field have often been developed in parallel and are often somewhat incompatible with each other.

New business model level – Sharing and re-using EHRs for eHealth services will not happen through sheer good will. There are several issues that impede scalable EHRs' re-use services. Financial incentives, intellectual property, platform tools, data flows, governance functions and accreditation mechanisms are all important matters that need to converge in practice. These issues highlight the need for developing sustainable multi-stakeholder business models by taking into account the specific unmet needs of the various actors involved so as to deliver meaningful benefits and tangible value (Kalra et al., 2011). Business models can be seen as new units of analysis, which emphasise a system-level, holistic approach towards explaining how business is done, including the overall organisational activities and interdependencies among businesses. A business model thus describes the overall organisational architecture and processes involved in optimising value creation, capture and delivery relevant to innovative products, technologies or services and defines the manner by which an organisation delivers value to customers, entices customers to pay for value and converts those payments into sources of revenue and profit (Zott, 2010).

Conclusion

Foremost, there is a lack of a viable – and sustainable – business model for the use of EHR data in Europe. This hampers any attempt at a solution. In the case of the current situation for EHR data re-use, to use a transportation-based metaphor, supporting clinical research in Europe very much resembles a monumental traffic jam. Not only are industry and public stakeholders stuck in the jam, but also everything around them contributes to the blockage. Current EHR systems are based on a wide variety of systems that remain incompatible with each other. A few clinical services using EHRs are also driving different models of cars. The range of different road systems, vehicles and traffic administration systems across the different countries and regions in Europe only exacerbates the problem. Substantial, but solvable, privacy and legal issues concerning the use and exchange of EHR data re-use also need to be addressed.

The re-use of EHR data reflects the way the life science industry can collaborate in new ways with different partners. It also shows how medical knowledge and clinical practice resulting from information sharing can benefit several actors. The strategic area of personalised medicine offers opportunities to support innovation in the life science industry for new drug development, as well as driving new cost containment models for clinical programmes. Moreover, personalised healthcare allows society to address the difficult financial questions of who is going to pay for bringing personalised medicine into therapeutic areas, and who will then seek a return on this very large investment.

Life science and healthcare have already entered a new paradigm. Within it, the potential winners are those who can implement a strategy that strongly connects the three areas of biological/science, information management and healthcare collaboration – not in sequence, but in parallel. The outcome will allow better science with new partnerships that can bring forward selected approval of drugs through careful introduction of real-life studies with shared risks and shared benefits (Olsson, 2011). This will allow lower costs, which, in turn, results in more therapeutic opportunities.

One of the implications of personalised medicine in life science is the need to conduct smaller but more data-rich trials with the appropriate patients. Clinical studies will be conducted in closer collaboration with hospitals, in which observational studies and data from EHRs inform the pre-design of studies and the way in which they are conducted. This could, as a consequence, involve considerably fewer patients, which will help address the extremely high costs that the organisers of studies face today.

The life science industry's need for scalable and sustainable eHealth services is undisputed. The timely access to high-quality health data can be seen as pivotal for a variety of needs, ranging from the discovery of disease mechanisms, and insight into specific biological events, biomarkers or pathways of disease, to a more systematic approach to personalised medicine. The latter approach can lead to improved therapeutic methods and drug products and, ultimately, support personalised healthcare. However, progress towards scalable eHealth services is still slow.

Now the time is ripe for eHealth to not only provide value to pharmaceutical companies and the biotechnology industry, but also to bridge and connect with healthcare. Making this step would address a variety of challenges: cost pressures; consolidation as well as break-up of value chains; disruptive transitions of core underlying technologies; the growing influence of new actors outside the traditional life science sector (e.g. telecommunications, sensor industry and the citizens/patients themselves); new expectations from funders of healthcare; and a change in the governing logics of science-based innovation. This new logic, and the associated business models, will involve many more diverse players who need to collaborate in a different way. The pharmaceutical industry, the healthcare domain, academics and new actors like the IT and telecommunications industries will all be involved in this shift. The key to success is collaboration, especially in the form of public/private partnerships – a new collaborative direction that will genuinely accelerate science and science-based innovation.

Notes

1. In this context, eHealth services are defined as scalable, sustainable and cost-effective services (for example, options to connect with hospitals or trusted third partners of choice). They include not only access to large amounts of health data, EHRs, but also the necessary technical interfaces, tools and interpretation/mining capabilities to bring value to the service receiver. EHR data re-use services can include patient recruitment services or comparative effectiveness services to support the value of new therapies.

2. In medicine, a biomarker can be a traceable substance that is introduced into an organism as a means of examining organ function or other aspects of health. It can also be a substance whose detection indicates a particular disease state: for example, the presence of an antibody may indicate an infection. More specifically, a biomarker indicates a change in expression or state of a protein that correlates with the risk of a disease or the progression of a disease, or with the susceptibility of the disease to a given treatment.
3. A randomised comparative trial is a specific type of scientific experiment that represents the gold standard for a clinical trial. A randomised comparative trial is often used to test the efficacy and/or effectiveness of various types of medical intervention within a patient population. Such a trial may also provide an opportunity to gather useful information about adverse effects, such as drug reactions.
4. There are many obstacles to be overcome when using EHRs in clinical research. Fragmentation of patient records and proprietary health information technology systems that do not adhere to standards are a challenge. EHR vendors adopt few, if any, health information standards, and they very rarely accommodate controlled terminologies. It is apparent that widespread incompatibility of the many data standards currently used by the clinical research and healthcare communities continues to hinder the efficient and rapid exchange of data among different electronic sources. It also compromises the quality of clinical trial results. Additional challenges that currently limit the use of, and potential value to be derived from, health ICT solutions in Europe include the regional diversity in healthcare practices and regulations, the emergence of multiple non-interoperable hospital EHR systems and inadequate and inconsistent clinical documentation within EHRs. These limitations currently prevent the optimal use of EHR patient level data and information (Jensen et al., 2012).

References

Bunnage, M.E. (2011), "Getting pharmaceutical R&D back on target", *Nature Chemical Biology* 7 (6): 335–339.

CMR International (2012), *Pharmaceutical Fact book* 2012. ISBN: 978-0-9551411-9-5.

Curtis, L.H., Weiner, M.G., Boudreau, D.M., Cooper, W.O., Daniel, G.W., Nair, V.P., Raebel, M.A., Beaulieu, N.U., Rosofsky, R., Woodworth, T.S. and Brown, J.S. (2012), "Design considerations, architecture, and use of the Mini-Sentinel distributed data system", *Pharmacoepidemiology and Drug Safety* 21: 23–31.

DiMasi, J.A., Hansen, R.W. and Grabowski, H.G. (2003), "The price of innovation: new estimates of drug development costs", *Journal of Health Economics* 22 (2): 151–185.

DiMasi, J.A. (2002), "The value of improving the productivity of the drug development process faster times and better decisions", *Pharmacoeconomics* 20 (Suppl. 3): 1–10.

"Medicine goes digital", *The Economist*, 18 April 2009.

Geissbühler, B., Safran, C., Buchan, I., Bellazzi, R., Labkoff, S., Eilenberg, K., Leeseh, A., Richardson, C., Mantasa, J., Murray, P. and DeMoor, G. (2013), "Trustworthy reuse of health data: a transnational perspective", *International Journal of Medical Informatics* 82: 1–9A.

Goldman, M. (2012), "The innovative medicines initiative: a European response to the innovation challenge", *Clinical Pharmacology Therapeutics* 91: 418–425.

Hermosilla, I., Kouskoumvekaki, I., Shublaq, N. and López Alonso, V. (2013) Prospective analysis on Biomedical Informatics enabling personalised medicine, *INBIOMED Vision Consortium*. (Available at: http://www.inbiomedvision.eu/PDF/Prospective.pdf.)

Jensen, P.B., Jensen, L.J. and Brunak, S. (2012), "Mining electronic health records: towards better research applications and clinical care", *Nature Reviews Genetics* 13 (6): 395–405.

Kalra, D., Schmidt, A., Potts, H.W.W., Dupont D., Sundgren, M. and De Moor, G. (2011), "Case report from the EHR4CR project: a European survey on electronic health records systems for clinical research", *iHealth Connections* 1 (2): 108–113.

Lehner, J-P., Epstein, R.S. and Tehseen, S. (2012), "Integrating new approaches for clinical development: translational research and relative effectiveness", *Journal of Comparative Effect Research* 1 (1) (Suppl. 1): 15–21.

Microsoft Research (2006), *Towards Science 2020*, Cambridge, UK. (Available at http://research.microsoft.com/towards2020science.)

Olsson, M. (2011), *The Data Explosion and the Future of Health: What Every Decision-Maker in the Health and Healthcare Industries Need To Know about the Coming Revolution*, Kairos Future, Sweden. (Available at: http://www.kairosfuture.com/en/publications/dataexplosion-and-future-health.)

Paul, S.M., Mytelka, D.S., Dunwiddie, C.T., Persinger, C.T., Munos, B.H., Lindborg, S.R. and Schact, A.L. (2010), "How to improve R&D productivity: the pharmaceutical industry's grand challenge", *Nature Reviews Drug Discovery* 9(3): 203–214.

Styhre, A. and Sundgren, M. (2011), *Venturing into the Bioeconomy: Professional Ideologies, Identity and Innovation*. London, UK: Palgrave MacMillan. ISBN: 978-0-2302383-6-7.

Sundgren, M. (2011), "Connection power in the new information landscape", *European Pharmaceutical Contractor Quarterly* June: 71–73.

Sundgren, M., Wilson, P. and de Zegher, I. (2009), "Making the most of the Electronic Age", *European Pharmaceutical Contractor* (3): 18–21.

Zott, C., Amit, R. and Massa, L. (2010), *The Business Model: Theoretical Roots, Recent Developments, and Future Research*. Working Paper WP-862, IESE Business School, University of Navarra, 1–45.

19
The European Virtual Physiological Human Initiative

Vanessa Díaz-Zuccarini, Rainer Thiel and Veli Stroetmann

Introduction

The personalisation, prediction and optimisation of treatment have always been at the heart of European efforts to realise the full potential of Information and Communication Technologies (ICT) for health. This chapter reviews the success story of the European Virtual Physiological Human (VPH) initiative, which is rooted in longstanding efforts of European Union (EU) initiatives in ICT for Health. This contribution outlines the origins of the VPH initiative in a European Union context and presents the work on the Digital Patient as an example of the VPH contribution to individualised and patient-centred medicine. A roadmap towards Digital Patient is outlined, presenting a vision and a trajectory for the way in which advances in physiological modelling could greatly enhance the quality and accuracy of healthcare and lifestyle interventions, thereby improving the health of patients and the effectiveness of clinicians and clinical teams.

From information technology for healthcare to knowledge technology for health

Ideas for a more personalised approach to health research and funding have evolved since the Fifth Framework Programme for Research, Development and Demonstration (FP5, 1998–2002). In the early phase of the ICT funding for health-related projects, summarised under the "societal problems and needs" objective, the focus was placed on the main "societal needs" of three types of stakeholders: health professionals (the need to optimise the human, technical and financial resources allocated to the healthcare systems); citizens (the need to stay healthy and to protect general wellbeing); and patients (the need to receive the best possible quality of care).

This triad informed both the Fifth (FP5) and Sixth (FP6) Research Framework Programmes, which were accompanied by a set of horizontal themes: eEurope, information-ethics and legal issues, as well as common strategic tasks such as standardisation and certification.

In an outlook on FP6, delivered in Figure 19.1 (European Commission, 2004), the shift is illustrated from a focus on information technology (IT) for health-care to a knowledge technology for health focus in the ICT programme. In the words of Jean-Claude Healy, this knowledge is shared between the molecular level ("e-molecule", represented by the bio-informatics sciences), the cellular level ("e-cell", represented by the neuro-informatics sciences) and the classical medical information level ("e-individual", represented by the medical data in alphanumerical and images).

In line with this view, the discipline of biomedical informatics emerged in 2003–2004 with the aim of creating a common conceptual information space to further the discovery of novel diagnostic and therapeutic methods in the rapidly evolving arena of genomic medicine (Martin-Sanchez et al., 2004).

In the same vein, in 2005, a small group of European researchers met in Barcelona, Spain, to discuss a need that was emerging within multiple segments of applied biomedical research: namely, to better understand physiological processes in living organisms, particularly human beings. In order for such processes to be effectively explained, mechanistic hypotheses are required to explain and integrate observations made at radically different scales of both

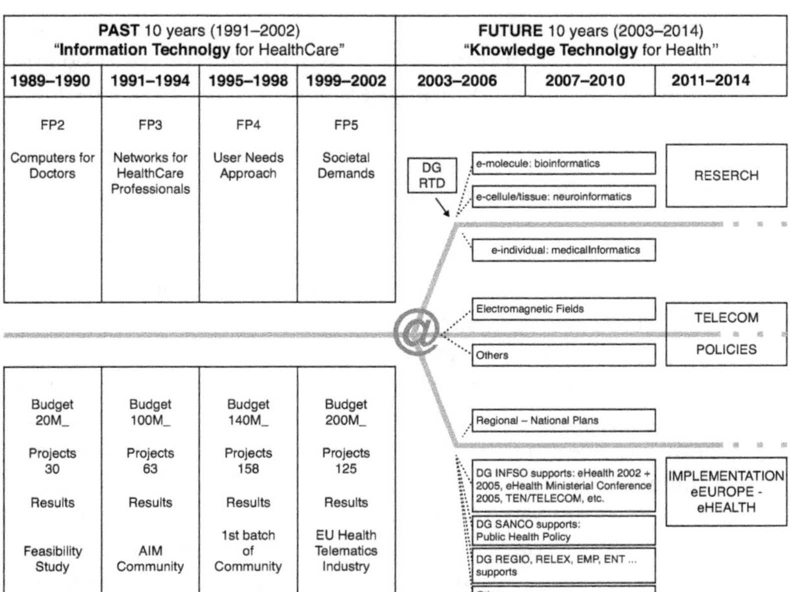

Figure 19.1 From information to knowledge technology for health

time and space, across cell to organ systems, and across the traditional sectors of biomedical knowledge (biology, physiology, medicine, biochemistry, physics and so on).

The discussion led to a consensus that the only way to cope with the underlying complexity this integrative approach required was to use computer models. Only computer models can capture the mechanistic knowledge generated at each scale and are able to combine individual models into new types of hyper or integrative simulation models.

It was first necessary to develop a framework of methods and technologies that would make it possible to investigate the human body using an integrative approach such as this. The research community called this framework the *Virtual Physiological Human* (VPH).

The VPH vision

The VPH vision, defined as "a framework of methods and technologies that, once established, will make it possible to investigate the human body as a whole" (Fenner et al., 2008), is fundamentally a multi-disciplinary development. It relies on trans-disciplinary research efforts, improved IT infrastructure, better communication, large volumes of high-quality data and tools superior to those available today.

The VPH community is relatively young; the first ideas for what is now known as the VPH projects were consolidated in a roadmap document, elaborated in the framework of the Europhysiome initiative between January 2006 and May 2007, and funded through a co-ordination action grant from the European Commission – *STEP: A Strategy for the EuroPhysiome* – which concluded in March 2007. The first European Commission-funded projects formally linked to VPH were then initiated in the summer of 2008. This roadmap was intended as the European contribution to the worldwide Physiome initiative, "an ... effort to define the physiome through the development of databases and models which will facilitate the understanding of the integrative function of cells, organs, and organisms" (Fenner et al., 2008).

By 2013, under the Seventh Framework Programme for Research, Development and Demonstration, a large number of projects received funding under the umbrella of the VPH, demonstrating a rapid development of the initiative, spanning from basic research to clinical decision support systems based on computer simulation models awaiting clinical trials. To date, 66 projects have been funded by the European Commission under the banner of the VPH. Of these, a third address the core development of the VPH: research roadmaps and networks, the IT infrastructures and specific information technology research. The remaining projects focus on one or more diseases, with the lion's share of these relating to cardiovascular disease, oncology, musculoskeletal disorders, neurology, infection and immunity.

This scientific concept has to date attracted approximately €200m of funding from the European Commission (primarily in the ICT for Health section of FP7), with additional support emerging from funding bodies within individual member states. The VPH initiative has been acknowledged worldwide as an endeavour that targets key diseases and major organ systems across many space-time scales (Interagency Modeling and Analysis Group, 2009). It has been estimated that today, in Europe alone, there are over 2,000 researchers who have selected development of the VPH as their primary research topic (Hunter et al., 2010). VPH researchers now constitute an established European and global community, working towards the systematic use of simulation models to better understand and explain life processes, including diseases and predictive models that can improve and personalise healthcare services.

Success stories: The VPH for osteoporotic patients' risk assessment

A specific visible result of how VPH research has led to a more personalised and predictive medicine is the technology developed in the *Virtual Physiological Human for Osteoporotic Patients* project (VPHOP).

A key challenge for clinicians working in the field of osteoporosis and treating patients with it has been the identification of those potential patients with a high absolute risk of fracture, and to base their treatment decisions on reliable predictors of probable impact of different prevention and treatment options. The widely applied forecast model, the World Health Organization-supported FRAX tool, is based on population data only; it demonstrates a high failure rate in correctly predicting the fracture risk of specific patients. In other words, it has a rather low sensitivity level, and misses a considerable number of patients who should have been identified to undergo therapeutic intervention in order to avoid fractures, making its specificity level also quite low. The FRAX tool also does not provide a great deal of decision support when selecting prevention and treatment options.

Furthermore, at the present time no agreed-on European or global evidence-based guidelines are available to support clinicians in their daily decision-making; there are only guidance documents available. When undertaking clinical trials in this field to test new drugs or other treatment options, the usual clinical outcome measure is whether a patient suffers a fracture, or not, within a given time period. This leads to somewhat lengthy, costly and inefficient clinical trial set-ups.

In contrast to this state of affairs, the advantage and key value proposition of the VPHOP approach is that it becomes possible to improve the general knowledge and predictive capability of decision support tools based on population observations, and to target them to the specific needs of each individual patient. This will lead towards a practical way of achieving the provision of truly personalised medicine (Box 19.1).

Box 19.1 Practical way for a truly personalised medicine

1. Every clinical decision is taken not based on knowledge about the "average" human being or a given population only, but on the specific person being treated, with his/her gender, age, phenotype, lifestyle and so on being known and integrated into the overall decision-making process. This will considerably increase the precision of the diagnosis as well as the appropriateness of the clinical treatment.
2. Initially, as the VPHOP technology starts from primarily population-based predictions, an early estimate for a specific patient can be obtained before more advanced and costly examinations are undertaken. Thus, it becomes possible to improve early selection of those patients at higher risk, to avoid unnecessary interventions for patients at low or no risk, and to arrive at more precise predictions for the higher risk patients.
3. Preventive interventions will not only be possible at an early (diagnostic) stage of the impending disease, but it can be expected that they will also lead to a high rate of success, due to the early and correct identification of citizens in need of them.
4. For those patients identified as having an immediate high absolute risk of fracture, the various treatment options available can be simulated. Thus, it will become possible to base the final decision regarding the further clinical process on highly specific, personalised evidence.

In summary, the VPHOP technology will allow for improved identification of osteoporosis patients with a considerable to high present or future risk of fracture. At the same time, it will support decision-making on both the probable success of preventive measures and on the optimal treatment path if indicated.

Defining the digital patient

A key feature of VPH research is the patient-specific simulations which are increasingly regarded as valuable tools in a number of aspects of medical practice, including surgical planning (Ballester et al., 2009) and medical intervention (Deligianni et al., 2004). The idea is that real data (usually in the form of an image) is obtained for the patient; this image can be of the whole anatomy of the patient (through 3D scanning or motion capture) or part of the patient (for example, the heart, trachea, skeleton and so on) using medical imaging technology. The data are then fed into an appropriate computer simulation program, where real-time simulations can be performed based on the image. Operations and procedures can be simulated and "practised" before the real procedure is carried out. From these simulations, predictions can be made about future events of the individual, based on the original image. Such predictions are rooted in classical physics and are typically made possible through the use of established mathematical (or mechanical) models. Patient-specific simulations are at the core of the Digital Patient vision outlined in a roadmap developed by the European Union-funded project Discipulus (as part of FP7/2007–2013, under grant agreement no. 288143, http://www.digital-patient.net/). The Digital Patient Roadmap is a Science and Technology roadmap: experts from Europe and beyond have come together, discussed and exchanged ideas of what is needed to reach a state of research and healthcare services in which the above activities are routinely carried out. The roadmap reflects the consensus opinion of over 200 key stakeholders from across Europe and the United States of America, from many different perspectives and disciplines.

The Digital Patient Roadmap follows the blueprint set out by the VPH, in that it is built around models of disease/organs/pathologies. Its approach is characterised by the term "middle-out" (Brenner et al., 2001). In debates over the best strategy for biological simulation, whether it should be "bottom-up", "top-down" or some combination of the two, the consensus is that it should be "middle-out" (Kohl and Noble, 2009), meaning that modelling starts at the level(s) at which there are rich biological data and then reaches up and down to other levels (Noble, 2002). This is the fundamental driver behind this roadmap and the path that has been followed.

While the term "personalised medicine" has been used to describe medicine based on "omics" (a field of study in biology ending in -omics, such as genomics, proteomics or metabolomics, and usually referring to the characterisation and quantification of pools of biological molecules), there is a more encompassing view emerging: personalised medicine must address the challenge by taking a holistic view. There is clearly a need to integrate information at the gene scale within a wider context (Baker, 2013), and this is the approach that has been advocated in the Digital Patient Roadmap. This "integrative aspect" is highlighted as the fundamental element of systems medicine (Regierer et al., 2013), where molecular data (especially genomic information) is integrated with anatomical, physiological, environmental and lifestyle data in a predictive model approach, in order to produce "virtual patients".

The Digital Patient will make it possible to create, for each citizen, a computer representation of his or her health status that is descriptive and interpretive, integrative and predictive.

- *Descriptive* – providing unified access to all information about the patient's health determinants, including those related to lifestyle, such as physical activity; and interpretive – helping to gain new understanding.
- *Integrative* – automatically combining all the available information so as to provide better decision support based on a large volume of information.
- *Predictive* – the integrated information is used to inform individualised simulations able to predict how specific aspects of a subject's health will develop over time, as a function of different interventions.

Digital Patient technologies provide individualised (person-specific) future projections, systemic predictions based on mechanistic understanding of the disease process in an integrative and holistic way. It is envisaged that all medical professionals (nurses, general practitioners, hospital specialists and so on) will be able to access Digital Patient technologies for prevention, diagnosis, prognosis, treatment planning, monitoring and rehabilitation purposes.

The Digital Patient provides clinicians (and patients) with highly visual and integrated views of relevant health and wellness information relating to the patient. These integrated views are combined with predictive models and simulations to provide projections of future possible health status, the course of illness and the outcomes of healthcare interventions. The Digital Patient technological framework includes VPH models, decision support tools and patient data records and, once fully developed and deployed, will make it possible to create for each citizen a descriptive, integrative, exploratory in-silico representation of his or her present health status as well as a predictive representation of potential future states, based on causal simulation models.

The complex territory of biomedical and technological research can be charted in the following dimensions:

- *Technological challenges*: the Digital Patient is a multi-disciplinary, multi-technological initiative, but each technological aspect must be discussed within a specialised context so as to ensure excellence;
- *Maturity levels*: the Digital Patient is a long-term vision, but we should be able to target short-, medium- and long-term goals, so as to ensure a progressive impact;
- *Exemplary clinical challenges*: we need concrete clinical problems around which the technological discussion can evolve, so as to ensure proper clinical rooting and engagement of clinical and industrial stakeholders.

Four maturity levels were identified for Digital Patient technologies as illustrated in Figure 19.2. Maturity levels indicate a measure of "what is achievable now" and "what will be achievable in the future", or, more simply, the different "ages" of the Digital Patient.

Once the Digital Patient technologies are fully deployed, every hospital in Europe will generate a volume of integrated clinical data about real individuals, on a daily basis. This "one million Digital Patients" database could subsequently be used for what-if simulations to inform public health decisions. The goal here is the *ePublic Health* (potentially the 4th maturity level), where policy decisions can be made on the basis of reliable computer simulations of the different scenarios.

In sum, a Digital Patient is a technological platform, which enables interactive health analytics (ICT support for the exploration and the understanding

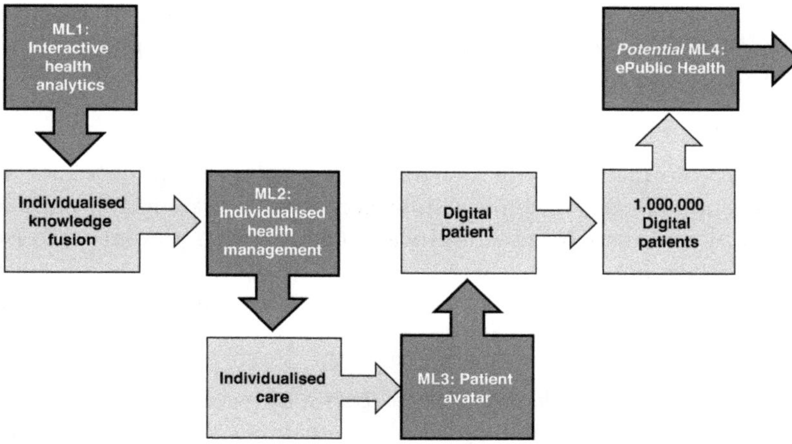

Figure 19.2 Digital Patient maturity levels

of a patient's health status from a large amount of digital data) together with individualised health management (individualisation of prevention, diagnosis and treatment). The platform, furthermore, allows personal health forecasting through a citizen-centric health management. ICT provides each of us with predictions of how our daily choices will impact our health and wellbeing.

The scientific and technological challenges

There are a number of major scientific and technological challenges on the path to clinical translation and adoption of the Digital Patient, as summarised here.

Generation of data for model construction, validation and application

The realisation of the Digital Patient vision is heavily dependent on the availability of large amounts of data for a range of purposes. These purposes can be ascribed to three categories: building models (gathering and structuring information to identify interactions and translating them into numerics); validating models (comparing the models against some "ground truth" to try and falsify/corroborate them); and populating models with patient-specific information (deploying and validating models in a clinical context).

On the one hand, in many cases of VPH research the stumbling block is not the modelling method but the lack of information with sufficient quality, extent and resolution to inform the model properly with quantitative data. On the other hand, the theoretical structure underlying both the creation and application of the Digital Patient provides arguably one of the strongest settings for generating maximal information out of biomedical data, irrespective of whether these data are sampled for specific research and development purposes or for primary and secondary healthcare purposes.

Biomedical information management

Biomedical information forms the basis for good scientific decisions, wise management and use of resources, informed decision-making and ultimately high-quality and cost-effective healthcare practice (from prevention to treatment and follow-up).

The most challenging facets of biomedical information management include:

- *The collection and the sharing of data*: tools and incentives are required to facilitate and encourage individual groups, teams or consortia to share their data with the rest of the scientific and medical community (while full compliance with legal and data protection requirements is guaranteed);
- *The standardisation of data collection and the question of ontology*: tools and frameworks have to be established and developed to align existing ontologies, and incentives have to be identified to cultivate a concept of unified ontology;
- *Dimensionality reduction*: methodologies have to be improved to deal efficiently with the heterogeneity and the complex structure of available data, and with differences in origin, quality and ontologies.

Mathematical modelling for the Digital Patient

The Digital Patient relies on the power of predictive modelling. In fact, it can be argued that modelling is at the core, and is the most fundamental element, of the Digital Patient, as it is able to seize observations, data and explanations to formulate them and/or capture them in a mathematical and numerical form, in order to achieve the goal of explanatory/predictive medicine. It is the extraordinary and compelling power of multi-scale predictive models that will help achieve the goals of the Digital Patient.

Ideally, we would have a full understanding of all biological processes in both health and disease, as well as of the relationships between structure and function on all scales, and this complete knowledge would be represented in a practical and useful manner, in a collection of inter-compatible mathematical models at all relevant scales. With this resource, it would be possible to simulate diseases and pathologies and to explore patient-specific therapeutic intervention strategies, including evolution over time and realistic evaluation of prognosis. In reality, our understanding at all scales is only partial. Nonetheless, current knowledge of anatomy and physiology is extensive on many levels and much of it has already been successfully represented in mathematical models, and relevant data is abundant, despite being incomplete and despite the many issues of standardisation, accessibility and interoperability.

There are two major modelling categories that represent two points in a large spectrum of mathematical models used in the Digital Patient research context (Box 19.2).

Box 19.2 Two major modelling categories for the Digital Patient

Phenomenological models are, on the one hand, *related to the empirical observations of a phenomenon*, where a phenomenon is understood as an observable fact or event. When considering how to achieve the realisation of the Digital Patient, these models occupy a central position whenever a quick means is needed to represent pathologies quantitatively for both basic science and practical applications.

Mechanistic models, on the other hand, aim at reaching a better understanding of the mechanisms that underlie the behaviour of the various endpoints of the biomedical process. Mechanistic models often investigate the molecular and cellular basis of biomedical processes through their physico-chemical properties. They are able to consider events at different orders of magnitude for both spatial scales (from intracellular to cell, tissue and organ) and time scales (from the 10^{-14} s of the molecular interactions to the hours, months and years of the biomedical processes).

To realise the Digital Patient, an initial scientific challenge that needs to be addressed is the selection of the most adequate mathematical modelling approach. In a broad sense, the choice might be between phenomenological and mechanistic mathematical models, but a recurrent topic when modelling any disease is the strong link and dependency between these two modelling approaches. Even though mechanistic models are complex in nature, some have already entered the clinical arena in the form of software applications embedded in diagnostic or therapeutic devices.

Clinical user interface

Currently working prototypes are available and allow the 3D exploration of large amounts of information on human anatomy, physiology and pathology, referred to an average subject in a fixed point of time (generic and static).

Designing clinical user interfaces for a framework that is intended for clinicians and clinical researchers comes with a number of challenges, including:

- The diversity of professionals likely to interact with the system;
- The constraints imposed by the ICT systems and the clinical and data workflows with which the Digital Patient framework needs to be compatible. Simulations in particular are very time consuming and limitations associated with computational power impose restrictions on the achievable resolution and accuracy;

- The numerous functionalities that the framework needs to offer. These include the access and retrieval of heterogeneous information from individual or populations of patients, body-centric and multi-scale visualisation of raw data and of simulated results, multi-scale and multi-physics simulation and modelling tools, visually assisted data analysis and post-processing tools for the extraction of clinically meaningful information and for treatment planning, clinical decision support, intervention support and so on.

As a general feature, any Digital Patient interface should allow access to the medical history of individual patients, to all the risk factors associated with the development of major diseases, and to all available data likely to serve the user's needs.

Translation and adoption

The area of translation requires the development or the adaptation of formal processes for verification, sensitivity analysis, validation (including clinical trials), risk-benefit and cost-benefit analyses, ultimately leading to product certification.

The feedback received from stakeholders (especially clinicians and patient representatives) suggests that the historic focus of VPH research on secondary care specialist decisions is only one of the possible opportunities. Considerable interest has been identified in supporting patients with lifestyle and self-management simulations and predictions, and guiding generalists on how to manage complex care in the community, and when to escalate treatment to specialists.

To allow for a better assessment of alternative exploration strategies and decision support when investing in Digital Patient applications, policy-makers, health system managers and clinicians need better data on the impact of the new technology and the respective "business" case. This requires the development of novel health technology assessment methodologies, cost-benefit approaches and exploration planning tools adapted for Digital Patient solutions. The rapid diffusion of Digital Patient solutions will call for their clinical assessment and economic evaluation against the current standard of care in realistic scenarios and routine application contexts.

To date there is little experience of real-life application of VPH models at the clinical coalface to support patient care decisions on any significant scale. As model formulations are now reaching maturity, there is an urgent need for clinical studies to validate the safety and relevance of the models in the context of real life care decisions. Such clinical trials are mandatory in order to give assurance to the clinical professions and to health services that these simulations and projections can be used in a trustworthy way.

The upcoming EU Horizon 2020 Framework Programme for Research and Innovation (Horizon, 2020) foresees as one of its core objectives to further the health and wellbeing of European citizens. The Digital Patient framework of methods and technologies as described earlier shows that the management of many human health issues can be greatly improved by the application of accurate predictive models. There have been great advances in modelling of physiological processes in recent years, as the various VPH initiatives show. One major step in capitalising on these advances will be to incorporate these models in a systematic way into the clinical decision-making process.

The Digital Patient will allow patients and clinicians to become more pro-active in instituting lifestyle modifications and clinical surveillance for the prevention of diseases, by providing tools for health prediction and simulation. The Digital Patient initiative aims to individualise the clinical decision-making process. It will promote discussion on how to migrate from population-based prediction towards truly personalised medicine, which will emphasise the acquisition, integration, processing and application of patient-specific information.

Future directions for the vision of personalised and predictive healthcare

The VPH initiative is focused on scientific challenges that cross the boundaries of many disciplines. It has already successfully translated concepts or methods that were originally developed in discrete branches of knowledge (such as engineering, mathematics and physics) into medicine. Ultimately, this will benefit the greater understanding of health and disease. In order to speed up the adoption of VPH technologies, it will, in the future, be necessary to conduct more clinically focused research.

At this juncture, it is also important to mention that some of these technologies are not mature for clinical translation *just yet.* It is first necessary to fully understand, develop and harness fundamental technological and biomedical problems. Joint developments in both clinical and computational research are of outmost importance to properly refine and validate the VPH tools that will shape the future of *in-silico* medicine.

The VPH community is convinced that, within modern healthcare, quality of care is intimately and firmly facilitated by and linked to technological progress. The inter-disciplinary co-operation of physicians, engineers, biologists, clinical professionals and other scientists has opened up new possibilities in medical diagnosis and treatment, as well as disease prevention and rehabilitation.

The Digital Patient concept presents an innovative domain for research and development efforts, offering significant clinical and commercial potential. It can play a key role within European Union innovation policy as it is aligned with all of its three main priorities – excellent science, industrial leadership and societal challenges (European Commission, 2011). In line with the core objectives of the Horizon 2020 societal challenge of "health, demographic change and wellbeing", the Digital Patient initiative enquires into novel applications fostering our understanding of lifestyle factor interactions with disease management, and advancing the developments of disease and decision support systems based on predictive computer modelling. The innovation thrust of Digital Patient technologies and VPH-related research will enhance our understanding of topics that are central to the main European Union societal challenges. To mention only a few:

- The determinants, risk factors and pathways of health, ageing and disease;
- Decision support systems based on predictive computer modelling used by the patient him- or herself, citizen engagement, mHealth and patient empowerment supported by ICT to promote self-management of health and disease;
- How to improve health information, data exploitation and the evidence base for health policies and regulation through a digital representation of health data, for improving disease diagnosis and treatment;
- Understanding diseases through systems medicine and systems biology;
- Advancing ICT systems and services for Integrated Care.

Depending on the respective technology readiness level, the Digital Patient initiative and its community of VPH researchers can realise the vision of personalised and predictive healthcare by: allowing for novel tools to facilitate individualised knowledge fusion, in other words interactive health analytics; providing for improved clinical applications fully supporting individualised care; and developing novel, advanced modes of visualisation of medical conditions and implementation of Digital Patient solutions for both clinicians and patients.

In the light of current challenges facing European healthcare systems, in particular the pressure of multi-morbidity, demographic change and spiralling costs, it is crucially important that the potential of technological innovation for the benefit of the individual patient is fully utilised and exploited.

Acknowledgements and disclaimer

This chapter is based on work performed by the EU funded FP7 project Discipulus [Grant Number 288143]. The Digital Patient Roadmap was drafted by key experts in consultation with the wider community; this support is gratefully acknowledged.

References

Baker, M. (2013), "Big Biology – the 'omes Puzzle", *Nature* 494 (7438): 416–419.

Ballester, M.A.G., del Palomar, A.P., Villalobos, J.L.L., Rodriguez, L.L., Trabelsi, O., Pérez, F., Canamaque, A.G., Cortés, E.B., Panadero, F.R., Castellano, M.D. and Jover, J.H. (2009), "Surgical planning and patient-specific biomechanical simulation for tracheal endoprostheses interventions", in Yang, G. Z., Hawkes, D. J., Rueckert, D., Noble, J.A. and Taylor, C.J. (eds) *Medical Image Computing and Computer-Assisted Intervention, MICCAI 2009*, London, UK: Springer, pp. 275–282.

Brenner, S., Noble, D., Sejnowski, T., Fields, R.D., Laughlin, S., Berridge, M., Segel, L., Prank, K. and Dolmetsch, R.E. (2001), "Understanding complex systems: top-down, bottom-up or middle-out?", in Bock, G.R. and Goode, J.A. (eds) *Complexity in Biological Information Processing*, John Wiley & Sons, pp. 155–159.

Deligianni, F., Chung, A. and Yang, G.Z. (2004), "Patient-specific bronchoscope simulation with pq-space-based 2D/3D registration", *Computer Aided Surgery* 9(5): 215–226.

Diaz, V., Viceconti, M., Kalra, D. and Stroetmann, V. (2013), DISCIPULUS – Digital Patient Roadmap, London.

European Commission (2004), Applications relating to health, fifth research and development framework programme 1998–2002, Information Society Directorate-General, Unit B1 – Applications relating to Health, Luxemburg.

European Commission (2011), Horizon 2020 –The Framework Programme for Research and Innovation, Brussels.

Fenner, J.W., Brook, B., Clapworthy, G., Coveney, P.V., Feipel, V., Gregersen, H., Hose, D.R., Kohl, P., Lawford, P., McCormack, K.M., Pinney, D., Thomas, S.R., Van Sint Jan, S., Waters, S. and Viceconti, M. (2008), "The EuroPhysiome, STEP and a roadmap for the virtual physiological human", *Philosophical Transactions of the Royal Society of London. Series A: Mathematical Physical and Engineering Sciences* 366 (1878): 2979–2799.

Hunter, P., Coveney, P., de Bono, B., Diaz, V., Fenner, J., Frangi, A.F., Harris, P., Hose, R., Kohl, P., Lawford, P., McCormack, K., Mendes, M., Omholt, S., Quarteroni, A., Skår, J., Tegner, J., Randall, T., Tollis, I., Tsamardinos, I., van Beek, J.H. and Viceconti, M. (2010), "A vision and strategy for the virtual physiological human in 2010 and beyond", *Philosophical Transactions of the Royal Society of London. Series A: Mathematical Physical and Engineering Sciences* 368 (1920): 2595–2614.

Interagency Modeling and Analysis Group (2009), The Impact of Modeling on Biomedical Research, http://www.vph-institute.org/upload/imag-futures-report_519244d3a0aa0.pdf.

Kohl, P. and Noble, D. (2009), "Systems biology and the virtual physiological human", *Molecular Systems Biology*, 5 (292).

Martin-Sanchez, F., Iakovidis, I., Nørager, S., Maojo, V., de Groen, P. and Van der Lei, J. (2004), "Synergy between medical informatics and bioinformatics: facilitating genomic medicine for future health care", *Journal of Biomedical Informatics* 37 (1): 30–42.

Noble, D. (2002), "Modeling the heart from genes to cells to the whole organ", *Science*, 295 (5560): 1678–1682.

Regierer, B., Zazzu, V., Sudbrak, R., Kühn, A. and Lehrach, H. (2013), "Future of medicine: models in predictive diagnostics and personalized medicine", in Seitz, H. and Schumacher, S. (eds) *Molecular Diagnostics* Berlin Heidelberg: Springer-Verlag, pp. 15–33.

20 Making the Economic Case for eHealth

Tom Jones

Introduction

Until around 2004, eHealth evaluations were limited in dealing with economic and financial aspects. Few included cost data, and those that did often relied on absolute numbers at points in time, not on the changing position over time. In 2002, the European Commission authorised an eHealth Impact (eHI) study (www.ehealth-impact.org). Since then, almost 60 economic evaluations on both good and weak economic performance have used this eHI methodology. Aggregated data from several eHealth evaluations now show the gap between good and weak eHealth, with this difference providing meaningful data on eHealth risks that are crucial for taking realistic decisions and planning mitigation strategies. The core concept underpinning the eHI methodology is socio-economic return (SER). This information now informs decisions on eHealth investment across many countries and continents. The reality is that eHealth is not an investment to save money; it is an investment in quality, access and efficiency. Awareness of the value of the socio-economic benefits of eHealth is slowly expanding, both as information for investment decision-making and as a tool for monitoring and evaluation.

Overview of eHealth economic evaluation

How Things Work is a popular children's book by Conrad Mason that describes how everyday devices work for people's benefit so that they can understand and appreciate them better. There are several reasons eHealth is not core content. One is that – as eHealth decision-makers moved into the 21st century – they only knew how bits of eHealth worked as an economic activity (Whitten et al., 2002); only 9 per cent of economic evaluations included cost and benefit data. Now that we are well into the second decade of this century, we know much more about economic evaluation. Perhaps future editions of the Mason book will indeed include eHealth?

Up until about 2004, eHealth evaluations tended to deal with a limited number of aspects, such as the numbers of users and some of the benefits and technical effects of information and telecommunications technology (ICT). Two aspects were missing in these very limited details about costs. The first was the cost of organisational changes to clinical and working practices, which is a considerable part of the total costs of an eHealth project (Dobrev et al., 2010); the second involved timescales that show how the economic and financial performance of eHealth differs at various points over time. A simple example is an eHealth project where benefits continue to accumulate as the number of users increases over time, but with costs that also increase over time as ICT capacity and capabilities expand and become obsolete.

Not all economic evaluations include these two aspects of organisational change and timescales, nor do they link estimated economic performance, or value for money, to affordability and financing. In all investment decisions, it is therefore crucial to optimise the relationship between value for money and affordability – a high-performance sports car, for example, may offer value for money, but few of us can afford one.

This approach to eHealth evaluation provides two main perspectives and comprises the economic case for eHealth: first, by identifying and estimating costs and benefits over time for all major stakeholders, and second, in providing an organisational model of healthcare stakeholders, resources and delivery that includes changes to clinical and other working practices over time. Put in a simpler way, it shows how things work both before and after the introduction of eHealth. Where these two views combine to provide a sound economic case for a planned eHealth initiative, they indicate an estimated positive net benefit over time. Conversely, an unsound case shows a low or negative return that looks much worse when adjusted for risk. The organisational aspect of the model helps to explain the result, and to understand hidden costs.

This combined view relies on the definition of eHealth as being ICT plus organisational change. The ICT component tends to operate directly at the point of care where patients and healthcare professionals meet, so consequently eHealth affects many stakeholders. Cost benefit analysis (CBA) offers an appropriate technique for identifying and valuing the positive or adverse effects on these stakeholders. Change is essential to realise benefits. However, change is always challenging – it needs resources, time and a viable change management strategy that all stakeholders who are affected can support.

A proven CBA model is the United Kingdom (UK) Treasury's Green Book (HM Treasury, 2011), a socio-economic methodology that provided the foundation of the eHealth Impact methodology of the European Commission's eHealth Impact study that reported in 2006 (Stroetmann et al., 2006). eHI is a methodology for eHealth evaluations, each one of which has its own custom-made socio-economic model. These eHI models reflect each eHealth initiative's specific, different characteristics and healthcare settings. Indeed, vaccination, telemedicine, order entry, ePrescribing and electronic patient records may all take place in different contexts even while present in the same health system. In the same way, similar eHealth initiatives can have different contexts created by their different health systems. Thus, a standard methodology together with bespoke eHI models, are both requirements of good economic cases.

The UK's Green Book separates the economic case – often called value for money – from the financial case, sometimes referred to as affordability. This is a distinction that Irving Fisher, an economist in the early 20th century, identified in his separation theorem (Fisher, 1930). A simple view is that an investment decision is independent of the preferences of the owner – in eHealth, often a healthcare provider organisation or Ministry of Health – and of financing options and decisions, a concept that is core to eHealth economic cases. Many healthcare organisations consider the financial perspective to be paramount, but economic cases of successful eHealth show that it is seldom a quick fix and rarely generates net cash savings (Dobrev et al., 2010). Instead, eHealth is an investment in better healthcare over time, offering better value for money in the long run. Adopting eHealth to save more cash than invested, especially in the short term, is a poor decision.

In 2006, the European Commission's 2006 study (Stroetmann et al., 2006) used the eHI methodology to provide measures of economic performance of ten eHealth initiatives already judged as successful. Several valuable features of the results of the study are:

- The more complex the eHealth, the longer it takes to reach a net benefit.
- When net benefits start to emerge, they rise and accumulate rapidly in successful eHealth initiatives.
- Healthcare professionals need to be engaged in the changes from the outset.
- Effective leadership is essential.
- Net cash savings over time are not the norm.

Since 2006, the eHI methodology has been developed further. Its use has expanded beyond the European Commission's requirements, with almost 60 eHealth evaluations now using eHI in 20 countries across three continents. Some 84 per cent of the evaluations show positive results, with negative results appearing in 16 per cent of the cases. Taken together, these results provide the knowledge and insights needed for rigorous evaluations of new, proposed eHealth initiatives.

Not all economic cases need a full CBA or use the eHI model. Some clinical eHealth initiatives can change the use of healthcare resources significantly, such as fewer hospital admissions and shorter lengths of stay. For these, a more manageable cost-effectiveness analysis is sufficient to demonstrate the economic case: thus, the eHI methodology provides this as a subset.

The content of eHealth economic cases is explained in Box 20.1. The differences between economic and financial cases are explained in the next section of the chapter.

Box 20.1 Content of eHealth economic cases

The content of eHealth economic cases extends across stakeholders, timescales, costs and benefits components.

Stakeholders: These include citizens, patients and carers; healthcare professionals and other health and care workers; healthcare provider organisations, such as hospitals and primary care centres; and third party payers.

Timescales: For smaller-scale eHealth, such as telemedicine and specific clinical information, a timeline of up to seven years is usually suitable, but when considering larger-scale eHealth, such as electronic patient records (EPRs), approximately ten years are necessary. In addition, timescales must include two main phases, the development and implementation phase, with extra costs for the engagement and development, as well as the phase following implementation, where benefits are expected to be generated. As a generality, for larger-scale eHealth, such as EPRs, diminishing returns set in after about 15 years. This provides a guide to the life cycle of these initiatives and the maximum timescale for realising and optimising net benefits.

Costs: The three main types of costs are resources needing extra finance, costs generated by the redeployment of resources, and intangible costs, where there is no market price. The extra and redeployed costs include: ICT of all types; procurement; post-procurement services; time of healthcare workers allocated from existing budgets for engagement, planning and development, as well as for training, implementation and change; trainers; obsolescence; and changing clinical and working practices.

Benefits: The three main types of benefit are quality, access and efficiency. Quality benefits include better-informed patients, patient-centred healthcare and healthcare that is safer, more effective, timely and consistent. The quality definition is broadly similar to the United States (US) Institute of Medicine quality initiatives (Institute of Medicine, 2001). Access is for citizens who are not yet patients and who were, or will be, unable to take up healthcare. Finally, efficiency (OECD, 2010) consists of cash savings, improved productivity and better resource utilisation. Similar to costs, there are benefits that need extra finance, some circumstances where existing finance and resources become available for redeployment, and intangibles, where there is no market price for the benefits. All values for costs and benefits are at constant prices in each valuation, excluding the estimates of the cost of general inflation, and showing real cost and benefit changes over time. This requires that all the estimates of monetary values for each year need adjusting to a common present value by using discounted cash flow, thus converting all the estimated costs and benefits to present values in order to adjust for the differences in the value of money over time.

How an economic case differs from a financial case

It is clear that there is a need for both an economic and a financial case. Pursuing unaffordable value for money is not a sustainable position, so both aspects of an evaluation help decision-makers to address the following key question: What is the maximum value for money that is affordable over time? An economic case measures value for money, with the net benefit over time for all stakeholders as the core measurement. The eHI model calls this the socio-economic return (SER) to distinguish it from return on investment (ROI), which tends to measure an impact on one entity, usually the entity paying for the eHealth initiative.

Affordability draws much of its data from the economic case, but also includes items excluded from an economic case. Value added tax (VAT) is a transfer payment, so it is not part of an economic case; where it is not recoverable it is a financial cost, so it does need adding to the affordability estimate. Depreciation of equipment, if it is applied, is another example of an accounting cost that needs to be included in the financial but not the economic case. This results in a total affordability requirement that complies with an entity's financial and accounting regime. Both economic and financial cases need adjusting for risk.

The economic and financial cases share much of the same data. Investing more to improve value for money can impair the affordability position. Improving the affordability requirement can reduce the resources needed for a satisfactory value for money goal – this is the essential search for an optimal, demanding solution.

A critical feature of the financial case is that its timescale must match that of the economic case, in order to ensure that the affordability and financing models extend into sustainable benefits realisation. It is a common error to finance the implementation costs of eHealth for too short a timescale without financing benefits realisation fully. This short-term perspective results in the need for additional finance coming as a surprise, or not being available when the requirement is predictable.

What is important for a net benefit?

Net benefits derive mainly by using eHealth to improve healthcare quality and efficiency, with many components combining to realise a net benefit for an eHealth initiative, as listed in Box 20.2.

Box 20.2 Components needed for a net benefit

- Clinical, executive and political leadership;
- Continuous engagement with healthcare professions and other stakeholders;
- Meeting users' information needs;

- Making working life better for healthcare professionals;
- Usability, often referred to as user-friendly applications, software and hardware;
- Functionality, the range of operations in a computer system;
- Achieving the critical mass of utilisation by users, not just the number of users, but also the extent to which they use a new eHealth initiative;
- Rapid take-up of utilisation from the time that a new information system is operational;
- Information architecture that sets the design and structure of information shared by several users;
- Interoperability, so that separate information systems can exchange information and work together efficiently and effectively;
- Making the changes needed to realise the quality gains redeploying existing resources liberated by eHealth;
- Change management;
- New skills needed to use and share the information, achieve change and deal with complex activities such as information architecture and interoperability;
- Rapid take-off for benefits realisation;
- Sharing information among healthcare professionals;
- Giving up replaced systems, such as paper medical records, as soon as possible;
- Sustainable finance for benefits realisation;
- Mitigating risks;
- Effective procurement;
- Controlling costs.

It is not enough for the components from Box 20.2 merely to be present in an economic case; they must be resourced, sustained and effective. Negative eHealth economic cases show negative net benefits over time, largely due to certain essential features being missing.

Some of these features are not directly consistent with modern methods, such as agile project management, which suppliers prefer. For example, iterating users' information needs may not offer the same levels of completeness and usability as a conventional needs statement.

There are two main measures of net benefit: one is the first year that the annual benefits exceed the annual costs, and the other is the first year that the cumulative benefits exceed the cumulative costs. The cumulative net benefit provides the SER, and the annual profile shows how the relationship between costs and benefits changes over time.

Several other techniques combine to build a complete eHI model for an economic case, including estimating. Estimations are crucial because much of the data in healthcare organisations' information systems are for financial and performance control; the knowledge from retrospective eHI evaluations provides a valuable source of estimation and assumptions. Optimism bias is a common feature of estimating. The effect is understating costs and timescales and overstating benefits, so rigorous reviews of estimates and assumptions are essential in order to limit any bias. This is often challenging when healthcare organisations are seeking unfounded, unrealistic financial gains from eHealth.

Intangible costs and benefits do not have market prices, and although the willingness to pay technique helps to provide monetary values for these, its use must be controlled and monitored.

Risks (Hopkin, 2010) are a large cost item for economic cases for planned eHealth. They require two parallel economic cases, one without risk, and one adjusted for the estimated cost of risk. At a superficial level, cost and time overruns are major risks, but these are manifestations of numerous specific risks, examples of which can be found in the list in Box 20.3.

Box 20.3 Examples of risks

- Unexpected difficulties with engagement;
- Utilisation which undershoots the required critical mass;
- Software that has limited usability;
- Key people with specialist but scarce skills who leave the project part way through;
- Inadequate hardware specifications;
- Hardware capacity which is insufficient for peak utilization;
- New technologies that result in unplanned increased costs;
- Training that is not effective enough;
- Suppliers who fail to perform as required, and so need replacing, and suppliers who are dissatisfied with their clients' performance, and so withdraw from the contract.

This list is by no means exhaustive, and it is not impossible for these factors to conspire to damage the planned economic performance of an eHealth project. Each identified risk has two components, its maximum estimated cost and its probability of materialising, which taken together provide a measure of risk exposure. There are very few data available on the probability for eHealth economic cases, and the section of this chapter on "Risk and Mitigation" provides the overall annual check values.

An example of an economic case

The European Commission requested evaluations of successful interoperable electronic health records (EHR) (www.ehr-impact.eu), later referred to simply as the EHR impact study. The resulting study outcomes (Dobrev et al., 2010) identified a substantial difference between the positive SER for all stakeholders and the narrow ROI for the cash position. Accomplishing a positive SER needs large injections of cash in most cases. There are a few exceptions in special circumstances, such as a significant reduction in drug stocks during the evaluation period.

In Spain, Andalucía's Health Ministry EHR initiative, called Diraya, was one case examined by the European Commission study (Dobrev et al., 2010). At the time, Diraya was used across healthcare provided by pharmacists, general practitioners, outpatients and accident and emergency departments. It is now linking to inpatient services.

Figures 20.1 and 20.2 show the annual and cumulative socio-economic evaluations, as well as the long timescale for planning, development and engagement up to implementation; and the steep build-up of benefits to exceed costs over short timescales.

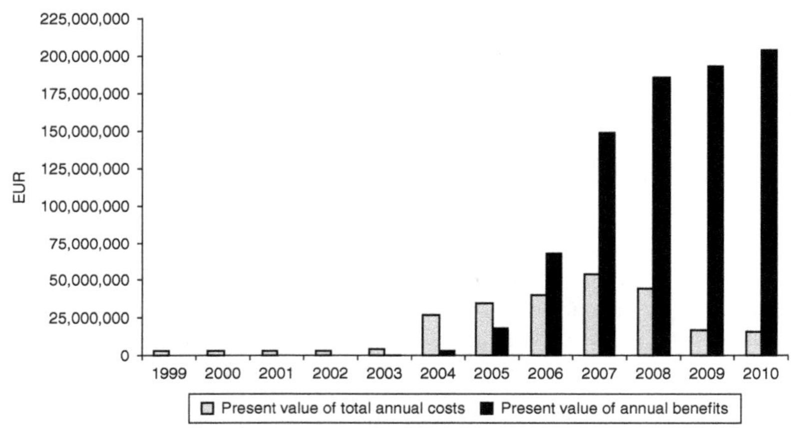

Figure 20.1 Annual estimated costs and benefits

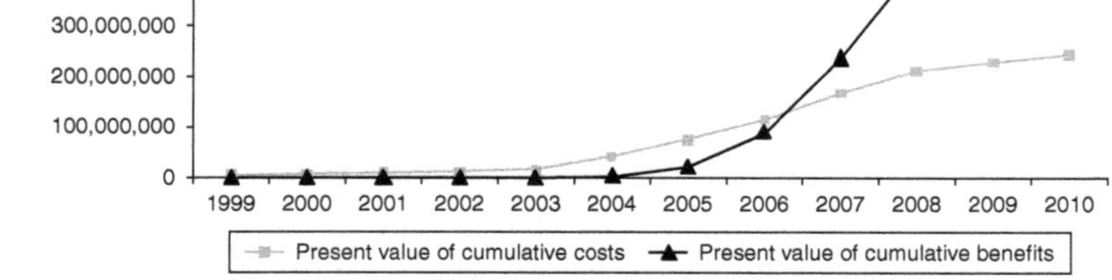

Figure 20.2 Cumulative estimated costs and benefits

Figure 20.1 shows the annual costs and benefits over time and the clear investment that needs to be made during the implementation period. It also shows an important success criterion, which is that benefits realisation begins during implementation and not when implementation is complete – in other words, these two activities are parallel, not sequential (Figure 20.2).

Figure 20.2 shows that the cumulative costs begin to level off after about 10 to 12 years whereas the benefits rise over time. Diminishing returns have not yet set in over such a 12-year timescale, but they do occur not much further into the future.

Diraya's cash position is typical of the EHR impact evaluation findings: about 61 per cent of Diraya's total economic cost needed extra cash as finance, with some 18 per cent of the benefits yielding extra cash.

What a combined view shows

The result of the EHR impact study (Dobrev et al., 2010), which undertook nine evaluations, is illustrated in Table 20.1.

Essential features of these findings for complex eHealth initiatives point to a number of findings: a long timescale for EHRs and ePrescribing for cumulative net benefits; more than half the costs are for change and less than half for ICT; and that EHRs need considerable, sustained financing.

A review (USA Congressional Budget Office, 2008) supports this need for finance. It found that studies significantly overstate savings for the healthcare system, by tending to identify potential savings rather than likely savings.

TinTree International eHealth's (Jones, 2012) database has findings from almost 60 studies, and Figure 20.3 shows the net SER from some of these. Whereas a good SER curve begins to rise towards positive as shown in the good eHealth curve in Figure 20.3, the curve for weak eHealth initiatives is stuck in negative for several years: it eventually slips into positive as shown in the far right-hand side of the curve in Figure 20.3. It cannot reach the same scale as successful initiatives.

Table 20.1 EHR Impact Study for nine evaluations

	Minimum	Maximum	Mean
Years to first annual net benefit	4	9	7
Years to first cumulative net benefit	6	11	9
Cumulative socio-economic return	–0.2	1.92	0.78
ICT costs as share of total	14%	68%	42%
Change costs as share of total	32%	86%	58%
Costs needing extra finance	21%	83%	49%
Benefits creating extra finance	0%	58%	13%

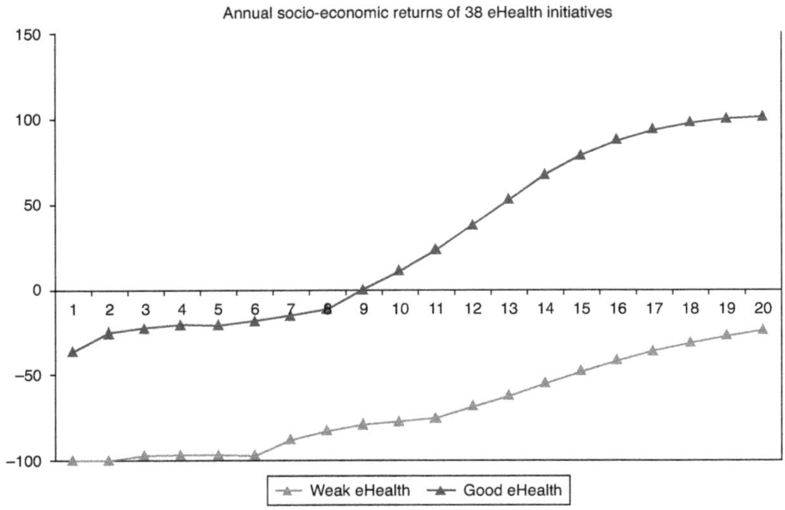

Figure 20.3 Net socio-economic returns of good and weak eHealth initiatives

Weak eHealth is mainly EHRs, and includes telemedicine that have suffered the high risks of eHealth and not realised sufficient net benefits, if any. Good eHealth is a wide range of eHealth initiatives, including EHRs, and smaller-scale eHealth initiatives such as telemedicine and vaccination. Smaller-scale eHealth shows a positive SER on a much shorter timescale than complex EHRs. Compared to the European Commission studies, the TinTree data extend its observations to a 20-year timescale to identify the estimated effect of diminishing returns.

These trends contain two correlations that show the difference between good and weak eHealth. The correlation between net benefits and costs is about +0.9, whereas for weak eHealth it is about −0.9. Although the ranges are different, measures reveal the different constructions of good and weak eHealth. The challenge is to achieve a positive correlation of net benefits and costs.

Another example of an economic evaluation is England's "Whole System Demonstrator" (Henderson et al., 2013). The importance of this economic evaluation is that it is one the few that includes data from randomised clinical trials to support estimates of benefits. The results suggest that the benefits for people using telehealth and standard support and treatment were similar to those obtained from receiving conventional care, and the total costs for the telehealth group that was evaluated were higher than for the usual care group.

Risks and mitigation

All eHealth economic cases carry significant risks, with their manifestation being a combination of cost and time overruns. Costs and time overruns are not in themselves risks; rather they reflect the effect of each risk coming to fruition. The eHI model includes over 40 risk factors, some of which have been outlined earlier in this paper. If these risk factors are not mitigated sufficiently, costs and time overruns can be considerable. Consequently, risk is a large cost.

Figure 20.4 includes two important features. As a struggling eHealth initiative continues, its risk accumulates up to possibly 200 per cent of the annual net benefit at the peak year, and about 140 per cent for the cumulative performance. Ignoring risk mitigation and management is a proven bad idea.

The first four years of a project present the largest challenge. During the planning, development and engagement period, good and weak eHealth broadly follow similar curves. It is not a simple matter to distinguish precisely which curve an initiative is pursuing. These years are when risk management and mitigation are most important in order to avoid pursuing a high-risk curve inadvertently.

All the items listed in Box 20.4, 'Components needed for a net benefit', are also some of the risk factors. If they are not properly in place, they will malfunction and manifest themselves as the extra cost of risk. Their effectiveness needs to be assessed rigorously in the first four years or so of an economic evaluation to establish the curve that the initiative is pursuing. It is not essential that they are all in place simultaneously, but those in place must be effective. The plans for the other components must be relevant, viable and implemented on time.

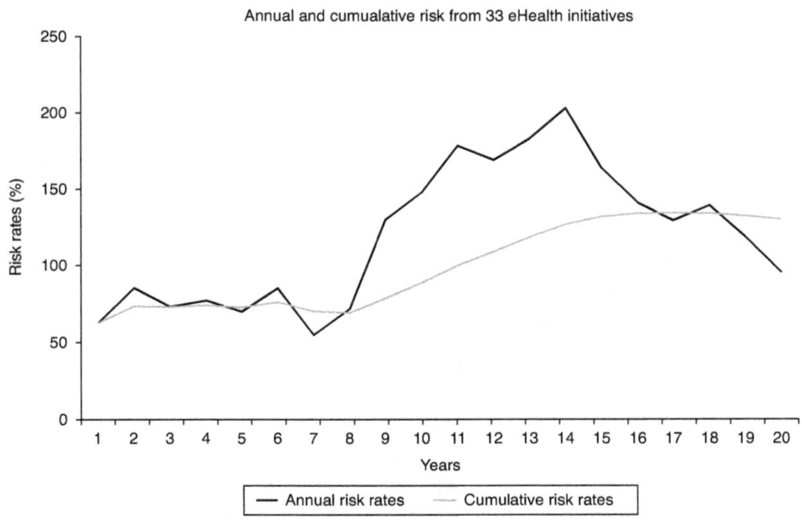

Figure 20.4 Annual and cumulative risk rates

Using economic and financial evaluations for decisions

Evaluations provide invaluable insights for decisions on eHealth, both for new initiatives and for monitoring and evaluation. There are three main types of economic evaluation. Retrospective evaluations are of completed projects to provide knowledge for decisions for future eHealth initiatives, or for corrective action needed to improve net benefits. Prospective evaluations of new projects assess the probable costs, benefits, net benefits and affordability over time. Combined retrospective and prospective evaluation of projects still underway provides the information needed for corrective action. All three kinds of economic evaluation can provide information about value for money, the economic performance and with additional information about affordability, they can show the estimated financial performance. Both perspectives are needed for effective decisions. All prospective evaluations need adjusting for risk.

Completing these evaluations requires two activities: the first being to collect the available, actual data; and the second to use a methodology for reliable estimates where actual data is not available. Even retrospective studies have to rely on estimates because healthcare entities do not keep all the information needed in their conventional records.

Clarity on the difference between methodology and models is also important: a methodology, such as the UK Green Book methodology, is generic; however the eHI models that apply the methodology are always custom-made to match the specific context of each case. Each eHealth initiative has its own specific characteristics, so the methodology and models are seldom the same. An example is a standard vaccination system, which can have different economic and financial features in conditions where the conventional pre-eHealth context is different. For example, one initiative may replace an obsolete vaccination system, while the other may replace a manual system.

Economic evaluations need estimates of costs and benefits for all types of stakeholders, as well as data, such as the numbers of patients affected, numbers of carers affected, user numbers and users' utilisation rates. Because estimates are always based on a combination of data and assumptions, the assumptions are stated explicitly in the eHI models. Although the data can be awkward to model, it can all be handled using a basic spreadsheet, leaving time to deal with the challenging aspects. These include constructing a bespoke eHI evaluation model; collecting the data; applying the data in an eHI model; adjusting the findings for exposure to risk and seeking a realistic monetary measurement of performance for all stakeholders – good, bad or indifferent.

For these tasks, the most important specialist skills needed for eHealth evaluation are knowledge of the impact of ICT for change, analytical skills such as CBA and investment appraisal. These include a combination of economics, finance and risk analysis, and support the role of eHealth socio-economic and financial evaluation for the decisions facing healthcare executives and leaders.

Need for the economic case in monitoring and evaluation

A survey of 300 US healthcare leaders showed that they want economic cases, and ROI in particular, to start earlier in the planning stages (FierceEMR, 2012). Accordingly, 40 per cent use performance measures to evaluate ROI, 36 per cent are satisfied with using this approach, and 32 per cent use performance measures after implementation for at least one patient care service. These results follow on from an American article (Soumerai and Koppel, 2012) stating that EPRs do not save money: this is consistent with the findings of the aggregated eHI evaluations. Taken together, these studies support the need for a realistic prospective economic assessment of eHealth initiatives that incorporates the scale of risk to be included in the proposition and the actual effect of its mitigation.

Using eHealth economic findings for successful eHealth

The two economic evaluations commissioned by the European Commission (Stroetmann et al., 2006; Dobrev et al., 2010) have spawned a valuable source of knowledge about how good and weak eHealth initiatives work over time. These evaluations provide the platform and incentive to use a consistent methodology to collect data from other eHI initiatives, and discover more insights into how eHealth economics work. The knowledge gained from up to 60 different eHealth evaluations helps to show how eHealth functions, either successfully or not. It provides the information and data needed for rigorous socio-economic assessments of planned eHealth initiatives, thus improving their chances of success.

Using economic cases well requires decision-makers to set aside their preliminary views about short-term projects and rapid returns, especially with regard to seeking unrealistic, dominant financial returns. Economic cases provide information to help make better decisions about any competing bids for resources, such as the need for more doctors or for better information to enable doctors to work more effectively. Probably the most important features that should be considered are the feasibility of the economic case, the requirements for change management and the effect of risks.

The potential of economic cases in setting a foundation for monitoring can enable healthcare organisations to focus on what they need to do to succeed. This should secure the required net benefits over time, lead the needed organisational changes, set longer-term affordability and establish the realistic timescales necessary for sustainability. An increasing emphasis on this approach in the US, Europe and other regions around the globe supports more realistic eHealth opportunities.

Box 20.4 Core requirements for success

- Excellent clinical, executive and political leadership;
- A focus on long-term benefits for patients, citizens, healthcare professionals and healthcare provider organisations;
- Continuous engagement with stakeholders;
- Long-term vision, strategies, plans and projects that include both costs and benefits;
- Excellent change management (Harvard Business Press, 2003; Burnes, 2009) and benefits realisation strategies and plans;
- Excellent ICT solutions that can build up over time;
- Realistic, medium-term affordability and financing plans;
- Effective risk mitigation;
- Avoiding unrealistic and dominant goals for excessive and rapid financial gains.

The value of economic cases for monitoring and evaluation is more than just corrective action; it provides new knowledge of how healthcare delivery and organisations can work well and differently in an eHealth environment. Securing sophisticated quality gains from sharing eHealth information and redeploying resources liberated by healthcare professionals' time savings from eHealth are complex management and leaderships goals, but are essential for realising net benefits. Core requirements for success can be found in Box 20.4. Increasing the knowledge of how these key factors work, the actions needed to achieve them, and how long this takes, are essential for eHealth effectiveness as an investment in better healthcare.

References

Burnes, B. (2009), *Managing Change*, 5th edn. Harlow, UK: FT Prentice Hall.

United States Congressional Budget Office (2008), *Evidence on the Costs and Benefits of Health Information Technology* http://www.cbo.gov/sites/default/files/cbofiles/ftpdocs/91xx/doc9168/0--20-healthit.pdf. [Accessed 26 November 2013].

Dobrev, A., Jones, T., Stroetmann, V., Stroetmann, K., Vatter, Y. and Peng, K. (2010), *Interoperable eHealth Is Worth It – Securing the Benefits from Electronic Health Records and ePrescribing*, Luxembourg: Office for Official Publications of the European Communities http://www.ehr-impact.eu/downloads/documents/ehr_impact_study_final.pdf.[Accessed 26 November 2013].

FierceEMR (25 October 2012), Healthcare Execs: EHR return-on-investment measurement should start earlier, *FierceEMR* http://www.fierceemr.com/story/healthcare-execs-ehr-return-investment-measurement-should-start-earlier/2012-10-25.

Fisher, I. (1930), *The Theory of Interest, as determined by Impatience to Spend Income and Opportunity to Invest It*, New York: Macmillan.

Harvard Business Press (2003), *Managing Change and Transition*. Boston, MA: Harvard Business School Press.

HM Treasury (2011), *The Green Book: Appraisal and Evaluation in Central Government*. London: The Stationery Office. http://www.hm-treasury.gov.uk/d/green_book_complete.pdf. [Accessed 26 November 2013].

Henderson, C., Knapp, M., Fernández, J.-L., Beecham, J., Hirani, S.P., Cartwright, M., Rixon, L., Beynon, M., Rogers, A., Bower, P., Doll, H., Fitzpatrick, R., Steventon, A., Bardsley, M., Hendy, J. and Newman, S.P. (2013), "Cost effectiveness of telehealth for patients with long term conditions (Whole Systems Demonstrator telehealth questionnaire study): nested economic evaluation in a pragmatic, cluster randomised controlled trial", *British Medical Journal* 346: f1035. doi: 10.1136/bmj.f1035.

Hopkin, P. (2010), *Fundamentals of Risk Management: Understanding Evaluating and Implementing Effective Risk Management*. London: Kogan Page.

Institute of Medicine (2001), *Crossing the Quality Chasm: The IOM Health Care Quality Initiative*. Institute of Medicine of the National Academies. http://www.iom.edu/Reports/2001/Crossing-the-Quality-Chasm-A-New-Health-System-for-the-21st-Century.aspx.[Accessed 26 November 2013].

Jones, T. (2012), Costs, Benefits and Economics of eHealth, TinTree International eHealth Leadership and Development, www.tintree.org.

Organisation for Economic Co-operation and Development (2010), *Improving Health Sector Efficiency: The Role of Information and Communication Technologies*. Paris: OECD Publishing. DOI:10.1787/9789264084612-en.

Soumerai, S. and Koppel, R. (2012, 17 September), "A major glitch for digitized health-care records", *Wall Street Journal* [online], http://online.wsj.com/article/SB10000872396390443847404577627041964831020.html?mod=googlenews_wsj#articleTabs%3Darticle.

Stroetmann, K.A., Jones, T., Dobrev, A. and Stroetmann, V. (2006), *eHealth Is Worth It. The Economic Benefits of Implemented eHealth Solutions at Ten European Sites*, Luxembourg: Office for Official Publications of the European Communities. http://www.ehealth-impact.org/download/documents/ehealthimpactsept2006.pdf. [Accessed 26 November 2013].

Whitten, P.S., Mair, F.S., Haycox, A., May, C.R., Williams, T.L. and Hellmich, S. (2002), "Systematic review of cost-effectiveness studies of telemedicine interventions", *British Medical Journal* 324(1434). doi:10.1136/bmj.324.7351.1434.

Index

www.ingramcontent.com/pod-product-compliance
Lightning Source LLC
Chambersburg PA
CBHW070026190225
22175CB00004B/122
9781137379429